The Arts in Philosophical Practice

Philosophical Practice

Series Editor
Lydia Amir, Tufts University

The last decades have witnessed a renewed interest in the power of philosophy to address everyday problems on both individual and social scales. The outcome has been a theoretical and practical field called "philosophical practice," an original approach that highlights the timely and perennial need for philosophy. This series aims to bring to the academic public the best reflections that bear on the relation of philosophy to everyday life and the contemporary world as grounded in experience or arguments or both. It honors the founders of this innovative field while calling for new ways of empowering philosophy by demonstrating its relevance to individual and social concerns both inside and outside academia. It thus hopes to strengthen philosophy by bringing its potency to the attention of philosophers and scholars from other disciplines as well as to students and the general public.

Titles in the Series

The Arts in Philosophical Practice: Prospects, Perspectives, and Practices, edited by Jeanette Bresson Ladegaard Knox

Precarity, Trauma, Addiction, and Love in Philosophical Counseling, by Ross Channing Reed

Philosophical Praxis: Origin, Relations, and Legacy, by Gerd B. Achenbach, translated by Michael Picard

Philosophy in Philosophical Counseling: Unasked Questions, Open Answers, by Ora Gruengard

Wonder, Silence, and Human Flourishing: Toward a Rehumanization of Health, Education, and Welfare, edited by Finn Thorbjørn Hansen, Solveig Eide Botnen, and Carlo Leget

The Philosophy of Practical Affairs: An Introduction, by Joseph Agassi

The Arts in Philosophical Practice

Prospects, Perspectives, and Practices

Edited by
Jeanette Bresson Ladegaard Knox

BLOOMSBURY ACADEMIC
NEW YORK • LONDON • OXFORD • NEW DELHI • SYDNEY

BLOOMSBURY ACADEMIC
Bloomsbury Publishing Inc, 1359 Broadway, New York, NY 10018, USA
Bloomsbury Publishing Plc, 50 Bedford Square, London, WC1B 3DP, UK
Bloomsbury Publishing Ireland, 29 Earlsfort Terrace, Dublin 2, D02 AY28, Ireland

BLOOMSBURY, BLOOMSBURY ACADEMIC and the Diana logo
are trademarks of Bloomsbury Publishing Plc

First published in the United States of America 2026

Cover image: *Reflections: The Seine at 7AM* by Hayden Knox

Library of Congress Cataloging-in-Publication Data
Names: Knox, Jeanette Bresson Ladegaard editor
Title: The arts in philosophical practice : prospects, perspectives and practices / edited by Jeanette Bresson Ladegaard Knox.
Description: New York : Bloomsbury Academic, 2026. | Series: Philosophical practice | Includes bibliographical references and index.
Identifiers: LCCN 2025050716 (print) | LCCN 2025050717 (ebook) | ISBN 9781666947007 hardback | ISBN 9781978760851 ebook | ISBN 9798216262596 pdf
Subjects: LCSH: Art and philosophy
Classification: LCC BH39 .A7225 2026 (print) | LCC BH39 (ebook)
LC record available at https://lccn.loc.gov/2025050716
LC ebook record available at https://lccn.loc.gov/2025050717

ISBN: HB: 978-1-6669-4700-7
ePDF: 979-8-2162-6259-6
eBook: 978-1-9787-6085-1

Series: Philosophical Practice

Typeset by Amnet

Contents

Figures

Preface

The Arts in Philosophical Practice: Prospects, Perspectives, and Practices

Philosophical practice is no longer a virgin term. As an experiential practice, it permeates a variety of professions into which philosophers infuse their knowledge and skills with the earnest intent to philosophize with people and assist them in developing their own thinking and moral imagination. It is a practice that for over the past forty years has gained much success and sustained interest within education, management, correctional facilities, rehabilitation, and hospice care programs to mention a few. Other philosophers have followed in the footsteps of the ancient Greeks to bring the act of philosophizing to the public arena through offering philosophical counseling to individuals or by inviting people to discuss philosophical topics in informal *philo cafés* in coffee shops and other public places such as libraries and community centers.

As a contextual, situated activity, philosophical practice defies the ideals of some contemporary understandings of academic philosophy. When philosophy leaves people "unmoved," it leaves philosophy with a serious disability. Confining it to a question of logical thinking, rational calculations, and airtight argumentation speaks to the mind of people, not the inquiring soul and body of people living in a vast and perplexing world with no existential road map. It becomes lame and disembodied, dislocated from lived experience, and preoccupied with outmaneuvering opponents in the battle for winning an argument. Privileging conceptual logic over creative expression and imagination removes philosophy from "the problems of men" (Dewey 1946) who live from cradle to grave in the shadow of uncertainty, unpredictability, and impermanence. If philosophy is to be helpful in the art of living—and flourish—it needs to dialogue on values, virtues, and vulnerabilities that can abet loving attention (Murdoch 2001), champion reflection as rooted in the flow of life (Marcel 2001), and kindle human connections (Levinas 1979), not just theoretically but in actuality.

In philosophical practice, practitioners draw on the jewels of philosophical thought through the ages. The plethora of philosophical traditions resonate with people in their human questioning and quest for purpose. The traditions add perspective while forcing people engaging in philosophical practice to visit new avenues of thought. Understanding the human experience, the interactions between subjects, and the pursuit of truth are at the core of philosophical practice. In recent years, an increasing number of philosophical practitioners have included art forms in their work, which begs the questions: How may the life-giving rays of thought embodied by the works of authors, musicians, painters, playwrights, poets, sculptors, and others inspire philosophical practice? If the arts speak to the human condition and explore the multifaceted fabric of human existence, how may this inform the work of the philosophical practitioner when working with schoolchildren, juvenile and adult offenders, or seriously ill patients? How can creativity and imagination shape the methods, attitudes, and perspectives of philosophical practice? In essence, in what way may the arts be used in philosophical practice, and what may the combination offer other professions?

Philosophical practice concerns itself with the matter of living a human life. The arts too. In the continual process of human self-examination, the arts have played and still play an important role as reflective, embodied activities in what it means to lead a human life, what it means to be a human being, and how humans (dis-)connect with each other. Though the arts can be a mere distraction like enjoying a night out in the theater, concert hall, or museum, the arts can equally engage the human mind and body in pondering the existential paradoxes and puzzles of being. We learn from Aristotle to Martha Nussbaum that the value of art has mattered for the practice of philosophy. This anthology will detail *how* the value of art matters and what role and relevance the arts play and can play in the practice of philosophy today. The anthology will delve into the interfaces between philosophy and art forms and show theoretical and practical perspectives and imagined prospects for the relation between philosophy and arts as well as demonstrate how philosophical practice interacts with and employs the arts. In this book, the arts refer to—but are not limited to—the *performing arts* (drama, dance, music), the *literary arts* (prose, poetry), and the *visual arts* (painting, sculpture, design).

Philosophical practice and art connect in their questioning the fundamentals of life (e.g., what is beauty, what constitutes a good decision, or how to live with suffering) while abstaining from proposing final answers. Their joint exploratory aspect embraces openness, creativity, and freedom that is unparalleled by most other human activities. The arts provide a unique and expressive medium through which dense philosophical ideas can be examined and exhibited. The arts can in this way help give abstract ideas a tangible and holistic form. From literature to visual arts, art can encapsulate complex notions about human existence, morality, and the nature of reality in ways that are both accessible and profound. Throughout history, the arts have involved an emotional and sensory engagement with lived experience and the world. A drama such as *Othello* by Shakespeare portrays moral dilemmas and the obscure, fluid distinction between right and wrong; Munch's painting *The Scream* shows the essence of existential anxiety and human despair; Mozart's *Requiem* takes its listener to the heights of the sublime; and a musical like Lin-Manuel Miranda's *Hamilton* can invoke the question of who gets to "tell my story" and thus who defines my identity, whether it be an individual's, such as Alexander Hamilton, or the story of a nation, like the United States. The arts can evoke emotions and thoughts that take philosophers hundreds of pages to depict. Existing in the sensory, embodied world of humans, the arts can bridge the concrete with the abstract world of philosophically thinking, equally expanding experience and thought. This embodiment, if incorporated into philosophical practice, is what can make philosophy more relatable and impactful and make it emerge from opaque books to become vibrant and potent in human existence.

While art, with its emphasis on the concrete particularity of the sensuous and the richness of perception, serves as a corrective to philosophy's tendency toward excessive abstractness, philosophy, in turn, plays a crucial role in relating art to the larger discourse of human expression, inserting broader themes and questions about human existence and adding intellectual depth. Together, they create a more comprehensive understanding of the human experience. There is a mutually beneficial interaction between philosophy and the arts, and the chapters in this anthology illustrate how. It explores how the combination of the two can inspire and inform each other and other professional fields to provide new and enriching perspectives on these fields and their contributions to society. It does so by exploring themes pertaining to the uses of art forms in philosophy, showcasing interventions employing the arts in a professional arena and artistic exercises in educational settings. It rethinks philosophical practice through the arts and unfolds ethical issues and other philosophical issues by implementing art forms within philosophical practice. This anthology is therefore not a book on aesthetics or the philosophy of art, in which prominent philosophers through the ages have been engaged, for example, Plato (2008), Hegel (1935), Nietzsche (1968), and Adorno (1997). Much is still written on the philosophy of art, yet no book has taken up the task to investigate how philosophical practice and art forms relate or may interact.

The aim of the anthology is threefold: first, to demonstrate the role and value of the arts for philosophical practice through an array of examples from prominent philosophical practitioners around the world, some of whom also engage in artistic activities; second, as a consequence of the first, to conceptualize a novel vision for philosophical practice that exposes its use of creativity and imagination; and third, to establish the relevance of combining philosophical practice and the arts in society and propose how these disciplines can serve as a medium for social commentary and a vehicle for a Socratically inspired care of self.

The anthology is intended for professional philosophers, practicing philosophers, artists with an interest in employing philosophy in their artwork, graduate students, and other professionals interested in philosophical practice and the arts. Contemporary philosophers should find the material valuable, offering panorama and detailed analysis of the act of philosophizing and how to draw on the arts to enhance this act. Philosophy students who are interested in understanding how an abstract discipline can translate into practice and play an integral role in society will find concrete examples in the chapters of this book. Students may find the methodologies explored and developed in the book readily applicable—whether in classrooms, training curricula, or in different areas of philosophical practice—and be inspired to use the arts in their philosophical thinking and future practice. Students of the arts and artists may be inspired by philosophical practice and infuse it in their artistic activity.

Second, the collection will appeal on a conceptual level to people involved in applying philosophically based practices that incorporate the arts in, for example, civic communities, educational institutions, and health care and art settings. The book may inspire other professionals who are interested in employing the creativity of the arts and philosophical practice in their own field. Last, as the book broadly addresses the use of philosophy as an art of living where life is thoroughly examined, as Socrates taught us, it should captivate readers who are deeply engaged in bridging imagination and reflection.

The anthology consists of eleven chapters. The chapters engage with an array of art forms and philosophical methods, parading a multiplicity of outlooks on the relationship between philosophical practice and art. The chapters oscillate between the conceptual, the sensuous, and the creative in varying degrees. Readers will find discussions on art as a medium for philosophy and on philosophy as a critical, yet creative activity. The chapters are structured as follows: Starting with chapters on children, young adults, and adults in educational, learning, or pedagogical settings, it transitions into chapters on existential health, followed by chapters on fiction, music, and design. The book concludes with a chapter arguing that art can be viewed as a form of philosophical practice. The progression mirrors a lifespan perspective, from early stages in life to the contemplation of death and loss. It also captures the creativity and free spirit of the anthology, showcasing the various ways it combines philosophy with different artistic expressions. By doing so, the book lives up to its title: *The Arts in Philosophical Practice: Prospects, Perspectives, and Practices.*

Opening the anthology, Tomoko Masaki explains in "Phenomenology of Very Young Children and Picturebooks" how to use picturebooks as a tool to cultivate character development and promote self-awareness in children of all ages. Drawing on her many years of running a private, voluntary library in Osaka, Japan, Masaki focuses in her chapter on her library project that involves reading stories to the very young children, from babies to age three. First, she clarifies what kind of book a picturebook is before she demonstrates how picturebooks can be nurturing for these very young children. Her demonstration takes the reader through four examples with classical picturebooks: two Japanese and two American. Throughout the chapter, Masaki leans on, and integrates into her argument, the phenomenology of Merleau-Ponty and his thoughts on the importance of identifying one's particular I in this particular body.

Seeing Socratic dialogue as originating from the *Bildung* tradition, Ann Pihlgren chronicles her longtime experience working to enhance reflection skills and learning among pupils and mentoring teachers and principals in the Swedish educational system. Literary, visual, and the performing arts are frequently used by her to support and boost the dialogue about important philosophical ideas for the formation of children. In her chapter, "Art as a Resource in Teaching: Using the Arts to Reflect on Critical Ideas in Different Subjects," she describes how Socratic dialogue is performed and how different forms of art can be used. The chapter presents examples from actual dialogues held with pupils from preschool to grade 9 to visualize how philosophical dialogues are performed and what kind of art references might be used to philosophize on important ideas. Her use of different kinds of artworks as a reference point in Socratic dialogues has proven to make it easier for a philosophically unskilled teacher to use philosophizing dialogues as means to promote an open mind to new ideas, critical thinking, and analysis in the classroom.

Having developed and worked for many years with *art-based philosophizing*, Pia Houni describes in her chapter, "Rethinking the Yellow Sun," different ways that art can be an integral part of philosophical practice. With a background in theater, she draws on drama and performance art without ever losing sight of other art mediums such as literature, fine art, and photography, as her point of departure is creativity. The chapter explains her approach through two case studies that demonstrate *art-based philosophizing* in her work as well as briefly presenting the theoretical background for the practical exercises. Houni shows the reader how she, in her workshops, follows a similar basic structure, starting with art-based activities, questioning, and choosing a topic for a reflective dialogue, and, finally, reaching a conclusion.

The chapter "Cathartic Care: Otherness in Doctoring and Dialoguing," by Jeanette Bresson Ladegaard Knox, explores how Aristotle's idea of "catharsis," Emmanuel Levinas's notion of "face," and Marcel's concept of "mystery" can inform the communication between health care providers and patients to form more wholesome relationships. Using Margaret Edson's play *Wit* as a reference point throughout the chapter, she carves a horizontal and compassionate rapport between patient and health care provider in contrast to the dehumanizing experience of the play's protagonist. While art can evoke a sense of catharsis in humans, Levinas's concept of the face reveals the essential elements that define humanness, which philosophical curiosity and dialogue can accentuate while illuminating the mystery of being. Holding space for the vulnerability, fear, and uniqueness of a diseased person can launch a cathartic process that adds meaning and fullness despite chaotic and incomprehensible circumstances. The author argues that the conceptualization of face-to-face encounters in the clinic may be transferable to philosophical practice to strengthen not only its reflective processes but also the cultivation of virtues such as empathy, presence, and courage.

In "A Theoretical and Creative Life," Luis de Miranda weaves biographical and philosophical reflections into a wholesome chapter on how philosophy and creativity/poetry/art have merged and co-pollinated in his life. In this co-pollination, de Miranda writes poetically on philosophy and philosophically on fiction while outlining creative and personal moments that have formed his philosophical practice and philosophical novels. The chapter is a reflective memoir, delving into the role of metaphor and fiction in nurturing philosophical health, dedicating a large portion of his chapter to how the creative sources of the arts have informed his philosophical health approach that he calls *crealectics*, or the practice of *Creal* (combining creativity and reality), which is a philosophy rooted in fiction. Based on *crealectics*, de Miranda has developed the method SMILE-PH, an acronym for "Sense-Making Interviews Looking at Elements of Philosophical Health," which consists of six elements that he meticulously explains in detail.

Philosophy and poetry have had a long and interesting relationship. Two chapters engage in this relationship. As a seasoned philosophical practitioner, Vaughana Feary's chapter, "The Use of Poetry Therapy in Philosophical Practice. A Case Study: Ivan Petrovich and His Crisis of Faith," illustrates the effectiveness of using poetry in philosophical counseling. Through a close examination of a case in which selected poems by Emily Dickinson serve as the main vehicle for counseling an individual client experiencing what he called "a crisis of faith" as he was facing his own death from cancer, the reader is taken through conversations about the meaning of the poems, revealing underlying philosophical perspectives in the process. By talking about the philosophical perspectives revealed by the poems, the client expressed how his conception of faith had been transfigured and how he had become sufficiently reconciled to his spiritual struggles to be able to "die in peace."

Although Socrates claimed that a lover of wisdom must become a lover of poetry and many outstanding philosophers connect poetry with their work, these have generally gone unheeded not only by academic philosophy but also by philosophical practice. In "Pursuing Wisdom in Riddles: Practicing Philosophy with Poetry on the Puzzle of Our Existence," Sebastian Rehnman argues that to love wisdom is to consciously pursue an understanding of one's whole life and living from birth to death as well of the meaning of one's existence. But that very love is seeking to comprehend the incomprehensible. From a case of practicing philosophy in dialogue with a poem by R. S. Thomas, Rehnman demonstrates the importance of poetry in pursuing a comprehensive understanding of one's life and living. And finally, Rehnman shows that Thomas's poem embodies the reflective practice of many wisdom traditions to lead a life of expressing the inexpressible experience by analogy and metaphor.

Being the author of two philosophical novels, Detlef Staude reflects in "Fiction in Philosophical Practice" on the reasons why stories and novels are compatible with and suitable for philosophical practice. His argument is threefold. Staude starts out his position by describing how philosophical novels can transform data from the history of philosophy into a coherent idea. Next, he argues that philosophical novels reflect on the significance of actual situations, and finally, he explains how the use of philosophical novels stimulates questions and dialogue. In the chapter, he also compares ethics and the thought experiments often used in academic philosophy with narrative fiction and advocates that knowledge and an understanding-promoting effect are results of the latter. In comparing thought experiments with philosophical novels, he describes what is important in a dialogue about narrative fiction in philosophical practice.

In recent years, philosophy of music has received keen attention by the academic world and has been investigated under various perspectives due to its interdisciplinary nature. However, the connection between philosophy of music and philosophical practice still remains strongly underexamined. The chapter "Philosophers of Music: Imaginary Counselors for Musicians," by Manos Perrakis, fills this significant gap. The chapter sketches a map of possible implications of music philosophy for philosophical practice. In sketching this map, its core interest lies in the use of music philosophy for professionals of music, mainly, but also for everybody who plays music. Furthermore, the chapter is a plea for making philosophy of music take on a stronger presence at music and art universities.

In her chapter, "Sculpting Space: Philosophical Practice Through Design," Lydia Amir presents a new activity in philosophical practice. It involves a philosophic process whose final outcome is the design of a space—smaller or greater—which is conceived and sculpted in one's house or elsewhere as a living memory of a deceased loved one. The process involves the choice of objects that undergo transformations to better represent what the deceased was or now means for the living person. Designing a space is philosophical in that the mourning is processed and transformed through discussions about the relation with the memory and the restoration of the deceased. It is artistic in that it uses objects representing these relations in a creative way whose outcome is the design and actual construction of that memorial, which can be exhibited to others, either for some time or indefinitely or privately kept in one's home.

The collection ends with Lou Marinoff elucidating in "Art as Philosophical Practice: Ten Responses to Folly, Tyranny, and War," how art implicitly embodies or explicitly reflects active philosophical principles, in whose light one can view (some) artists as philosophical practitioners. Taking his reader into the artistic missions of a series of historic figures in the world of thought and art, Marinoff interprets their artistic endeavors as philosophical ways of living. Through ten existential responses to cathartic circumstances, these historic figures come to life as do the eras that marked them. We meet the likes of Goya and Beethoven, Tennyson, and Rand in their art and life. In seeing art as an activity that exercises philosophical practice, Marinoff also provides the reader with an insight into a broader understanding of the field, one that transcends traditional philosophical counseling to permeate individual responses to the challenges of the day.

Philosophy and art become rivals when philosophy is understood as a purely intellectual project, a rationalistic logic. This collection serves as an argument for philosophy and art as partners. The anthology showcases eleven examples of how philosophy and art can partner to reflect on human experiences and lived challenges. Collectively, the chapters demonstrate the depth and width of experimenting with the arts in philosophical practice. They show how philosophy and art can positively contaminate each other to the benefit of each individual form of human expression through which the pursuit of (self-)discovery and purpose and the experience of adversity and suffering as well as the wrestle with and wonder of everyday life can inspire greater understanding and new ways of thinking, being, and belonging. The juxtaposition of philosophical practice and the arts opens new avenues for inquiry into the human condition in all its complexity, particularity, and commonality.

Jeanette Bresson Ladegaard Knox
March 14, 2025
Copenhagen, Denmark

References

Adorno, T. J. (1997), *Aesthetic Theory*, University of Minnesota Press.

Dewey, J. (1946), *The Problems of Men*, Philosophical Library.

Hegel, G. F. (1935), *Aesthetics: Lectures on Fine Arts*, vol. 1, trans. T. M. Knox, Clarendon.

Levinas, E. (1979), *Totality and Infinity*, trans. A. Lingis, Kluwer Academic.

Marcel, G. (2001), *The Mystery of Being*, vols. 1 and 2, trans. G. S. Fraser, The Gifford Lectures 1949–50, St. Augustine's.

Murdoch, I. (2001), *The Sovereignty of Good*, Routledge.

Nietzsche, F. (1968), "The Birth of Tragedy," in W. Kaufmann (ed. and trans.), *Basic Writings of Nietzsche*, The Modern Library.

Plato (2008), *Republic*, trans. R. Waterfield, Oxford University Press.

1

Phenomenology of Very Young Children and Picturebooks

Tomoko Masaki

Introduction

For the past fifty years, I have been reading many picturebooks[1] with people of all kinds and age-groups: babies, young children, elementary and junior high school children, university students, nursery schoolteachers, librarians, senior citizens, and picturebook volunteers who visit libraries, nursery and elementary schools, and care homes for senior citizens. Through the course of my life, I have realized that the world of picturebooks as a whole is remarkably broad and deep and also that the world of a single picturebook is amazingly broad and deep. I have reached the idea that the picturebook is a designed and crafted art form in our daily life. It is in most cases impossible for us to buy an original painting by Picasso, Cézanne, or Van Gogh, but it is easy to purchase a picturebook, or we can borrow one from a library.

There are two ways you can appreciate picturebooks: You can read one of them by yourself, or you can read one with another person or people, and so share them with others. What is interesting about picturebooks is that we may appreciate them more when they are read aloud by someone else, whether you can read or not. It is true that very young children cannot read, so adults need to read picturebooks aloud to them. And it is generally considered that picturebooks are only for this age-group anyway. But I can quote many experiences when picturebooks have given happiness and joy to much older people and age-groups. For instance, when I read aloud some picturebooks to university students in class, they admitted that they greatly enjoyed them, even though they had previously thought that picturebooks were only for very young children.

Nevertheless, the group that surprises me most is that of very young children, from infants up to the age of three, because it seems to me that they can appreciate picturebooks in their own way, perhaps even more than older children or adults. Of course, they cannot express their feelings and thoughts in verbal language but do so through their body language. They spontaneously behave just as they want to. Their eyes sparkle, their faces beam with happiness, their bodies bounce up and down on their mother's lap when they listen to me and look at the picturebooks. On one day, they will utter some sounds to express their feelings. On another day, they will get down from their mother's lap and dance. And yet on another day, they will step down to point out something in the picturebook, as if they have found something important in the picturebook for the first time in their life. On another day, they will sit captivated in front of me as if they are living in the world of the picturebook, while I am reading the picturebook aloud, showing its pages with its pictures. What has happened to them? That question led me to the phenomenology of Merleau-Ponty.

In this chapter, I would like to describe my experiences with very young children, together with their growth and development in the first three years of their life, during which I shared picturebooks with them, and they taught me how picturebooks could work in their minds and bodies or in their imaginary world. Maurice Merleau-Ponty (1908–61), a French philosopher of phenomenology, writes in his main work, *Phenomenology of Perception*, that "phenomenology involves describing" (Merleau-Ponty 2012: ixxi), and I will describe what I have experienced with very young children. First, I will discuss the characteristics and potentials of picturebooks to help the reader understand what picturebooks are and how children can engage with them deeply. Following that, I will introduce my project "Very Young Children and Picturebooks." After that, I want to describe the process of children growing from infants to three-year-olds using four picturebooks chosen from among the many books that I have shared with them.

In this chapter, my approach aims to reveal the dynamic interplay between abstract theory and practical application.

Characteristics and Potentials of the Picturebook

In this section, I will expound on the various aspects of a picturebook to help widen the reader's understanding. This inclusion of picturebook analysis serves to illustrate these concepts in a creative and engaging way, demonstrating how philosophical ideas can be discovered and appreciated within the pages of a picturebook.

I would like to introduce a definition by Barbara Bader (1927–2021) in her voluminous work, *American Picturebooks from Noah's Ark to the Beast Within*, in which she writes about American picturebook history. She writes:

> A picturebook is text, illustrations, total design; an item of manufacture and a commercial product; a social, cultural, historical document; and foremost, an experience for a child. As an art form it hinges on the interdependence of pictures and words, on the simultaneous display of two facing pages, and on the drama of the turning of the page. On its own terms its possibilities are limitless.
>
> —Bader (1976: 2)

The picturebook consists of not only pictures and words but also other elements that, when combined together, make the picturebook a work of art. Here I want to describe the characteristics of a picturebook plainly to give the reader a better understanding.

First, a picturebook is a tangible object: you can look at one, you can touch it, you can smell it, or you can try to bite it if you want (I have seen several babies chew picturebooks). What's more, it can be held in our hands and embraced in our arms. It can be passed down from generation to generation and can form a connection between those generations.

Second, a picturebook is a book. It has a front cover (which can be seen as a door), a back cover (an exit), and between them, the content (a new world). We can experience an imaginary world of various lives and cultures in the book.

Third, the picturebook has a narrative, in which readers can find and experience the flow of time. Page turning conveys the passing of time: from the past to the present and to the future. Even very young children can recognize that time is flowing through the pages of a book, and this helps them understand that there is a story inside. This experience leads them to form stories of their own life. Life is not a mixture of diverse accidents but a kind of narrative that helps keep our memories alive. As Merleau-Ponty (2012: 414) says, "[T]he old man remains in contact with his childhood."

Fourth, a picturebook is a form of integrated art within an overall design. A picturebook is made by various people: artists, authors, editors, publishers, paper makers, ink producers, binders, designers, and even readers whose tastes are reflected in the picturebook. It can be said that a picturebook is a cultural object crafted by many human hands unlike a digital object.

Fifth, a picturebook can be appreciated when it is read aloud to you by someone else while you are looking at it. It is a matter of fact that we cannot look at two things simultaneously; we cannot look at words and pictures at the same time. Two people or more who meet in the "here and now" at an intersection of their individual lives can appreciate a picturebook together: One is reading aloud, and others are viewing—for instance, children and parents, children and teachers, and very young children and very old people. You can share a picturebook and create memories that last until the end of your life. In the case of children read aloud to, they remember their parents' voices and warm bodies. So a picturebook can be seen as a form of art that brings people together. I believe it can contribute to helping heal the fragmented society I will mention later in this chapter. For young children, especially, a picturebook read aloud by their parents can become a treasure that remains with them throughout their lives. Moreover, a picturebook can become the parents' treasure, too, because the parents can remember the happy times in sharing the picturebook. An American psychologist, Ellen Handler Spitz (1999: 13), emphasizes the importance of parents reading picturebooks aloud to their child in her book *Inside Picture Books*: "We care to know a great deal about what goes into our children's bodies; we need to be no less attentive to what goes into their." By sharing picturebooks with children, she believes that an adult reader "can provide a psychological embrace as well as a physical one" (Spitz 1999: 16).

Sixth, the picturebook has pictures and words that help people understand diverse cultures. In this modern world, it is hard for people to cross the borders and boundaries of cultures and nations. If children have been read picturebooks of other cultures when they were very young, they will be familiar with those cultures, and they will hopefully have warm feelings for them. I may be idealistic when I say that picturebooks can help foster peace and cross-cultural understanding in the world, but I believe it to be true and worth studying in detail.

The Project "Very Young Children and Picturebooks"

I have been running my own private, voluntary library since 1973 in Osaka, Japan, sharing picturebooks, poems, stories, and workshops with children aged from infants to teenagers once a week while at the same time lecturing in colleges about picturebooks to students who will become nursery or elementary schoolteachers.

In my library, I started my "Very Young Children and Picturebooks" project in 2001 when I returned to Japan after an absence of six years. I had been living in England to research Victorian picturebooks and write my doctoral thesis about the history of their printing and design, which was published in English in Japan as *A History of Victorian Popular Picture Books* (Masaki 2006).

The year 2000 was noteworthy for being designated the "National Year of Reading for Children" by the Japanese government. In cooperation with the Japanese government's advocacy, the Bookstart Japan scheme started in 2001, following the Bookstart UK scheme, which began in 1992. The idea of the Bookstart UK scheme is—by providing free packages of picturebooks—to raise the childhood literacy rate as well as to nurture a positive relationship between parents and babies through experiencing the joy of sharing books, while in Japan the aim is to fill the gap in reading development between children's ability to recognize words and their book-reading ability. Japanese children have a high literacy rate. They can read individual words but have difficulty appreciating the stories emanating from the words and sentences. This tendency may be called an inability to understand the deeper meaning of words or read between the lines.

On my return to Japan in 2001, I was shocked by the societal changes in the country. Several brutal crimes committed by teenagers had occurred around that time. I found that children were surrounded with digital devices, not with warm human beings, and that parents were not sharing picturebooks or storybooks with their children. Parents were keener than ever for their children to get high grades in school and gain places at prestigious universities. They even sent their very young children to private classes. Making their children assimilate difficult knowledge was more important than sharing picturebooks with them. They assumed that the earlier their children started lessons, the better they would learn. The education industry was infiltrating the lives of even very young children.

Greatly shocked by these situations, I wondered what I could do for children, and I came across the books of Japanese psychologist Natsuki Okamoto (1926–2009), who was deeply worried about the aforementioned problems. He writes in his book *Kodomo to Kotoba* (Children and Language): "Babies are born into human society, they learn and acquire the culture of their society and they form their own personality from the world around them through relationships with others" (Okamoto 1982: 5). In another book, *Yojiki* (Infanthood), he writes: "[C]hildren in their very young childhood try to grasp the meaning of the world, human beings and themselves, giving significance to each and forming an idea of the way of life they will lead" (Okamoto 2005: 2). Okamoto (2005: 2) reached the conclusion that a lack of unconditional love in their very young childhood had been causing social problems for adolescents and adults. He advocated that human beings should be able to look back on their experience during infanthood as a time when they were deeply loved by a parent or carer.

I later noticed this change in society was happening on a global scale. I read in the newspaper and saw on the news that families and societies were becoming disjointed all over the world. A poor infanthood is only one reason of the many that contribute to a dysfunctional society, but we know it is the first stage in one's life and forms a foundation for the rest of one's life.

Around 2001, I encountered Merleau-Ponty through his book *Phenomenology of Perception*, which was originally published in French in 1945. In it, he writes: "I am the absolute source. My existence does not come from my antecedents, nor from my physical and social surroundings; it moves out toward them and sustains them. For I am the one who brings into being for myself" (Merleau-Ponty 2012: ix–xii).

The idea of "I am the absolute source" tells us that it is important to establish "I" as a person, and this person should act with responsibility and in cooperation with others. Merleau-Ponty (2012: 455) also writes: "[I]t is not just essential that I have a body, but I have this particular body." The encounter with Merleau-Ponty's phenomenological thought gave me an idea of what I, as a picturebook researcher, could do for children in this situation.

I believed that picturebooks could help children understand the world and that picturebooks could also bring people together. I decided to begin the "Very Young Children and Picturebooks" project in April 2001, in which I would invite mothers to come together with their babies (I use the term "mothers" to represent all child carers). Their children would come to my class twice a month for three years, during which they would grow from the age of four months to three years old. In Japan, most children enter kindergarten when they become three years old.

Since then, more than twenty fruitful years have passed, and my project is still ongoing. During this time, I have learned much about young children in the early years of their life, and the important relationship between children and picturebooks. I wrote my second doctoral thesis about very young children and picturebooks with the phenomenological theory of Merleau-Ponty. It was published as the title *Merleau-Ponty to kodomo-to-Ehon-no Genshogaku* (*Phenomenology of Children and Picturebooks*) (Masaki 2018).

I will now explain how very young children are nurtured by picturebooks in my project. I have selected four picturebooks, among the many that I have shared, which illustrate the developing stages of children. By incorporating personal experiences, I aim to offer relatable, real-world contexts that make the theory of phenomenology more accessible and tangible.

Babies Meet Their First Picturebook, *Inai-Inai-Baa* (Peek-a-boo)

Inai-Inai-Baa (Peek-a-boo) (Figure 1.1) is the picturebook I have read aloud to infants at the beginning of every session.

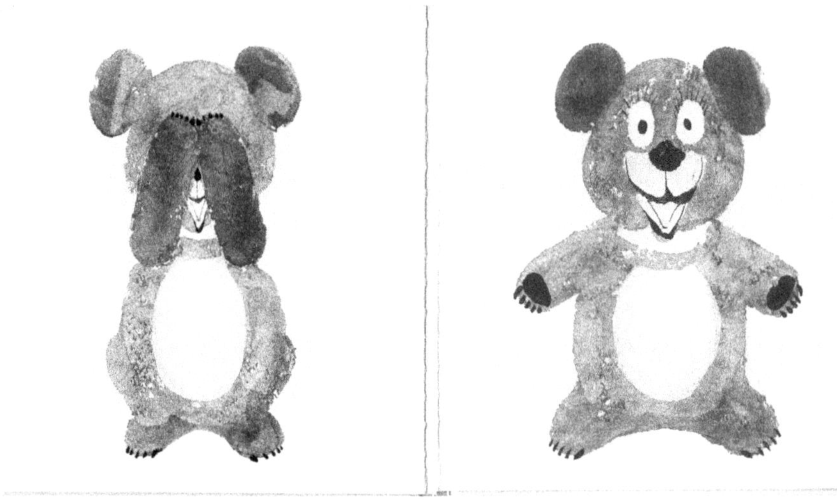

Figure 1.1 Illustrations from Y. Segawa, *Inai-Inai-Baa* (Peek-a-boo), text by M. Matsutani (Doshinsha, 1967).

"Inai-Inai-Baa" is the Japanese name for "Peek-a-boo," one of the best-loved games for parents to play with their babies in Japan and all over the world. The Japanese phrase "Inai-Inai" sounds like "nowhere-nowhere" for babies. So it seems to me that when a mother covers her face while saying "Inai-Inai," she is lost from her baby's point of view, her face being what the baby needs to identify her. The baby will pull at his or her mother's hands, trying hard to get her back. I would say that a mother covering her face while saying "Inai-Inai" means darkness, sorrow, and loss of love for a baby, whereas saying "Baa!" while revealing the face means light, joy, and the regaining of love.

The picturebook *Inai-Inai-Baa*, written by Miyoko Matsutani (1926–2015) and illustrated by Yasuo Segawa (1932–2010), is considered to be one of the first Japanese picturebooks. More than seven million copies have been published since its first publication in 1967. There is a substantial difference between the game and the picturebook: the *Inai-Inai-Baa* game is performed by babies with their mother, while the *Inai-Inai-Baa* picturebook is read aloud, with the children being introduced to the imaginary world by their mother.

The picturebook *Inai-Inai-Baa* has nine double-spreads[2] with five characters: a cat, a bear, a mouse, a fox, and a girl. The first double-spread shows a cat saying "Inai-Inai" while covering its face with its paws; then, on turning the page, the cat appears again, saying "Baa!" uncovering its face. As soon as the cat's face appears, all the children smile, and some utter what could be their first vocal response to a picturebook, saying something like "Baa!" When a picturebook is read aloud repeatedly to children, it can invite them to utter sounds like "baa," "oh," or "ah."

My experiences of reading picturebooks with very young children have shown me that they can imagine what the following page will be—that is, they have the ability to imagine what happens next. This potential is surely enhanced by picturebooks, in which the act of turning pages is one of the most important and enjoyable elements. Turn the page, and you will meet a new scene, expected or unexpected. The series of turned pages, from the front cover to the back cover, imparts the idea of cause and effect to readers through repeated double-spreads. Therefore, when being read a picturebook, babies come to expect a following page. This ability is very important to live in the real world: We will do this at any given moment, imagining the effect that will follow. In this sense, I recommend picturebooks with a story, in which each double-spread has an individual meaning linked to the previous and following double-spread, forming a simple storyline that runs through the book. Storybooks with gentle storylines allow infants to acquire the skill of understanding causality while enjoying the story.

American psychologists Jerome Bruner and V. Sherwood (1976) wrote in the book *Play: Its Role in Development and Evolution* about a project that was conducted using the Peek-a-boo game. In another book, *Making Stories: Law, Literature, Life*, Bruner (2002: 31) makes a significant point about very young children, taking Peek-a-boo as an example: "For example, children easily grasp and delight in wordless dramas of the unexpected performed for them by adults, like Peek-a-boo, and they do so before they have words enough to tell or understand stories." The theory states that young children can appreciate stories before they have words. Bruner (2002: 99) mentions the importance of early childhood, with the young childhood being "the opening chapter in a lifelong story of how we struggle to strike a balance between autonomy and connectedness. . . . We nourish our identities by our connections yet insist that we are something more as well—ourselves." It is true that we struggle in life to find a balance between "I want to be myself" and "I want to be with others." Both the game *Inai-Inai-Baa* and the picturebook *Inai-Inai-Baa* may give us a way to find a balance between this lifelong struggle. We should understand that the game and the picturebook require a connection between two living and breathing human beings.

The experience of sharing the picturebook is an experience of the imaginative world. We live in the "here and now." Our life is confined to the body, and we live "here" in our personal space and "now" in this time. No matter wherever or whenever you want to be, you cannot go immediately there. Yet in the world of the imagination, you can be anywhere and anytime. In this world of the imagination, you may play the game Peek-a-boo with a bear while never being able to do so in the real world.

Very Young Children Acquire an Understanding of the Passing of Time with Page Turning in Picturebooks

In my library, I often read the picturebook *Chocho Hayaku Konaikana* (Butterfly, when will you come to me?) (Figure 1.2) to two-year-olds. This picturebook has text and illustrations by Nobue Kai (1930–2023), who is famous for her pictures of plants and wildflowers. The picturebook shows a speedwell plant with little blue flowers as a main character. It has been waiting for a butterfly to come to

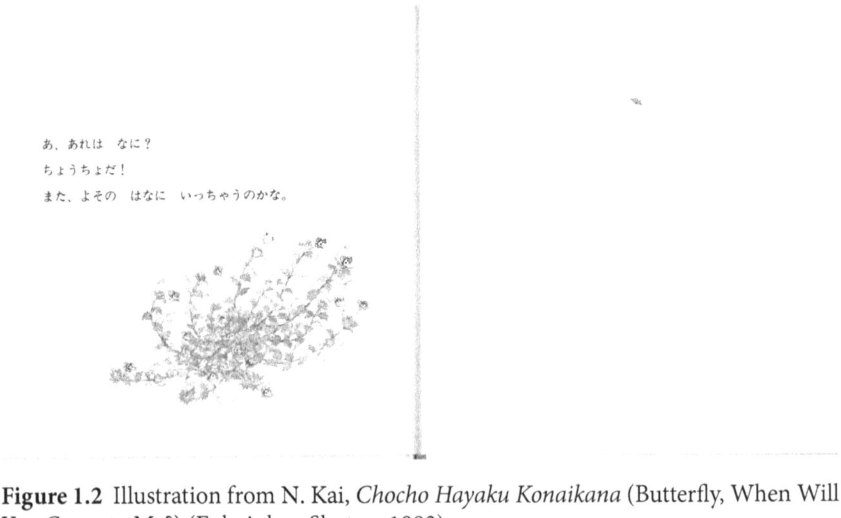

Figure 1.2 Illustration from N. Kai, *Chocho Hayaku Konaikana* (Butterfly, When Will You Come to Me?) (Fukuinkan Shoten, 1992).

it and suck nectar from it. Butterflies appear but visit the other surrounding flowers. It waits and waits. Finally, a little blue butterfly comes to it and stops on one of the little blue flowers.

Adults who read the picturebook aloud to young children normally just look at the words. They do not look particularly at the pictures. The sentences are short, plain, and straightforward—in short, too simple, undramatic, and uninteresting for adult readers. And finally, they say, "The end," and close the picturebook. One day, a two-year-old boy, after being read this book aloud, came to me, handed me the book, and said, "Please read it to me again." I read the book to him, and he asked me to read it once again. And once more. I could not understand what he found so interesting in this book. The book seemed too simple to be read several times.

I was reading the picturebook slowly to him, looking at the pictures in it and observing him. I realized that the speedwell plant was alive in the pictures. It was extending its small stems toward the butterflies, hoping longingly they would come to it. But again, they went to the other flowers. When I read the sentences toward the end, "What is it? A butterfly! But it may go to the other flower, too" (20–1), I suddenly felt that the two-year-old boy was weeping inside because of just listening to the text. He imagined himself as the plant feeling that no butterfly would come to him anymore although he had been waiting for hours, and he would always be alone. But when he saw the picture, he noticed that the butterfly was actually flying to the little flower. He could "read" in the picture what the text did not say. Actually, in my project, "Very Young Children and Picturebooks," two-year-old children come up to the picturebook and point to the little butterfly in the book. They cannot help but point to the butterfly one after another. They want to think that this butterfly will surely visit the wildflower.

Picturebooks consist of two kinds of expressions: literary and artistic. It is generally thought that pictures are easy to understand by anyone, while how to read words needs to be learned. However, it seems to me that very young children are born with an ability to "read" artistic images deeply. Merleau-Ponty (1964: 150) writes in *The Child's Relations with Others* that "[i]t is altogether startling to see certain children much more apt to understand this drawing or that painting by Picasso than the adults around them. The adult hesitates before this kind of drawing."

When I am sharing picturebooks with very young children, I am startled by how deeply they can read pictures—more than can older children or adults. They try to do their best to read the characters in picturebooks, doing so with the same level of focus they use when they look at real people in their actual life. In our daily life, we often see very young children staring at people so fixedly that we adults feel embarrassed. It seems to me that this strong tendency to stare, especially at human beings, may show that very young children would like to know what this world will be, whether this world is worthy to remain in to live, whether this person confronting them is a good one to live with, and so on. And so when looking at picturebooks, very young children employ exactly the same instinctive modus operandi: staring at characters such as children, animals, toys, and even flowers in picturebooks with an intense level of scrutiny.

A picturebook is a valuable tool through which children can encounter various kinds of people whom they may not meet in their real life. A picturebook has a door, and when you open the door, you can find a world in which you have various experiences.

The boy who asked me to read the picturebook several times asked me another thing. He wanted to look at previous pages. He turned the pages back and forth. I interpreted his act as trying to make the story flowing through the picturebook more coherent. He wanted to find consistency of time in past, present, and future. The picturebook *Chocho Hayaku Konaikana* is a story of the passage of time. The sun depicted in double-spreads clearly shows the course of time, and the speedwell has little blue flowers, each of which blooms for one day only. Both the pictures and words tell the story of one day during which the plant was waiting for the butterfly to come. The two-year-old boy could live in the picturebook as the plant, waiting for a visitor all day long. Page turning taught the boy about the passing of time.

Children Go to "Where the Wild Things Are"

The picturebook *Where the Wild Things Are* (Figure 1.3), written and illustrated by American artist Maurice Sendak (1928–2012), must be one of the most famous picturebooks in the world. It also provides a valuable insight into the psychology

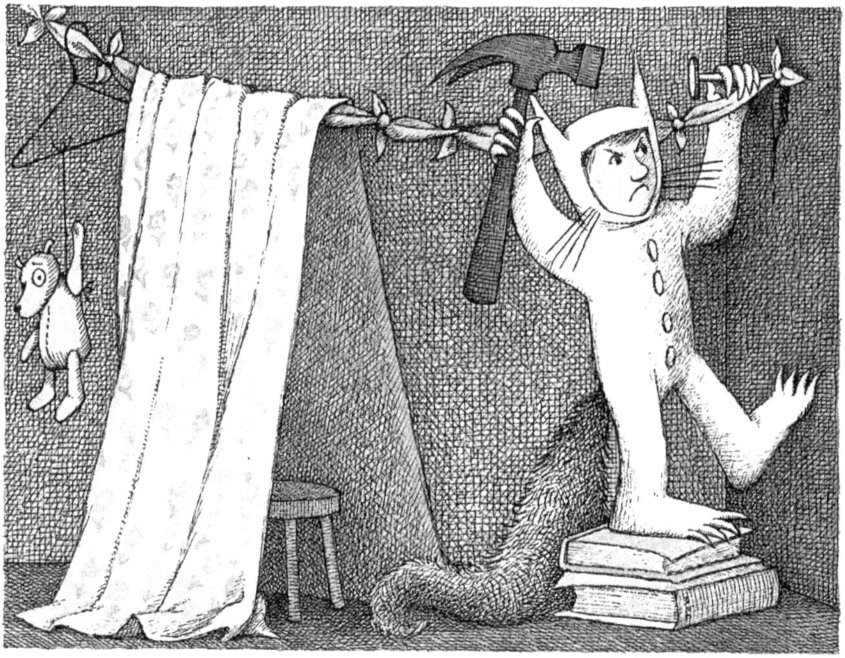

Figure 1.3 Illustration from M. Sendak, *Where the Wild Things Are* (HarperCollins, 1963). The Japanese version was published under the title *Kaijutachi-no Irutokoro*, trans. T. Jingu (Fuzambo, 1975).

of a child. The main character, Max, is a boy of around five years old, and he is pictured wearing a wolf-suit, which serves the purpose of showing his "wild" emotion. The most challenging task for the picturebook creator is how to depict a character's feelings such as frustration, anger, and fear. In the picturebook, Max is being mischievous, which is not mentioned in the text but implied by the pictures. The first picture shows him using books to reach high up the wall, holding a big hammer with which he is making a big crack in the wall. The wall can be interpreted as the frame made by adults with whom he seems to be angry.

We do not know why Max is acting mischievously. A little stuffed dog in the picture hanging by a thread gives us a clue. It is reproachfully looking at Max. It may symbolize a recently born baby brother or sister. And though Max himself cannot explain his feelings clearly, his present frustration is possibly caused by the baby.[3] He cannot help being naughty. He is sent to his bedroom without supper by his mother, who calls him a "WILD THING."

At this point, the boy begins to imagine another world where wild things live. A forest "grew and grew—and grew until his ceiling with vines and the walls became the world all around" (Sendak 1963: 10–15). Interestingly, as the pictures in each double-spread grow in size, his imaginary world grows too. Eventually, he arrives at the island where the wild things are. What are the wild things? Sendak provided a commentary himself about his picturebook in his Caldecott Medal Acceptance Speech[4] in 1964. The commentary appears in his book, *Caldecott & Co.*

> They are the necessary games children must conjure up to combat an awful fact of childhood: the fact of their vulnerability to fear, anger, hate, frustration—all the emotions that are an ordinary part of their lives and that they can perceive only as ungovernable and dangerous forces. To master these forces, children turn to fantasy: that imagined world where disturbing emotional situations are solved to their satisfaction. Through fantasy, Max, the hero of my book, discharges his anger against his mother, and returns to the real world sleepy, hungry, and at peace with himself.
>
> —Sendak (1988: 151)

The last scene offers a suggestion as to why Max can return home: Supper is waiting for him on a table. He knew his mother loved him even though she was angry with him, and she will always love him.

When I read this picturebook to children, I want to convey my hope that they will have wild things in their minds, such as anger, fear, hate, and frustration. Sendak understood these emotions well. And he thought that children needed fantasy to master these emotions. He received a letter from a seven-year-old boy who had written to him. Sendak happily introduced the letter in the abovementioned book.

> *Where the Wild Things Are* was not meant to please everybody—only children. A letter from a seven-year-old boy encourages me to think that I have reached children as I had hoped. He wrote: "'How much does it cost to get to where the wild things are? If it is not expensive my sister and I want to spend the summer there. Please answer soon.' I didn't answer the question, for I have no doubt that sooner or later they will find their way, free of charge."
>
> —Sendak (1988: 154–5)

I too hope all children find their way to where the wild things are, where they need fantasy or the imaginary world to master their strong emotions. I think it is not only children but also adults who need fantasy or imagination to control their violent emotions.

Children Meet the Troll or the Trial in Their Life in the Picturebook

In the project "Very Young Children and Picturebooks," I usually share the picturebook *The Three Billy Goats Gruff* (Figure 1.4), illustrated by the American artist Marcia Brown (1918–2015) with children in the last session. They have attended the class for three years, have grown to three-year-olds, and will soon go to kindergarten.

The three billy goats called "Gruff" try to cross a bridge over a mountain stream one by one, going from one bank to the other to survive. But lurking

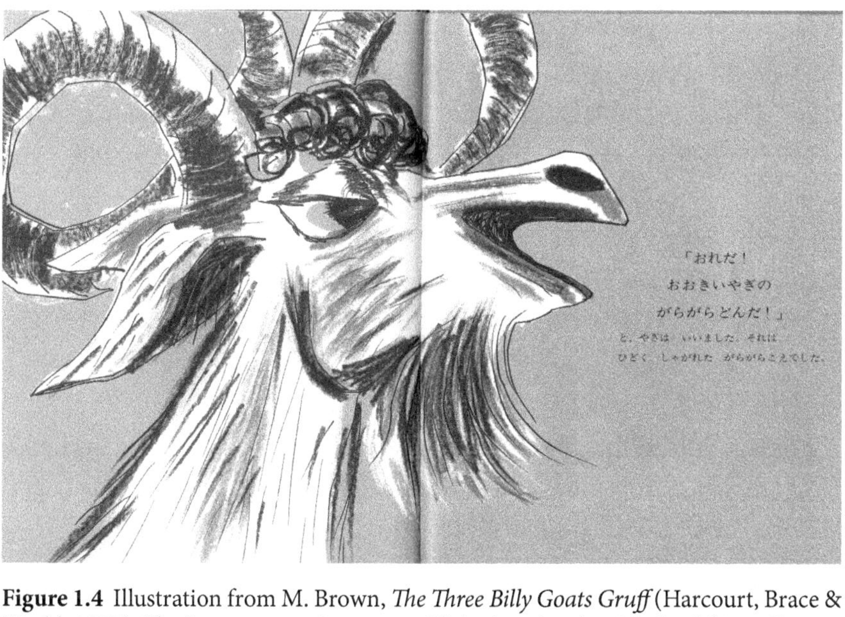

Figure 1.4 Illustration from M. Brown, *The Three Billy Goats Gruff* (Harcourt, Brace & World, 1957). The Japanese version was published under the title *Sanbiki-no Yagi-no Garagaradon*, trans. T. Seta (Fukuinkan Shoten, 1965).

under the bridge is a frightening troll. The first and the second goat confront the troll but are not mature enough to overcome it head-on. However, they do manage to cross the bridge using the best of their abilities. The third goat, being big enough to fight the troll, conquers it with a single run against it.

This picturebook tells a violent story and shows fierce pictures. The first few times I tried to share this picturebook with children under three, they rejected the book, turning their faces away or purposely running around the room. It meant they were not yet old enough to understand and appreciate this book.

On the last day of the class, all the children, who by then were older than three and a half, were ready to enjoy the picturebook. They were sitting in front of me when I began to read the picturebook aloud. Soon they were gripped by the story. They showed tension on their faces and in their shoulders, and they put their clenched fists on their knees, and they never turned their heads toward their mothers. They each were by themselves in the world of the picturebook. When I closed the picturebook, all of them let out a long breath and returned to the real world. They were old enough to enjoy the book.

Having considered in detail the relationship between the billy goats and the troll through the picturebook narrative, we can tell that this folktale is a story about the billy goats growing mentally and physically. "The tiniest Billy Goat Gruff" appears on the bridge looking tiny and weak with "such a small voice" (Brown 1957: 12). "The second Billy Goat Gruff" appears on the bridge looking more lively, and "his voice was not so small" (18). The third Billy Goat Gruff roars on the bridge: "It's I! The Big Billy Goat Gruff!" with "an ugly hoarse voice of his own" (25). The illustrations show the billy goats' physical features changing from being tiny, frail, and pale to being big, heavy, fierce, and dark. The words mirror their voices, changing from "such a small voice" to "an ugly hoarse voice." These changing bodies and voices tell us he is growing from a very young child to an adolescent youth.

I have to confess that, even though I had read this picturebook many times, I had not noticed that this is a story of a goat growing up, until children taught me. One day, having read this picturebook with three-year-old children, I noticed that the children were living in the picturebook, and they were growing in it, becoming the tiny creature first, then growing to the little lively one, and last to the biggest one, making themselves as big as they could. It can be said that the three goats represent one goat's growing up.

What is the role of the troll? What does the bridge mean? If the billy goats can cross over the bridge easily, smoothly, and without mishap—that is, if they live an easy life and never face hurdles and difficulties—they may not know how to confront hardships by themselves. The troll is a keeper of the bridge, and his presence in itself gives the bridge importance. The troll represents the trials that we all meet in our long journey through life.

When the children look at the picture of the climax (with the large head of the biggest billy goat) and they hear his hoarse voice, "It's I! the BIG BILLY GOAT GRUFF," they themselves become the biggest billy goat and puff out their chests proudly like the goat in the picturebook, as if they emerge from their chrysalis of young childhood and transform into the stage of being a big child. Even three-year-old children follow the narrative, "living" the passage from the tiny goat to the biggest, and at the end, their faces and bodies show their proud feeling: that is, "It's I!"

Just around this time, when they have been listening to me over three years, from being infants speaking no words to being three-year-olds running, speaking, and connecting with others, they begin to call themselves "I." Merleau-Ponty acknowledges in *The Child's Relations with Others.* He writes:

> "Use of the pronoun "I" comes still later than use of the proper name, at least as it is understood in its full meaning, i.e., in its relative meaning. The pronoun "I" has its full meaning only when the child uses it not as an individual sign to designate his own person—a sign that would be assigned once for all to himself and to nobody else—but when he understands that each person he sees can in turn say "I" and that each person is an "I" for himself and "you" for others. It is when he understands that even though others call him "you" he can nonetheless say "I," that the pronoun "I" is acquired in all its significance.
>
> —Merleau-Ponty (1964: 151)

It is interesting to know that young children call themselves "I" at the same time as they understand the concept of past, present, and future and that they are members of the people of the world. They start their life when they are born. After three years have passed, they stand at another starting line as an individual person proclaiming their own identity among others. The age of three and a half is a sort of watershed point that a child must overcome to grow further.

I want to add an unexpected result from the project "Very Young Children and Picturebooks." When some years had passed, I noticed a change in the mothers too. Ten mothers with babies visited my library twice a month for three years. I gave them some questions to answer in writing to find out why they wanted to participate in this project, such as whether there were any changes to their feelings or motivations after joining this group or whether they were still happy to attend classes.

The mothers wrote that the first motivation to come to the class was that they wanted to raise their children to be clever. They visited my library to make their babies love books and to read books well. However, they gradually came to be fascinated with picturebooks, which they now perceived to be so beautiful and profound. They even thought that they enjoyed picturebooks more than their children did.

There was another interesting comment about the project. One of the mothers wrote that the happiest moment for her was when her son stepped down from her lap and sat in front of a picturebook listening to the story and looking in fascination at the pictures by himself. She had been waiting for that day because the other children had done so earlier than her child. But, at last, the day came when I showed the front cover of *The Three Billy Goats Gruff* to the children. As soon as her son looked at the front cover, he got up from his mother's lap, walked a few steps to the picturebook, sat there, and stayed through the story from cover to cover. This episode of the child who stepped down from his mother's lap is illustrative: He was three-and-a-half years old, he called himself "I," and he could appreciate the picturebook *The Three Billy Goats Gruff*. All these developmental stages were reached at the same time.

And, moreover, these stages all happened in a situation of picturebook reading in a social place, where a mother and her child sit together. The mothers can also listen to the reader and look at the pictures, like their children, which means they can simply enjoy picturebooks just as much as their children.

The mothers can relive their own infanthood. And just as their children have passed a stage in their development, the mothers have also passed a stage in their maturing lives.

Conclusion

From sharing picturebooks with very young children between the ages of four months and three years old, I have learned many valuable lessons. They have taught me how they use their own body, which seems to me to be the phenomenological declaration by Merleau-Ponty (2012: ixxii) in *Phenomenology of Perception*: "I am the absolute source." The best way to grasp the world is not from taught knowledge or from digital machines like AI (artificial intelligence) but from "this particular body" (Merleau-Ponty 2012: 455). Descartes's famous proposition says, "I think, therefore I am." However, "I" should include the living body, if "I" exist in the world. We are born into the world with this body, and we come to confront things and people with this body. We are going to lose any hope for the future, if we lose the idea that we exist with the living body that is breathing—that is, we have a living, breathing body on a breathing earth in natural surroundings. My particular body is "the absolute source," even though it is vulnerable.

A picturebook is an experience similar to the one that Merleau-Ponty writes about when he talks about Van Gogh in *Phenomenology of Perception*: "Van Gogh's painting is forever established in me, a step has been taken that I can never take back, and, even if I hold no precise memories of the paintings that I have seen, my entire aesthetic experience will from then on be that of someone who has known Van Gogh's paintings" (Merleau-Ponty 2012: 413). If so, similarly, our entire aesthetic experience can be that of someone who has known a picturebook—and moreover who has shared it in our childhood with someone dear.

A picturebook can be an experience for children. When they are read *Inai-Inai-Baa* (Peek-a-boo) in their infanthood by a parent, they learn the concept of cause and effect. If they are read aloud the picturebook *The Three Billy Goats Gruff*, in which a bridge over a deep gorge is crossed, they learn that they will come across a trial in their own life: for example, a rite of passage such as becoming an older sibling, failing an examination, or having their heart broken. Children cannot live together with parents all their lives, but the memory of parents reading aloud to them will live with them forever.

A picturebook is a work of art available in our everyday life, unlike a painting by a famous artist, beyond the reach of ordinary people. I would like to end with a quotation from Merleau-Ponty about works of art. He writes:

> A novel, a poem, a painting, and a piece of music are individuals, that is, beings in which the expression cannot be distinguished from the expressed, whose sense is only accessible through direct contact, and who send forth their signification without ever leaving their temporal and spatial place. It is in this sense that our body is comparable to the work of art. It is a knot of living significations.
>
> —Merleau-Ponty (2012: 153)

My work over the years with picturebooks and very young children has convinced me that picturebooks are not only like works of art but that they carry the same, or even a greater, potential impact on the development of a child. My latest work *Ikirutame-no Ehon* (*Picturebooks for Life*) that was born from my long picturebook researching life is my gift for children and adults (Masaki 2023).

In this chapter, I aimed to deepen the reader's understanding of the importance of picturebooks in a child's life. I hope my discussion encourages readers to recognize the relevance of philosophical inquiry in various aspects of our existence and to appreciate the nuanced insights that can emerge from such interdisciplinary exploration.

Notes

1 The words "picturebook" refer to the kind of books in which pictures simply repeat the information contained in the words. Therefore, in the academic field of picturebooks and children's literature, the term "picturebook" was coined to refer to the more creative kind of books in which words and pictures are connected and designed parallelly or ironically and that make the narrative flow. One of the

earliest books that used the term "picturebook" is Barbara Bader's *American Picturebooks from Noah's Ark to the Beast Within* (1976), which was followed by that of various researchers, like Maria Nikolajeva's and Carole Scott's *How Picturebooks Work* (2001). I myself contributed one chapter to the book *New Directions in Picturebook Research* (2010), which was edited by Teresa Colomer, Bettina Kümmerling-Meibauer, and Cecilia Silva-Díaz.

2 A "double-spread" is a pair of facing pages in a picturebook.

3 Before the publication of *Where the Wild Things Are* (1963), Sendak had published a picturebook, *Very Far Away* (1957), in which a young boy Martin leaves home to be "very far away" because his mother is too busy taking care of a new baby.

4 Randolph Caldecott (1846–86) was a Victorian illustrator in England. His sixteen picturebooks, made in collaboration with the engraver-printer Edmand Evans, are recognized as the birth of modern picturebooks. The Caldecott Medal, the prize for the most prominent picturebook published in the preceding year in America, was named after him. The Caldecott Medal has been awarded every year by the American Library Association from 1938.

References

Bader, B. (1976), *American Picturebooks from Noah's Ark to the Beast Within*, Macmillan.

Brown, M. (1957), *The Three Billy Goats Gruff*, Harcourt Brace & World. Translated into Japanese by T. Seta as *Sanbiki-no Yagi-no Garagaradon* (Fukuinkan Shoten, 1965).

Bruner, J. (2002), *Making Stories: Law, Literature, Life*, Harvard University Press.

Bruner, J. S. and V. Sherwood (1976), "Peekaboo and the Learning of Rule Structures," in J. S. Bruner, A. Jolly, and K. Sylva (eds), *Play: Its Role in Development and Evolution*, 277–85, Viking Penguin.

Kai, N. (1992), *Chocho Hayaku Konaikana* (Butterfly, When Will You Come to Me?), Fukuinkan Shoten.

Masaki, T. (2006), *A History of Victorian Popular Picture Books*, Kazamashobo.

Masaki, T. (2010), "A Strawberry? Or the Planet? Children's Aesthetic Response to the Picturebook *Strawberries* by Susumu Shingu, Moving Art Sculptor," in T. Colomer, B. Kümmerling-Meibauer, and C. Silva-Díaz (eds), *New Directions in Picturebook Research*, 151–64, Routledge.

Masaki, T. (2018), *Merleau-Ponty to Kodomo-to-Ehon-no Genshogaku: Kodomo to Ehon wo Yomu-to-iukoto* (Phenomenology of Children and Picturebooks: Reading Picturebooks with Children), Kazamashobo.

Masaki, T. (2023), *Ikirutame-no Ehon* (Picturebooks for Life), Kazamashobo.

Merleau-Ponty, M. (1964), "The Child's Relations with Other," trans. W. Cobb, in J. M. Edie (ed.), *The Primacy of Perception*, 96–155, Northwestern University Press.
Merleau-Ponty, M. (2012), *Phenomenology of Perception*, Routledge. Translated by D. A. Landes from *Phénoménologie de La Perception* (Gallimard, 1945).
Nikolajeva, M. and C. Scott (2001), *How Picturebooks Work*, Garland.
Okamoto, N. (1982), *Kodomo to Kotoba* (Children and Their Language), Iwanami Shoten.
Okamoto, N. (2005), *Yojiki: Kodomo-wa Sekai-o Do-Tsukamuka* (Infanthood, How Children Comprehend the World), Iwanami Shoten.
Segawa, Y. (1967), *Inai-Inai-Baa* (Peek-a-boo), text by M. Matsutani, Doshinsha.
Sendak, M. (1957), *Very Far Away*, Harper.
Sendak, M. (1963), *Where the Wild Things Are*, HarperCollins. Translated into Japanese by T. Jingu as *Kaijutachi-no Irutokoro* (Fuzambo, 1975).
Sendak, M. (1988), *Caldecott & Co*, Farrar, Straus and Giroux.
Spitz, E. H. (1999), *Inside Picture Books*, Yale University Press.

2

Art as a Resource in Teaching

Using the Arts to Reflect on Critical Ideas in Different Subjects

Ann S. Pihlgren

Far down in the depths of the ocean on the sand lay an unread book. No one could tell how it came to be there. Perhaps it had accidentally fallen from a ship passing from one harbor to another. Or someone who didn't like the title had dumped it. Anyhow, there it was. The book moved slightly in the currents, but mainly it stayed in the same area between some rocks and stones. Fish would swim between its pages. Every now and then a crab sought shelter under the book's covers. Over time, the gilded title of the book got increasingly fainter until it was almost illegible. But the book remained in its place, waiting for its reader.

The teacher closes the notebook she has been reading and looks up at the class of fifth graders: "Please take a thinking pause and formulate a question that you would like to discuss based on what you are thinking now after hearing the story."

The Socratic seminar and other thoughtful dialogue methods explore ideas through a process of philosophizing (Pihlgren 2008). In this chapter, I will describe how artwork can be used as a way of discussing central ideas within every subject area throughout the school system by using Socratic dialogues. The examples of dialogues in the chapter were recorded as field notes during a project for the Swedish National Board of Education (in Swedish *Skolverket*), where I was constructing materials for teachers in different subject areas (e.g., Pihlgren 2012, 2014, 2023). The observations were carried out in different schools, with teachers using Socratic dialogues with students in grades K–12. The chapter will start with a brief account of the history of this kind of interlocution, discuss the use in classrooms, and finally end with providing some common methods to use in education.

General Education and the Socratic Dialogue

The Socratic methods have their origins within the *Bildung* movement, enhancing general education with the aim of becoming a thoughtful and well-educated human being. The *Bildung* movement spread widely during the beginning of the twentieth century in several countries, including Germany (*Bildung*), Denmark (*dannelse*), Sweden (*bildning*), and Greece (*paideia*). *Bildung* is most often referred to as "general education" in English, although this translation does not cover the full meaning of the concept.

Over time, several different methods stemming from the ideas of Socrates were developed to enable students to philosophize and think deeply about literature and artworks. Referring to Socrates is always problematic. Did he in fact exist? We know about him mainly from the works of Plato, but Plato uses the Socrates-figure as a main character in his writing for over forty years, and the person depicted in the early works of Plato is hardly the same person depicted in the later ones. However, the *Bildung* traditions rested on some of the features and statements of Socrates in Plato's early works, mainly these analogies (Pihlgren 2008):

- The self-stinging stingray analogy in which Socrates uses questions that will sting the participant with perplexity, getting him or her confused, but in the end also having the same effect on the questioner. The puzzle that has been investigated will not have a final answer but will continue to puzzle.
- The midwife analogy in which Socrates compares the role of the facilitator to that of a midwife—not giving birth to the facilitator's own thoughts but supporting the participants to deliver the best they can.

- The gadfly analogy in which Socrates compares himself to a gadfly sitting on the back of a big horse (the Greek state) and stinging it with annoying questions to make it move and change for the better.

These three analogies presuppose that what is sought is not a method but rather a thinking disposition and process in which the willingness to ask questions, analyze, and critically examine ideas lead to new insights and new questions for further investigation.

In the *Bildung* traditions, the Socratic idea of authentic discussion influenced a formal approach for group discussions with working-class men and women—for example, those in the free church or workers' union movements—as well as philosophy students at universities. A facilitator led the interlocution, mimicking the one used by Socrates in Plato's early dialogues. The participants strove to build a culture of dialogue that was permissive and open while also being critically scrutinizing and exploratory. The activity hence leaned on dialogic virtues, including listening to others and behaving civilly while supporting and referring to others. At the same time, it is an exploratory activity that will also scrutinize all statements closely and value their use in the dialogue.

In the preamble to this chapter, you get a glimpse into how a teacher employs these virtues. It is an account of how a teacher moves a dialogue through a series of questions using philosophy with children (PwC), a method that will be described later in this chapter. In the preamble, after reading the story that she has written as a starter, the teacher asks students to think about what they have just heard and formulate a question during a short one- or two-minute thinking pause. In this case, she asks students to confer in pairs to decide on a mutual question. They then share the questions with the rest of the class, and the teacher notes them on a whiteboard so that everyone can see them. Questions suggested by the students are "Why was the book dumped?" "Is a book a book if no one reads it?" "Is it a book or a house for crabs?" "What kind of story is this?" and "Can a book have feelings?" The questions tend to be more or less sophisticated, but the teacher writes them all down, reformulating them if necessary to make the meaning clear to all. She is acting as a midwife in this part of the dialogue, helping the students to think further and formulate their thoughts.

In a second thinking pause, the teacher asks that each student choose one question from the class list that he or she wants to discuss, and then a vote is taken. The teacher poses the chosen question "Why was the book dumped?" to start the dialogue and adds a follow-up question: "What different reasons can we think of?" Later, in the dialogue, the teacher centers the dialogue around particular concepts—such as "What is a book?"—to help students investigate more nuanced ideas. At this stage in the dialogue, the teacher aims at making the students question and reformulate their ideas, like in the gadfly analogy. In the evaluative dialogue held after the main discussion, some students comment that the dialogue really has made them think about ideas, including what it is to be a human being. The dialogue has functioned as a stingray, confusing and perplexing the participants but also helping them to find new ways to think about the subject in question.

Even though the students here chose a fairly simple question in the beginning, the core of the dialogue revolves around a more complex thought process: how to define and explore concepts. Literature helps students focus on the idea of defining, and the teacher's questions help students to probe deeper into the subject.

Socrates in the Classroom

In the classroom, Socratic methods are used to teach comprehension, particularly those involving discerning the meaning of a text or an artwork and exploring its ideas (Pihlgren 2008). Today, Socratic methods are used throughout school systems, from preschool to university levels, in several countries. An example is Sweden, where the National Board of Education includes Socratic seminars and other thoughtful dialogues in educational materials to enhance thinking and reading comprehension in all subject areas and with all ages. These materials include seminar materials and questions that involve students in topics such as student democracy and political influence and reading comprehension and teach about relationships, sexuality, and consent.

When a Socratic method or disposition is introduced into the classroom environment, something happens—it becomes a tool for teaching and learning and for enhancing personal intellectual growth and democracy throughout the curriculum. As you see in the following seminar examples, the key to Socratic dialogue is the act of questioning, as it is the power of questions that promote the quality of thinking and responses in a dialogue. Of course, the classroom is not purely democratic, as teachers always have a fostering role, but over time, students develop as proficient participants in an egalitarian dialogue. That is, they learn to act on the virtues of Socratic dialogue—of discerning meaning and questioning through discourse—when learning any subject. Socratic thinking and discourse, when they occur throughout the curriculum, create democratic opportunities for students to learn cooperative and supportive dialogue in their endeavor to better understand the knowledge and ideas in any subject area, something that has been shown in research (cf., Robinsson 2006; Orellana 2008; Pihlgren 2008).

In any seminar, in any subject area, the teacher plans by choosing the text or artwork and developing questions that accomplish the goal of the seminar. When using artwork, planning should focus on questions that help students analyze what central ideas the artwork evokes. The following is an example of a plan for a seminar with students in primary school using Wassily Kandinsky's painting *Black Spot* (Figure 2.1). The seminar starts with an opening question directed at all students. Then the plan includes analytical questions to use

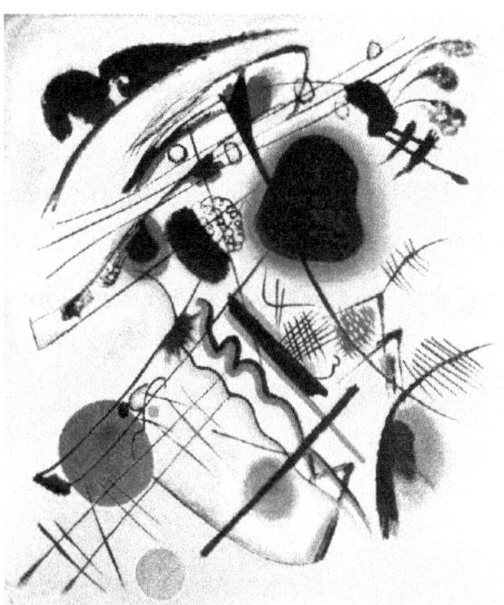

Figure 2.1 *Black Spot* by Wassily Kandinsky, 1921.

if needed to make the dialogue go forward. At the end of the seminar, an evaluative question helps students draw conclusions about what has been discussed. The plan has also identified some central ideas in the painting and connected it to further lessons in making music.

Plan for Socratic Seminar: *Black Spot* by Wassily Kandinsky

Central Ideas

Element, relation, form, feeling, alike and different, signs and symbols, art and music.

Opening Question

Which part of the picture seems important to you? Choose one and one that you think seems less important. Explain your choice.

Possible Questions of Analysis

- Of the parts that you chose, which ones seem harmonious (calm, happy), and which ones seem disharmonious (anxious, aggressive)?
- What role do the shapes play when you identify them as harmonious or disharmonious?
- What role do colors play? What would happen if we changed the colors? Will the feeling be different?
- If you were to put a sound to the shapes that we picked, how would they sound?
- The painting is called *Black Spot*. Why do you think that is so? Could it have had another name?

Possible Evaluative Questions

- Is the painting beautiful? Is it supposed to be beautiful?
- If you made a music piece, illustrating the painting, how would it sound?

- Why do different shapes and colors evoke different feelings? Are these the same to all humans?

A seminar can lead to additional activities. In this case, extension activities introduced the primary students to abstract art and contemporary music. For example, the students engaged in activities in which they illustrated the shapes with sounds, constructed symbols for the sounds, and wrote these down as a score. They later played the music for an audience. As the series of lessons was part of a longer thematic project, the activities later were connected to using Modest P. Mussorgsky's music piece *Pictures at an Exhibition*, in which the music illustrates a promenade at an art gallery, displaying different works of art.

Learning Through the Socratic Way

As stated earlier, when philosophizing methods enter the classroom, they do so in the service of teaching and learning. However, not only do students change their approach to learning, but teachers also change their approach and methods when teaching. For one, the teacher's role changes from being didactic—knowing the answers to the questions raised—to a role closer to Socrates' midwife, a first among equals. As facilitators, teachers do not give or evaluate students' answers. Instead, they support the exploratory and critical dialogue by asking questions, aiming toward deeper thinking, and by letting students elaborate on the answers collectively. However, not all statements can be accepted without motivating or substantiating the positions. For the facilitator, it is a balance between creating a culture that is permissive and respectful and at the same time allowing for the questioning of ideas and values. For many teachers, this takes practice and reflection (Pihlgren 2008). The teacher may have to guard his or her speech, gestures, and facial expressions by:

- asking questions, not giving answers,
- asking students to substantiate and motivate their points of view,
- finding counterarguments if the group does not so that the issue is illuminated from multiple angles, and
- not preventing contradictions and differences from being discussed.

My research shows that students also pass through different stages of development (Pihlgren 2008). When the group is beginning to understand the nature of the dialogue, some students intentionally break the rules to test them—by protesting too aggressively against something said or making disturbing noises, jokes, or provocative statements. One way to deal with this is to actually take the statement seriously: "I heard you said X. How does that solve the problem we are discussing?" This conveys to the students that they're allowed to think outside the box and that what they say will be taken seriously and scrutinized. Students may also make personal, revealing, or sensitive statements that should not be discussed in the group. This may involve private family relationships or personal feelings, such as "I hate my dad!" It is important to protect the student's privacy by bringing the conversation back to philosophical discussion by asking a more general question, such as "Is hating a parent the same as hating a friend?" The thoughtful dialogue is a philosophical conversation, not a therapeutic or psychological one. If the facilitator can handle possible disruptions in a constructive way, the chances increase that the student group will experience the conversations as meaningful. If not, the anticipated outcomes may not be achieved.

Accordingly, it is important that teachers nurture learning behaviors through open dialogues in a cooperative culture. One way a teacher can do this is by introducing dialogic rules that guide students to create the openness and cooperation necessary for a Socratic dialogue:

- We share our thoughts and ideas through thoughtful dialogue. The interlocution is an experience of shared inquiry through thoughtful dialogue. This means that students think carefully, and they collaborate to come to a better understanding—it is all about "group-thinking."
- We listen attentively to what others say: Listen to really hear what others are saying and what that means instead of just waiting for them to stop so you can start talking. Listening is one of the virtues that most students, who have participated in Socratic seminars, think is the main ability if you are to become a proficient participant.
- We respect that there are many possible answers. The questions asked do not have a single given answer; instead, responses call for interpretation and evaluation. However, some of the ideas presented might be more

useful or even truer than other ideas, and some ideas might be rejected when having been scrutinized.
- We can reconsider and change an opinion. This is the spirit in which the seminar should be held, with all students showing an open mind to new ideas and a willingness to adopt those that they find are better substantiated than others.

The Socratic dialogue in classrooms inevitably shows different features than the idealistic ones sought by the *Bildung* movement, as they become teaching and learning activities. Research shows that using the Socratic methods is an effective way, in fact one of the few, to enhance deep thinking and cognitive learning among students (Pihlgren 2008). The use of Socratic dialogues also has an effect on students' critical thinking, their language and social skills, and their character development, if they are used recurrently in the classroom (Robinsson 2006; Orellana 2008; Pihlgren 2008).

The kinds of learning that enhance thinking are illustrated in this example of a group of six-year-old students discussing eight reproductions of classic works of art. The seminar considers *Self-Portrait with a Bandaged Ear* by Vincent van Gogh, *The Scream* by Edvard Munch, *The Weeping Woman* by Pablo Picasso, *Water Lilies* by Claude Monet, *The Third of May 1808* by Francisco de Goya, *Imaginary Child* by Jean Miró, *We Hail Thee Mary* by Paul Gaugin, and *Self-Portrait with Thorn Necklace and Hummingbird* by Frida Kahlo. When conducting this seminar, it is not important what works of art the teacher chooses as long as they differ in expression and ideas. The works of art can be more or less contemporary.

- Step One: After introducing students to the eight pictures, which were spread out on the floor, the teacher directed each child to get four cards (illustrated in Figure 2.2): You may hear students make comments such as "I would like to have it at home," "I like it," "I don't like it," and "Anyone can make it."
- Step Two: The teacher asked each student to assess the works of art by putting each card under one of the pictures. They could put one or more under the same picture or all under different ones. They were told not to show each other what card they put where. When everyone had made their choices, the pictures were taken away and the cards were exposed,

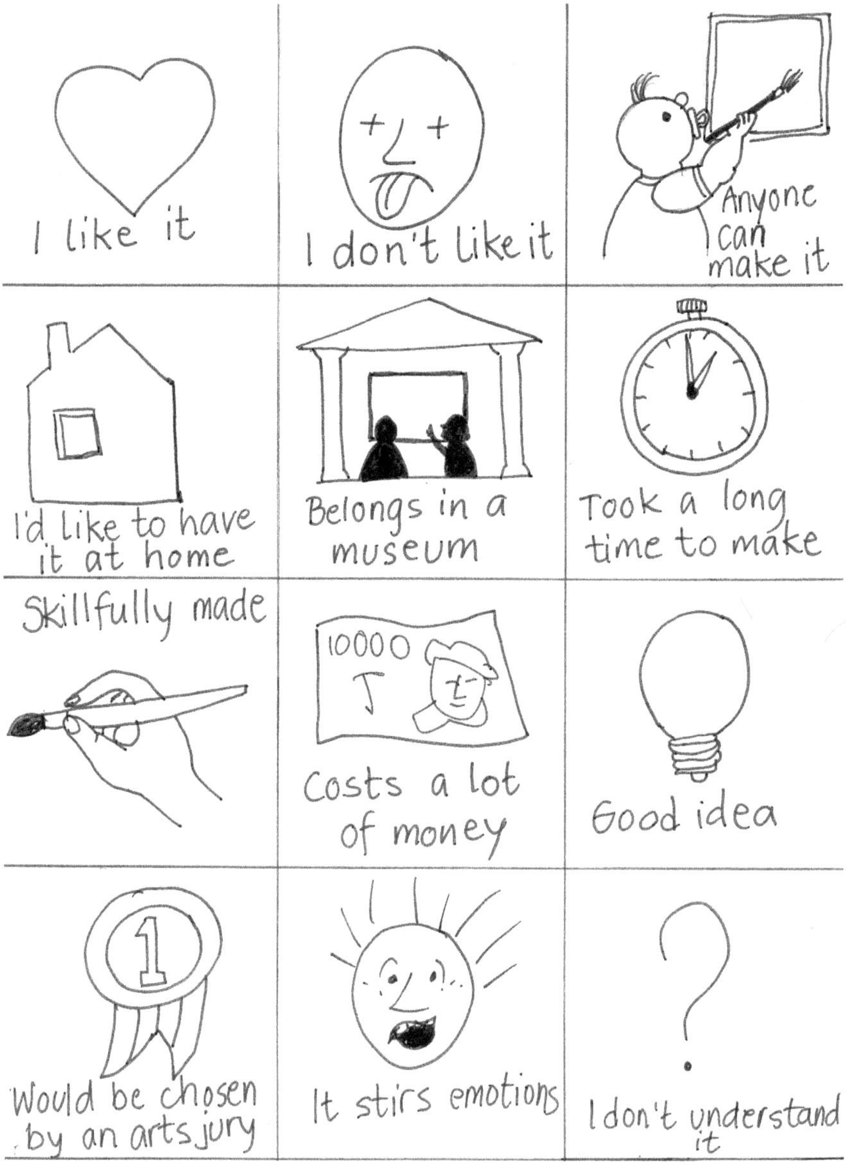

Figure 2.2 The sets of cards used to assess paintings. Illustration: Ann S. Pihlgren.

showing some patterns. Many of the students had put the "I like to have it at home" card under *Water Lilies*, "Anyone can make it" under *Imaginary Child*, and "I don't like it" under *The Scream*. The cards saying "I like it" were distributed on several pictures, without much pattern.

- Step Three: The first dialogue focused on why one would like something or not. During the dialogue, the students settled certain criteria for liking and not liking a painting: color, theme, and technique. They reasoned that the three paintings, chosen by many, had similar techniques, but the color and theme in *The Scream* made it unsuitable to have at home. *Imaginary Child* couldn't be considered art, the students argued, because they themselves had made similar (and better) drawings.
- Step Four: In a later second session, the paintings remained the same, but new cards were distributed with phrases including "Costs a lot of money," "Belongs in a museum," "Skillfully made," and "Took a long time to make." Several students put "Belongs in a museum" or "Costs a lot of money" under *The Scream* and *Crying Woman*. Many thought that *The May 3 Shootings* would have taken a long time to make and considered Kahlo's *Self-Portrait* skillfully made. This time the dialogue refocused, from discussing feelings to discussing what constitutes good art. The students argued that the art, considered good enough to go to a museum or worth a lot of money, was not always what they had judged as skillfully made.

This dialogue led to a third session where the cards included "It stirs emotions," "I don't understand it," "It would be chosen by an arts jury," and "Good idea!" In this session, all the pictures were chosen to illustrate some of the statements, and the choices were more diverse. The students also showed a deeper understanding of the essence of art in the third session, discussing how the idea of the artist might be more important than the techniques or the execution.

Using Art as a Resource for Philosophizing

Using artworks as a basis for philosophical dialogues may, for some, seem contradictory, since philosophy is often seen as a totally logical and analytical activity, while art is seen as something creative and perhaps even chaotic. However, the philosopher Michel de Montaigne([1580] 2008: 83), as early as 1580, pointed out that there is "nothing more airy, more gay, more frolic, and I had liked to have said, more wanton" than philosophy. Although artworks generally do not address facts, nevertheless artists, as well as scientists, use analytical and critical procedures during the creative process. Accordingly, artworks allow for a range of thinking, from discerning explicit meaning to interpretation (Lindström 2006). Knowledge and understanding cannot rely on scientific facts alone; human judgment also has to act on and be able to sort out the best way to act when no such facts are at hand (Bornemark 2020). Using art will give the teacher and the students possible ways to get closer to complex problems within each subject area by addressing them from a different, creative position (Shlain 1991; Roberts 2019).

Since school subject areas are organized as a part of that system of ideas, every subject has its own central ideas, and artworks can augment the understanding of key concepts and knowledge. In physics, for example, artworks help students understand key concepts, including force, power, and mechanics, and in language studies, they can explore central ideas in communication, grammar, and understanding (Pihlgren 2010). For the teacher, artworks in any subject can help him or her create opportunities for students to explore within subjects. It is while exploring these areas, supported by the questions from the teacher and the understandings of the fellow students, that a deeper understanding of the subject area evolves.

Socratic dialogues address the central ideas of humanity, those ideas that have been explored throughout the history of mankind (Adler 2000). Clearly the arts provide much material for delving into these ideas. There are several ways to work with art within Socratic dialogues. One way is to raise questions about the nature of art and its conditions or to interpret the message of the artwork. This purpose is closely connected to enhancing thinking and understanding in subjects concerning art, music, literature, dance, and other creative areas. The dialogue examples, represented in the text so far, can all be used in this way—the sunken book in literature; *Black Spot* in art, handicraft, and music; and the different artworks in art. However, there are also ways to use these dialogues in other school subjects, since they also focus on ideas that are general to human knowledge. The dialogue about the sunken book in fact raises questions of how to define and systemize, something that is an issue in all school subjects. The preschool dialogue about different paintings also raises the question of how choices are motivated, analyzed, and carried out—for example, questions in social science, general values, and to some extent, language. In the *Black dot* dialogue, the content could also apply to design and techniques, social science, and language, because the ideas center on interpreting expressions and conveying messages.

There is also a more direct way of choosing to use art as a starter in a subject area. Some artworks address particular events or recurrent, transferable historical happenings, as in *Guernica*, where Pablo Picasso depicts the massacre of the Basque town in 1937. The painting is used in history to discuss historical similar events and the dilemmas they present. In the ballet *The Rite of Spring* by Igor Stravinsky, the idea concerns human sacrifice. Teachers use this piece of music in social science to discuss modern equivalences, for example, the oppression of women in the name of honor or child marriages. Rembrandt's painting *The Conspiracy of Claudius Civilis* centers around loyalty and betrayal and is used to discuss contemporary parallels in social science, including uprisings and rebellion. In physics, there are several paintings that address central ideas like force, the law of gravity, and time, as does *Les Promenades d' Euclide* by René Magritte. In a Socratic seminar in physics concerning the laws of nature, a teacher used the painting *Time Transfixed* by René Magritte. The painting shows a steam locomotive forcing its way out of the wall in the middle of a fireplace. It seems to be steaming its way in full speed into an almost empty room except for a clock and two candlesticks on top of the fireplace. The questions asked during the seminar were: "How can we describe the room before the train enters?" "What happens to the room when the train enters?" "If we were sitting in the train, how would the experience be at this point?" "What physical laws seem to have been replaced here?" "How could the new laws be formulated?" and "How are living creatures dependent on the stability of the laws of nature and physics?" In the evaluation at the end of the seminar, the students stated that they had gained a different understanding of how the laws of nature operate at all times and how dependent their entire lives were on the reality that laws are stable.

Other artworks addressing ideas in physics include *Möbius Strip* and *Relativity* by M. C. Escher and *The Persistence of Memory* and *L'Enigme de Guillaume Tell* by Salvador Dalí. In biology, *Portrait of Siriaco* by J. L. da Rocha and *Tognina* by Lavina Fontana capture central concepts. *The Elements*, sung and written by Tom Lehrer, is a good choice for chemistry. And any music score can be used in mathematics as well as paintings, such as *The Sacrament of the Last Supper* by Salvador Dalí, which offers opportunities to consider perspective in arts and geometry.

The point here is that when teachers want to focus students on the big questions of humanity, many artworks are a good choice. There is much to draw on, as literary, visual, and performing arts can support and boost dialogues about the philosophical ideas relevant to each subject area. When arts are used, the discussion tends to open the mind to new ideas; it also helps students to enhance and widen dialogue and the ideas discussed. The use of art in the Socratic dialogues helps students to discard a stereotypical or prejudiced way of looking at problems (Pihlgren 2010). The dialogue starts in a general way, not directly connected to the problems or dilemmas of the participating students. Given time for inquiry and reflection, students will be able to see more than the surface of a problem. At the end of a philosophizing activity, the dialogue will inevitably get closer to the students' everyday life and to what could be learned from the dialogue and each other.

However, not all works of art serve as a basis for philosophizing. There has to be some ambiguity, a question raised, a dilemma, or a crack in the interpretation. Some wonderful works of art are beautiful and compositionally excellent but raise few relevant questions. An example is John Constable's landscapes with their overly romantic versions of rural life. Others, like Leonardo da Vinci's *Mona Lisa*, have undergone so many public analyses and references that students will end up mimicking the same ideas. If the teacher feels puzzled or even provoked by the artwork and if the work addresses more than one central idea, it is probably a good choice.

The use of art also makes it easier for a philosophically unskilled teacher to use philosophizing dialogues. Some artworks are so obvious they provide the seminar questions, and it will make it easier for the teacher to lead the students. This is especially true with literary texts when the text itself and the author often provide a clear voice in the dialogue. On the other hand, films, dances, and music can require teachers to identify obscure and hidden meanings and develop questions to engage students in those ideas. When using that kind of material, the teacher should give students opportunities to read, listen to, look at, and consider the material before the dialogue is held. For example, after watching the short film *Rebel Rocket Attack* by Banksy from 2013, as well as reading a newspaper article criticizing the film, students in a secondary social science class discussed questions related to how propaganda is used, the relationship between art and politics, and the limits of art. The students prepared for the seminar by looking at the video two times in class and once at home, reflecting each time over a question: "Who is depicted as good, and who is depicted as evil, and how is this done?" "What role does the boy play?" and "How is the technical quality, and why has the artist made that choice?" The repeated viewing and the questions helped the students to remember sequences in the film that they could later refer to during the dialogue. The teacher also had the opportunity to play parts of the film during the seminar for reference.

The Paideia Seminar

There are different versions of a Socratic seminar. One version is the Paideia seminar, which involves a structured way of discussing ideas embedded in a text or an artwork. Paideia, as do all Socratic seminars, employs literature, art, music, and artifacts in its seminars, and these materials serve as an additional "participant" in the discussion because the author, artist, or scientist are invisible but active members of the dialogue. The Paideia seminar is particularly useful when the teacher wants to direct the dialogue toward understanding a certain value or idea, as in the example of the plan for discussing Kandinsky's *Black Spot*, the sessions with the different paintings, and with *Time Transfixed* by René Magritte. Here, a dialogue about the poem by the medieval Persian poet Rumi, *The Chance of Humming*, is an illustration of the structure of the Paideia seminar. The poem was discussed in a secondary social studies class. The steps in the Paideia seminar are as follows:

1. The students study the poem closely by marking to identify specific reactions or questions. This could be done just before the seminar, as homework, or by the teacher reading a text aloud or showing the picture the day before. The important thing is that the students are given some time to study the artwork and think about questions that it might raise.
2. The seminar starts with the teacher posing an opening question. This is the only question that the teacher actually knows will be put to the group. The rest of the seminar will depend on what the students say. In the example, the following opening question was used: "What line in the text would you chose as the most important? Be prepared to explain your answer." After a short thinking pause, each student gives a short answer to the question.
3. At this point in the dialogue, students will have heard from others their ideas about the poem, and it is time to go deeper into the interpretation.

The teacher had prepared analytical questions to insert, if needed, into the dialogue. In this case, she had prepared questions such as "What is the most difficult: Being tied to the camel downstream, upstream, or to be standing on the two logs?" "What's the difference?" "Why does it say that all might be well with the world?" "What is meant by 'a reasonable plan'?" and "Why is the poem called 'The chance to hum'?" However, the questions are only used if the students are struggling to find questions or discussion topics themselves.

4. At the end, the teacher closes the dialogue by asking students to reflect on how the ideas in the poem and the dialogue might inform their everyday lives. Evaluative questions she had prepared and might ask are "What would you need right now to be humming in the present?" "Can you always live in the present?" and "What would be a reasonable plan for you, at this point?"
5. The seminar ends with the students evaluating their participation in the dialogue: "Did we think new thoughts? Did everyone get to speak?"

The steps of the Paideia seminar help students go from an intuitive pre-understanding and evaluation of the artwork and its meaning during the opening question to, when hearing the other students' ideas, gradually getting a sense of the different dimensions and ideas that the artwork evokes. This will in turn lead to a closer analysis, during the next stage of the seminar, when the material is scrutinized by posing questions about the material as well as to each other. At the end of the seminar, each student has come to a new understanding, though maybe still confused; though having considered ideas in a new light, students might not end in consensus. If the students as well as the teacher leave the seminar with more questions than they had when entering, it is a good seminar; it will provoke further thinking about the ideas in future seminars or when learning new material in other subjects.

PwC: Philosophy with Children

As in the Paideia seminar, PwC, detailed in the beginning of this chapter, uses a text as a starter for a dialogue, and it could be a work of literature, painting, sculpture, dance performance, or piece of music to set up the students' thinking and imagination. PwC is an open method, in which students choose the questions that they want to discuss (Haglund 2001). The teacher's role is to help students manage their questions and move through the steps in the dialogue process. She might also pose additional questions to enhance and deepen their thinking. A similar method, philosophy for children (P4C), uses prewritten texts and teacher materials complete with questions (Lipman et al. 1980; Børresen and Malmhester 2004). The teacher will have more help from the material, but the dialogues are also at risk of being less open to the students' ideas.

A PwC seminar where a local sculpture was used illustrates how this process unfolds. Students in grade 8 had just started studying a period of the emancipation of women, and the history teacher planned for a PwC dialogue outdoors at one of the local public art sculptures depicting women suffragettes. The students are seated on foldable chairs in a semicircle around the sculpture. The teacher conducts the PwC seminar sequence:

1. Introduction: A work of art is introduced, in this example, the piece of public art. The teacher here asked the students to study the sculpture by moving around and watching it from all directions.
2. A first thinking pause is introduced. Each student thinks about a question that he or she would like to discuss.
3. The teacher writes down the questions so that everyone can see them, for example, on a whiteboard or smart board. As the example dialogue was held outdoors, this was done on a big sheet of paper that the teacher eventually put in front of the semicircle. In the example, the students asked questions such as "Why are the women clenching their fists?" "Why are they dressed in fancy hats if they are out to fight?" "What is worth fighting for?" "What risks would you take and for what?" and "Are there suffragettes today?" The students might suggest questions that the teacher considers silly or provocative; however, it is important to write down all questions as if they are serious contributions. It is part of the PwC process of learning to take responsibility for mutual dialogue.
4. A second thinking pause is introduced. Here each student is asked to choose one of the suggested questions. They can choose their own question, but they might also find that a more interesting one has been suggested by someone else and pick that one.

5. The group then decides what question should be discussed. This might be done by voting, checking which question everybody has chosen, by discussing and choosing one in consensus, or by discussing all questions in turn. Even though the group chooses one question to start with, all questions might come in handy during the dialogue.
6. The dialogue starts when the students address the chosen question. In this example, the group chose "What is worth fighting for?" and the teacher added a second question to help the students sort out the problem: "What different reasons can we think of?" After listing to the reasons, the question "What risks might be considered?" was asked to help the group further investigate important criteria.
7. When the discussion is over, the students are given a third thinking pause, where they think about the conclusions they draw from the dialogue.
8. The dialogue is then evaluated, something that is done in all of the Socratic methods: "Did we think new thoughts? Did everyone get to say what they wanted?"

In PwC, teachers give students opportunities to choose what questions are discussed, making the dialogue more open to the ideas of the students, than in the Paideia seminar. On the other hand, the PwC method also puts a higher stress on logic. The teacher could promote this in the dialogue by asking students to reflect over things using questions such as these (Børresen and Malmhester 2004):

- Finding similarities and differences between the presented ideas. (How is Ana's idea similar to Ali's?)
- Find counterarguments and alternatives to what is said. (Could one think in a different way?)
- Separate truth and untruth. (Is this real or fiction?)
- Choose criteria. (If a fight should be successful, what criteria must it show?)
- Fantasize, doubt, and ask. (What would happen if …? What seems questionable or odd here? What questions would you ask if you hear …?)

Logical thinking is not about training students in mechanics or rote knowledge. Instead, it is about helping students think carefully and thereby get access to different ways of analyzing and understanding the world. A playful atmosphere, where omissions and flaws are permitted as long as one is prepared to reconsider one's ideas, nurtures the best culture for testing new, brave ideas.

Philozoo: A PwC Method

Another methodological approach to PwC is philozoo (De Schrijver et al. 2018). It was originally developed to be used in dialogues in the natural science subjects in preschools and schools. The group is introduced to one or several evaluative questions, varying with what subject area is targeted. Working with art as a subject area, questions like these could be selected:

- Could anything be art?
- Could an artwork be done by someone else than an artist?
- If a picture hangs in an art museum, is it art?
- Is a rubber duck art, or could it become art?
- If someone pays you a lot for one of your drawings, is the drawing art? Are you then an artist?
- Can an art object stop being art?

Similar questions could be used as starters when working with natural science: Can you measure a cloud? Can a rabbit be a scientist? May the water run out? or questions in social science or ethics: Who has the right to decide over others? Can a child tell a parent off? Do you have to be friends with everybody? To clarify different ways of expressing oneself, different animals are used as symbols, see figures 2.3–2.8:

- The questioning fox asks questions about what is being discussed.
- The argumentative moose argues for a certain point of view.
- The exploring octopus examines and explores what is being discussed.
- The fact owl states and tells facts about the area.
- The doubting sheep expresses hesitation or doubt about something.
- The fantasy butterfly fantasizes about what is said.

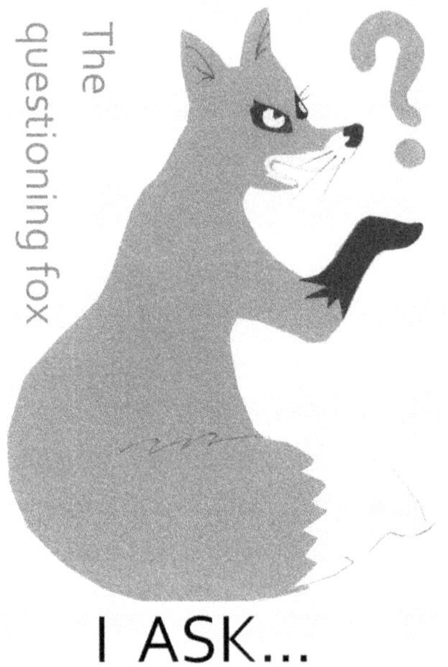

Figure 2.3 The questioning fox. Illustration: Ann S. Pihlgren.

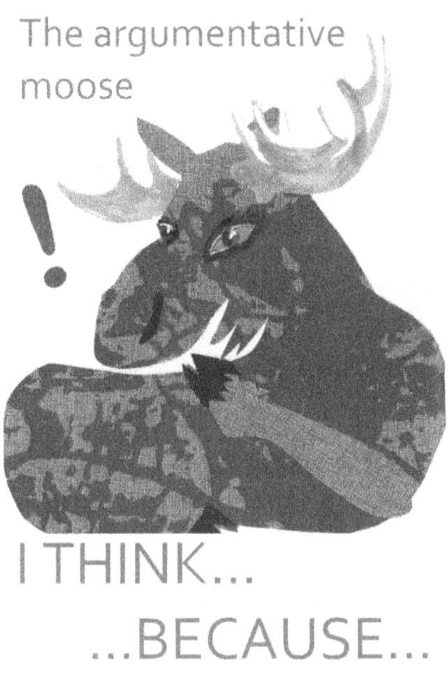

Figure 2.4 The argumentative moose. Illustration Ann S. Pihlgren.

Figure 2.5 The fact owl. Illustration Ann S. Pihlgren.

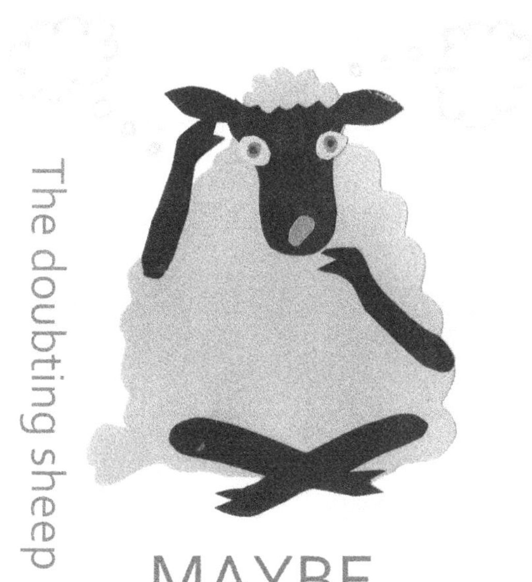

Figure 2.6 The doubting sheep. Illustration Ann S. Pihlgren.

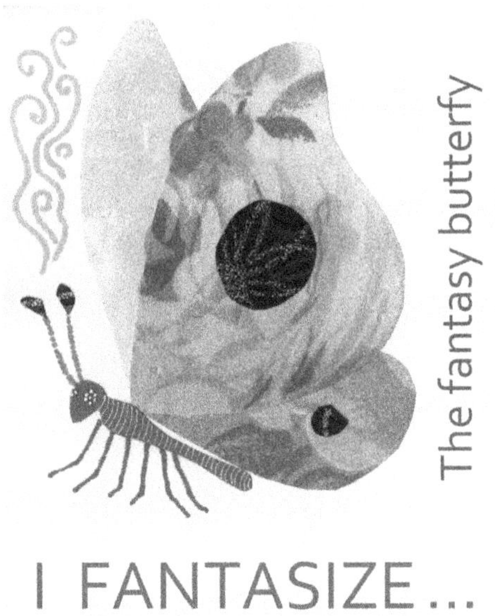

Figure 2.7 The fantasy butterfly. Illustration Ann S. Pihlgren.

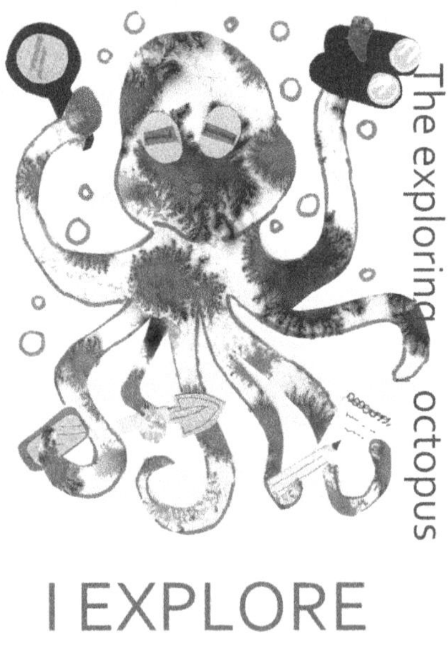

Figure 2.8 The exploring octopus. Illustration Ann S. Pihlgren.

The teacher introduces the animals to the students. During the dialogue, the students use the animals by pointing to them and saying things like: "I'm the octopus, I want to investigate if that is true"; "Now I am the sheep, I don't really know what to think"; or "I'm the fox, and my question is, What is art, really?" This way, the understanding of the different ways to express ideas in a discussion is broadened. With time, the students can also unveil patterns in their own approaches in dialogues. A progression in thinking can also be reached by letting the students pick an animal card and formulate a question, statement, doubt, and so on, depending on what card they picked.

PRI: Philosophy, Reflection, Insight

PRI—philosophy, reflection, insight—is a method in which philosophizing is combined with art production: drawing, painting, or clay modeling (Wrangsjö 2016). The art production is used to reach intuitive levels of understanding concepts and ideas. By using both head and hand, the participants reach the subject area from a less intellectual direction to start with, a way that helps to play down the somewhat intimidating notions of "philosophy."

The advantage to this method is that it can be used with any concept or idea in any school subject area. The concept used in this example is taken from a biology class in grade 7: "variation." These are examples of steps that a teacher might use with a group of students:

- The teacher presents an idea or a concept to be discussed, or the students might agree on an idea or concept. In this example, it is something that the students have been studying for a while: Darwin's theory and concept of "variation."
- The teacher asks the students to draw, paint, or clay-model individually their conception of the idea or concept, preferably not using words. In the example of "variation," the teacher chose to ask the students to clay-model their illustration.
- Students then share their works and ideas in pairs, concentrating on finding similarities and differences, for fifteen to twenty minutes (or shorter when the students are younger).
- The pairs are organized in groups of four to six students, and the teacher or group chooses a group facilitator. The students now present their ideas from

the pair discussion to the group of four to six students. The group looks for similarities and differences in the conceptions of the idea/concept in dialogue for around twenty to thirty minutes (or shorter when the students are younger). In the example, the students found that they all have depicted animals, some in several different stages of development. A difference was that some students had depicted the reason for the variation due to some outside factor (e.g., the giraffe needs to get to the leaves in the high tree and therefore develops a long throat), whereas some had depicted a variation as a developmental change due to a selection of individuals (e.g., it is more advantageous for giraffes to have long throats, because they can reach higher leaves. Therefore, high-throated specimens will survive better and carry on that gene to their breed).

- Each group presents the main ideas they have been discussing in the larger group, and these ideas are discussed by the whole class. In the example, the main discussion centered around the ideas of transition and development, and the different effects these would have on breeding animals or manipulating crops, for example.
- As in the other Socratic methods, students evaluate the dialogue in a meta-dialogue: "Did we think new thoughts? Did everyone get to say what they wanted?"

The PRI is an even more open approach than several of the other methods mentioned in this chapter, because it starts in the precognition and intuition of the participants, whereas the other presented methods provide materials to support new ideas. This openness can pose a risk, resulting in shallower reasoning if students or the chosen group facilitators are less experienced in philosophizing dialogues. However, the connection to art production, as well as discussing with other students and listening to others during the dialogue, puts the students in contact with the more intuitive aspects of philosophizing by giving students a deeper, more visceral insight than when only using critical reasoning.

Some Final Reflections

Philosophizing and art production have much in common. They both depend on hard intellectual work from the executor, and they both require creative and cognitive leaps. However, artists tend to start their exploration using a sort of brainstorming phase followed by critical analysis and evaluation (Lindström 2006), whereas philosophizing is intellectual and often starts with a critical analysis and evaluation before moving on to a creative phase. The two activities aim to achieve different goals even when working on the same subjects: Philosophizing aims at reaching better solutions and getting closer to what is true, whereas art aims at challenging established solutions or truths. Art thus takes philosophy by surprise, and opens the mind to new revelations.

Research has found that the kind of deep and interpretive analyses that students make in a Socratic dialogue can also help them when encountering difficulties and colliding values (Orellana 2008; Pihlgren 2008). Importantly, it can also help them make decisions in their lives (Pihlgren 2008). Having gained competence in the Socratic way of thinking, they have the means to understand themselves and the world better. This was also an important question for the *Bildung* movement: "How can I use art, music, dance, and literature to live a good life?" This is an experience with the arts I wish every student would acquire in preschool, school, and higher education.

References

Adler, M. J. (2000), *How to Think About the Great Ideas. From the Great Books of Western Civilization*, Open Court.

Bornemark, J. (2020), *Horisonten finns alltid kvar. Om det bortglömda omdömet*, Volante.

Børresen, B. and B. Malmhester (2004), *Låt barnen filosofera. Det filosofiska samtalet i skolan*, Liber.

de Montaigne, M. ([1580] 2008), *His Essays, Letters, and Journey Through Germany and Italy*, J. W. Moore.

De Schrijver, J., J. De Poorter, E. Cornelissen, and R. Anthony (2018), "Can a Rabbit Be a Scientist? Pilot Study on the Introduction of Philosophical Dialogues in Flemish Science Classes," in F. G. Moriyon, E. Duthie, and R. Robles (eds), *Parecidos de familia. Propuestas actuales en Filosofía para niños*, 238–50, Anaya.

Haglund, L. (2001), *Att tänka noga*, Tiden.

Lindström, L. (2006), "Creativity—What Is It? Can You Assess It? Can It Be Taught?" *International Journal of Art & Design Education* 25 (1): 53–66.

Lipman, M., A. M. Sharp and F. S. Oscanyan (1980), *Philosophy in the Classroom*, 2nd edn, Temple University Press.

Orellana, P. (2008), "Maieutic Frame Presence and Quantity and Quality of Argumentation in a Paideia Seminar," PhD diss., University of North Carolina.

Pihlgren, A. S. (2008), "Socrates in the Classroom. Rationales and Effects of Philosophizing with Children," PhD diss., University of Stockholm.

Pihlgren, A. S. (2010), *Sokratiska samtal i undervisningen*, Studentlitteratur.

Pihlgren, A. S. (2012), *Våra bästa samtal*, Norna förlag.

Pihlgren, A. S. (2014), *Fler eftertänksamma samtal*, Norna förlag.

Pihlgren, A. S. (2023), "Del 7. Eftertänksam dialog," *Läslyftet Skolverket*. Available at: https://larportalen.skolverket.se/moduler/M000/7 (accessed November 12, 2023).

Roberts, T. (2019), *The New Smart. How Nurturing Creativity Will Help Children Thrive*, Turner.

Robinsson, D. (2006), "The Paideia Seminar: Moving Adding Comprehension from Transaction to Transformation," PhD diss., University of Massachusetts.

Shlain, L. (1991), *Art and Physics. Parallel Visions in Space, Time, and Light*, Quill William Morrow.

Wrangsjö, S. (2016), *What Is Time?* Field notes from workshop held at the annual meeting of the Swedish Society for Philosophical Practice, January 13, Stockholm.

3

Rethinking the Yellow Sun

Pia Houni

Do you remember your first drawings in childhood? On a piece of paper, you drew some plants, the sun, maybe clouds, some birds, and of course yourself or family members.[1] We all drew a yellow sun on the paper because someone told us that the sun is yellow. Perhaps we had experiential knowledge about the sun and its strong rays on our faces. From our earliest days, we learned that the sun is yellow. Much later, we formulated a question: "What color is the sun?" Do you remember asking this question? At what age? Perhaps in childhood or in high school? From our very earliest days, we humans have a strong impetus to ask relevant questions about our own life and the environment in which we are living. Then, as we grow, an important time for this questioning is early adulthood, when many of us also discover an interest in philosophical thinking.

The yellow sun is a metaphorical example in this chapter, in which I study the possible relationship between art and philosophy. The metaphor I use here represents the idea of how art and philosophy can have the capability of teaching us to see life from new perspectives.

Questions provide power for philosophical thinking, and they stimulate the artistic mind and creativity. In both art and philosophy, there is an interest in exploring life through questions, perceptions, experiences, emotions, and reasons. There are hardly any theoretical approaches to looking at the crossing points of art and philosophy. Of course, on the perimeters of the topic, to name a couple, there is the philosophy of art, which studies from an aesthetic point of view, and art therapy, which works as a therapeutic model. One path to follow the possible relationship between art and philosophy is by understanding their roots from ancient Greece. After pre-Socratic philosophy, the ancient Greek tragedies were an important field for developing philosophy as well. These tragedies raised existential and moral questions for our viewing. After the golden time of tragedy, prominent philosophers such as Plato and Aristotle became important commentators.

Aristotle's first principle in his little book *Poetics* is *mimesis*. "Mimesis"—Socrates' word—means some kind of "representation" or "imitation." For Aristotle, human behavior is imitative and natural (*kata physin*, 1447a12); it is based on action, reaction, repetition, and adaptation through behavioral memes. After his first principle, Aristotle noticed that if mimetic arts imitate people in action, then such people are either virtuous or vicious, and the imitation will therefore be either elevated (*spoudaios*) or base (*phaulos*) (Aristotle 1448a2–5; Critchley 2019: 196–8).[2]

In this chapter, I will consider the theoretical and practical connections between art and philosophy. I understand this connection to be a potentially fruitful way to develop philosophical practice. This is also connected to my interest in developing *art-based philosophizing*.[3] Throughout this developing, I will present some theoretical views that I have found to be important to bear in mind when working with art and philosophy together. My purpose here is not to present one theoretical or practical model as to how to work in art-based philosophizing but rather to be open as to how to develop this way of working. My main argument in this chapter is the following: Art can help one's philosophical mind. Why is this important? In the action of philosophical practice, we underline diversity and equality. Traditionally, philosophical thinking is not easy, and people without education shy away from it. Art is usually nonformal and easier to approach without in-depth knowledge. The dialogue between art and philosophy can create a stronger impact than their separate activities. We also have important research evidence (e.g., Fancourt and Finn 2019) on how art impacts well-being but less knowledge on similar effects of philosophy—except for the emerging issue of existential health.

In this chapter, I will briefly describe the possibility of dialogue between art and philosophy. Subsequently, I will explore the learning points from ancient Greek tragedies, with particular emphasis on creativity. Next, I will examine art as "a strange tool" and how it can be a part of philosophical practice, focusing on cognitive, practical, and well-being aspects. Finally, I will share two case studies, employing a reflective mind, to demonstrate how art-based philosophizing is an interesting way to work in the field of philosophical practice. My cases aim to demonstrate what we can do when art and philosophy work in dialogue.

What Is Art? What Is Philosophy?

Lucia Berlin (1936–2004), the American author, used to say that the "most important thing in life is a good story" (Davis 2019: 7). This apparently lightweight motto is deeper than it seems. Since the earliest days of the history of literature, the idea of "story" has been one of the most relevant aspects to consider in the study of the human mind and behavior.[4] Our nature is to be organizers, and one example of an organized activity is conversation—the level of consciousness, we might say, when two people talk, express ideas, and pay attention to each other. Conversation has a function—or rather functions and purposes—and is a fundamental mechanism for relationship building, living together, and problem-solving (Noë 2015: 6–7).

In the moments when we are exploring our complex lives and hoping to find answers, we evaluate our meanings, knowledge, and experiences. Basically, this activity is almost the same as walking, eating, talking, perceiving, or driving—we do not take a jump from one to a hundred kilometers per hour to become good at, or become a specialist in, these activities; rather, we practice, repeat, test, and organize our experience to understand more deeply how to do things, what is most important, and how to adapt this information to daily life (see Nelson 1949).

It is difficult to define what *art* is and what *philosophy* is. A long heritage has created varied meanings and contents for these words. Generally, we have located these words, at least in Western history, in the ancient Greek period (around 500–300 BCE). At that time in ancient Greece, the concept of "art" was understood as the skill (*tekhne*) and talent of a person, but it did not represent an individual's creative expression as we understand it today. The artist was a person who was skilled in *mimesis* (imitation). The definition of "art," as we usually understand it, entered our modern English language repertoire much later. *Philosophy* literally means "love of wisdom," and it is the study of basic ideas about knowledge, truth, morality, ethics, religion, nature, and the meaning of life, to mention but a few. *Philosophical practice* is guided by the same issues. In philosophical practice, we are interested in *practical* elements and tools such as how to make wisdom and philosophical education part of daily life. For this reason, philosophy is something a person must exercise, as we have learned from ancient Greek and Roman philosophers and, of course, from our own contemporaries (see, e.g., Hadot 2002).

In the next short paragraph, I will propose standpoints that I understand to be important for the interaction between art and philosophy. Very often, people in public forums have various opinions about the essence of art and philosophy, as seen in common statements such as "Art is wild and creative" and, conversely, "Philosophy is rational" or "There is no historical connection between them" or comments like "Imagination and logicality cannot go together." We like to keep our thinking in boxes and within safe parameters. In rethinking the yellow sun, we can wonder what kind of creativity philosophy needs or if creative thinking is limited only to the world of art. Philosophical practice itself is a good example of this. From its early days, philosophical practitioners broke away from the academic, intellectual way of seeing philosophy. Leonard Nelson, Gerd Achenbach, Pierre Hadot, Lou Marinoff, Ran Lahav, and many others have developed thinking toward entirely new concepts in philosophy. Without creativity, this could not have happened.

Learning from Philosophical Dialogue in the Ancient Greek Tragedies

Many philosophers have written about how tragedies are important works of literature in history. It is relevant to say that philosophy is based on this literature. There are two good arguments for looking back on ancient Greek tragedies. The first one is its close ties to philosophy. These ties existed in the early days of philosophy, reflecting the significant influence of tragedies on philosophical thought. The second point is the method of dialogue. The tragedies, dated between 500 and 400 BCE, fall within the timeline from the pre-Socratics around 600 BCE to the period when classical philosophy was emerging, often considered the "birth of philosophy." These tragedies were, after Homer's time (approximately 700 BCE), a form of literature—dramatic performances in which their content (family stories, mythology), characters, and plots addressed strong emotions, moral issues, and the question of what it means to be human. All this happened in a new way—performed through a dialogical technique on the stage in front of the audience.[5] It is easy to empathize with the power of these experiences. Tragedy shows what is perishable and what is fragile. Tragedy provokes what snags in our being—the snares and booby traps of the past that we blindly trip over in our relentless, stumbling, forward movement (Critchley 2019: 3). Aristotle, who wrote his *Poetics* about a hundred years later (330–320 BCE) than the tragedies first played in Athens, approached drama philosophically. He thought that ethical principles constructed through drama made an emotional impact, and for this reason, the skill of the playwright was important. In his study of tragedy, Aristotle focused his attention more on textual details than on performances. This is an important research difference for classicist and theater scholars. Classicist scholars are mainly interested in language. In theater studies, people are interested in performances—what happens on the stage. I believe that for philosophers, both elements are interesting. Both theater scholars and philosophers have an interest in language and performances. I understand that the knowledge of tragedies might support us in our efforts to understand more deeply the heritage and connection between art and philosophy. Perhaps the ancient tragedies should be a basic reader for philosophical studies. To gain a deeper understanding of tragedies in the context of literature and philosophy, we need to look at the dialogue (like Plato, who used dialogue in a very dramatic and creative way). In learning more about the nuances of dialogue, we approach creativity and philosophical practice.

Aristotle wrote in the *Poetics* that all the ideas for tragedies are inside the family. Ancient Greek tragedies were the first dialogical lessons for us to learn about the dynamics of emotions, power, and relationships. One epistemological element that constructs our view is creativity. But how can we explain creativity? The history of philosophy, art, and science regards creativity as extraordinary and, in that sense, exceptional. Typical attitudes come in two variations: "creativity as realized by exceptional people or by exceptional cognitive processes" (Kronfeldner 2018: 213). We can even combine this with another attitude—that creativity is a mystery that cannot be explained (Kronfeldner 2018: 213). In the *Ion*[6] dialogue, as well as in the *Phaidros* and the *Menon*, Plato recognized that creativity is characterized by two aspects: originality and spontaneity.

Creativity: A Difficult Word

We can think of creativity as being the opposite of routine production and technique. It involves originality and spontaneity, and both these criteria (originality and spontaneity) can be fulfilled in degrees, and in that sense, creativity comes by degrees too (Kronfeldner 2018: 215). Creativity possesses value, and in contemporary life, we live in a creativity-obsessed society. Assumptions about what creativity is, why it is valuable, and how to promote being creative might be paradoxically misguided (Gaunt and Kieran 2018a: 1–21). Morgan and Nelligan (2018) call the creativity-obsessed attitude the "creativity hoax." The heart of the creativity hoax suggests that you are defined by your potential—you *are* what you *aim to become*—and that you can claim an occupational identity even when you make your living doing something else.

When we are thinking about creativity and philosophical practice, the next questions are important: Are we doing something to call up "new ideas," or are we studying something we already know? This is easier to understand in the context of art but more difficult in the context of philosophy. Do we accept that creativity belongs in philosophy as it belongs in art?

We naturally link creativity with art but not so often with philosophical thinking. We are not used to saying that, for example, Aristotle or Wittgenstein presented creative ideas—usually, we resort to more intellectual terms to describe a philosopher. I see this as a mistake because thinking is, generally, a creative process. In philosophical practice, we again have the space to explore these types of thinking mistakes and how the philosophical process could be creative as well. Maria Kronfeldner (2018: 225) tries to summarize the difficult task of explaining creativity with the following words:

> Creativity is hard to explain, like the weather. As science has made progress with the latter, it will make progress with the former as well. Complexity is a practical, transient obstacle not an in-principle one. It is also likely, given the ordinary process view, that creativity is not an ability that only few of us have. . . . Not everyone is a creative storm that changes the intellectual landscape. Yet, as we learned from the early Greek philosophers who started to emancipate philosophy from

> religion, even a storm operates on natural principles; these are the same principles that account for a mild, refreshing wind on a normal day. No exceptionalities or mysteries are needed to account for either of them. The same holds for creativity. No special process, no exceptionalities are needed to explain any of its occurrences, be it wild or mild.

When we are thinking of art and philosophy, we cannot forget the *philosophy of art* and research activities in this field. The philosophy of art is focused on topics such as aesthetics, artworks, art marketing, art in society, art education, and so on (Young 2001; Eldridge [2003] 2009). When I discuss the connection between art and philosophy in this chapter, my approach is generally to explore what kinds of benefits, tools, and practices we can develop for philosophical practice.

Art as a Strange Tool

Many people perceive philosophy as difficult, highly theoretical, and abstract—accessible only to those with extensive education. However, philosophical practice aims to break free from this perception, and art serves as an excellent partner in this endeavor. By engaging with art, we look at the yellow sun differently. Similarly, philosophy teaches us to shift our viewpoints and explore different ways of thinking. Art is, in many ways, a "strange tool" in our life, and perhaps for this reason, it has also attracted strong opinions, attitudes, and arguments around it. Anecdotally, at least in public, people seem to have much to say about artists' work and art in society (and this appears to be the case in Finland, where I reside). By this, I mean the public expression of commonly held opinions such as when people do not understand a piece of art, when they wonder why the government has to pay artists' salaries, and so on. Perhaps these are also partly an imaginary view of art in society. The term "strange tools" comes from a book by Alva Noë. In his book, he is considering what art tells us about ourselves. He clarifies the idea of art as a "strange tool" against the backdrop of technology. He writes, "Artists make stuff, after all: pictures, sculptures, performances, songs. And art has always been bound up with manufactures and craft, with tinkering and artifice" (Noë 2015: 98).

Noë's idea holds potential for my topic and work in this chapter. Of course, art is not itself one of our technologies, but technology, as a practice of making, is no contribution to art. It is its precondition. A work of art is a strange tool because it is an implement or instrument that has been denuded of its function. Art is an enemy of function; it is the perversion of technology—and this view provides a rich opportunity to look at philosophical approaches (Noë 2015: 98–9). Noë believes that there is an intimate link between technology and organized activities, and this means a tool (like a hammer or a computer) because a tool is the hub of organized activity. With four arguments, Noë (2015: 19, 98–100) tries to explain this: Technology is natural for us; the scope of technology is broader than clothing, utensils, and dwelling; tools help us solve problems (and also enable us to frame new problems), and tools are useful only against the background of our needs and capacities.

For example, when we think of the works of Shakespeare, Sarah Kane, Marina Abramovic, Florentina Holzinger, and many others, we might understand how important it is to consider what is meant by observation, experience, and emotion and how art can be our guide to the "essentialness" questions. Art does not represent the world for us. It demonstrates what we are not able to see. Art offers us an opportunity to see how we construct a life of consciousness. The brain, as an individual organ, does not make observations itself; rather, active humans or animals do so. In a natural sense, we are organizers and designers by nature, and art will cause these practices to start up and enable reorganization. Art is communicated through physical, bodily processes, as can even be observed or measured through the sciences of cognition and neurology; art is always an aesthetic experience, and it is through the language of aesthetic experience that art speaks to us (see also Fancourt 2017).

Benefits of Art to Our Well-Being and Health

In this chapter, I would like to highlight one important research area and discuss the benefits of art. We do not have much evidence-based data about the positive impact of philosophy toward well-being, though the data we do have shows much potential for well-being (see, e.g., Feary 2002; Knox 2020, 2023; de Miranda 2024). Additionally, projects that incorporate philosophy in prison settings have demonstrated the profound benefits of philosophical thinking as an important tool for personal development and well-being (Brune and Gronke 2010; Barrientos-Rastrojo 2023).[7] The meaning and position of art and culture in society have changed significantly over the last ten to twenty years. Economic growth and effectivity have forced us to look at art and culture in a new light. On one hand, this is a fascinating situation: When we focus our attention on the question of how art can be an investment in well-being, we are simultaneously looking back at history. The ancient Greeks understood the impact of art on people. For example, medical science was born in a very close connection with art and environmental aesthetics. The important name here is Asclepius. He is considered the founder of ancient Greek medicine and is depicted holding a rod with a snake coiled around it. In their chapter "Science in Greece: From the Age of Hippocrates to the Age of the Genome," Falagas et al. (2006: 1946) explain that Asclepius

> was sanctified during the 6th–5th centuries BCE and gave his name to the "Asclepiads" who were priest-healers serving in the "Asclepieia." Asclepiads exerted beneficial influence on patients suffering mainly from psychosomatic diseases. Asclepieia were both temples dedicated to Asclepius and healing centers. Asclepieia were located in scenic and rather isolated regions, near mountains or natural springs and can be imagined as modern spas. They were well organized and many of them included a library, a stadium and a theater. Moreover, medical schools existed within these temples. Proper diet, baths and exercise played key therapeutic roles.

It is not easy to define "well-being." Even in the medical field, there are various theories on this topic. One of the more prevalent understandings is the self-reported experience of one's own well-being. In other words, people tell their story about their understanding of their own well-being. As Foucault argues, modern Western medicine introduced clinical categories pertaining to mental health that produced specific types of deviant identities and enabled greater state control over the identification and separation—both spatial and ideological—of "ill" and "healthy" populations (Kokanovic and Stone 2018, referencing Foucault). In the ethical sense, there is always "good" autonomy of patient and "good" for medicine.

In November 2019, the World Health Organization (WHO) launched a report by Daisy Fancourt and Saoirse Finn (2019). This report quickly "went viral" on the internet due to its sheer size. The number of references cited in their report was enormous. They indicated around three thousand research references on the positive impacts of art on well-being and health. Even though these numbers are impressive, it is wise to understand the different categories these results fall into. In the report, the authors collected and analyzed key research data and produced evidence that art and cultural activities have a positive impact on well-being and health. Two years later, Fancourt's research group also published a new review article in *The Lancet* (2021) about how leisure activities affect health. In this report, the researchers identified over six hundred potential mechanisms of action through which leisure activities might affect health. Some of these mechanisms represent immediate responses to leisure activities, whereas others are proposed to emerge over time or through changes in broader aspects of human development and behavior. When people are healthy, the body can be bracketed off from their daily perceptual experience of themselves. In illness, however, the body interrupts the fantasy of mastery, making its presence known and felt, exposing itself for what it actually is—the material foundation of subjectivity. Illness interrupts comfortable certainties by forcing open the perceptual gap between doing and being, where the "doing" of life is restricted or confined when the body loses some or all of its capacity to function or is affected by serious psychological trauma: "It is only when something goes wrong with the body that we begin to notice it . . . the harmony between the biological and the lived body is disrupted and the difference between the two becomes noticeable" (Carel 2013: 31).

Gillie Bolton, the British pioneer of therapeutic writing, has talked about the important role of medical humanities. Bolton says that many professionals, such as therapists, argue that people do not need to *write* their stories. But once a story has been written, read, and discussed, these professionals understand how an artistic process can significantly develop a person's perceptions and understanding (see Parker 2018; Guttensen 2024). Why is this important? Bolton (2011) explains:

> We do not go to a particular section within a file, a drawer, a cabinet in our memories; we go to a particular place in a narrative—an association of events, faces, voices, places, foods and senses of roughness or softness. Since the Enlightenment we have suffered under mechanical metaphors that depict bodies and minds as "machines." Yet we are not machines. Our feeling, cognitive, physical, spiritual selves are intermixed; they condition and are conditioned by political and cultural contexts. All are experienced, understood and expressed as narrative.

Art-Based Philosophizing—Two Cases

In this part of the chapter, I would like to look more closely at two cases of art-based philosophizing workshops that I have facilitated. Over the last ten years, I have facilitated many workshops where art has been a key element in driving the dialogue. Because I am a trained Socratic facilitator, I am used to borrowing ideas from the Nelson-Heckmann tradition but also working flexibly within the structure of dialogue. My interest in finding a bridge between art and philosophy stems from my own art education, as well as art philosophy and extensive experience with how art and artists communicate philosophical issues in their work or in public. The American philosopher Vaughana Feary wrote an article nearly ten years ago, in which she introduced seven models for understanding the role humanities play in philosophical counseling and consulting. Her seven models are the representational, the expressive, the phenomenological, the narrative, the developmental, the transformative, and the revolutionary (Feary 2005: 95–112). What I find interesting here is how theoretical approaches can be useful together with art to serve clients in counseling or participants in Socratic dialogue.

The term *art-based philosophizing* describes the main idea of my workshops, where art techniques connect to or serve as an impulse for philosophizing. In my workshops, I use different types of art mediums: literature (poems, ancient tragedies, short novels, creative writing), fine arts, theatrical tools, photography, sound design, and so on. All the workshops follow a similar basic structure: starting with art-based activities, questioning, choosing a topic, dialoguing, and reaching a conclusion. The workshop ends with a meta-dialogue. Generally, I do not give too much information beforehand—only basic instructions such as bringing a specific item with you or wearing comfortable clothes.

First Case: Art and Philosophy Workshop—Berlin, Germany

Fifth Colloquium on Dialogical Philosophizing. August 11–15, 2017, Berlin, Germany.

"The Logic of Question and Answer"—this was an international conference, where philosophical practitioners offered lectures and workshops. The organizer of the conference was PPA (Philosophisch-Politische Akademie).[8]

The Theory

In the beginning of the workshop, I shortly addressed how art can benefit our thinking processes. To clarify some ideas for the participants, I lectured briefly in the beginning of workshop. I introduced a few perspectives on how art benefits our thoughts. I will briefly describe these perspectives. One important view is to see that the creative process can manifest memories, feelings, and illogical ideas, like imagination. Art can be a way to see unusual elements together, and this in turn might cause new thoughts in our minds. In philosophizing processes, we are looking for a logical structure of thinking, and art can help us understand this more deeply. Also, art can give us ideas for thinking processes themselves. Finally, art can be used as an impulse to support dialogue. One of my theoretical views behind this workshop was "the schemas" introduced by the French philosopher Alain Badiou. He wrote from a historical perspective that connection between art and philosophy can be understood in three schemas via a question of truth: the didactic schema, the romantic schema, and the classical schema (Badiou 2005). I believe

Badiou's schemas are relevant pedagogically for my workshops and also in understanding the different views of philosophy vis-à-vis art.

The Practice

We started the workshop in Berlin with some easy body improvization, like walking and shaking hands. After warming up to being in the same room together, I introduced a group collage work. I had asked people to bring objects from their room or bags, something belonging to them. The objects were placed on a side table. The items included things such as an umbrella, a small bottle of sparkling wine, running shoes, pencils, a lipstick, and a book. We assigned a space on the floor, and I instructed everyone to take one object from the table and set it on the floor in a spot of their choosing. The goal of the process was to make one collective collage work. Every participant knew that they would make a collage artwork without talking and negotiating with each other. They were allowed to change places between any objects but not use any words. After a reasonable time, I checked if the art piece was ready or not. When they accepted it to be ready, we moved to look at the final version, and I asked participants to name this art piece, like artists do for their works. Suggestions were written down, and then the participants voted on the final name. The piece this group created was called *Memorial*. After this point, activities turned toward philosophizing, and we loosened the artistic view. Participants formulated a question from the name of the art piece. The question guided us to the dialogue. The allocated time of the workshop was not enough to follow the correct structure of Socratic dialogue in the Nelson-Heckmann (1949) tradition, but we covered a few perspectives of the question; we shared examples and made arguments against or on behalf of these points. Because of the name *Memorial*, the dialogue handled aspects such as eternity, memories, and remembering. At the end of the dialogue, we tried to write down a sentence or short comment about the question.

After the dialogue, we returned to the beginning, the artistic part. I asked participants to compare their sentence with the art piece and share some thoughts. Generally, people were surprised at how strongly these two

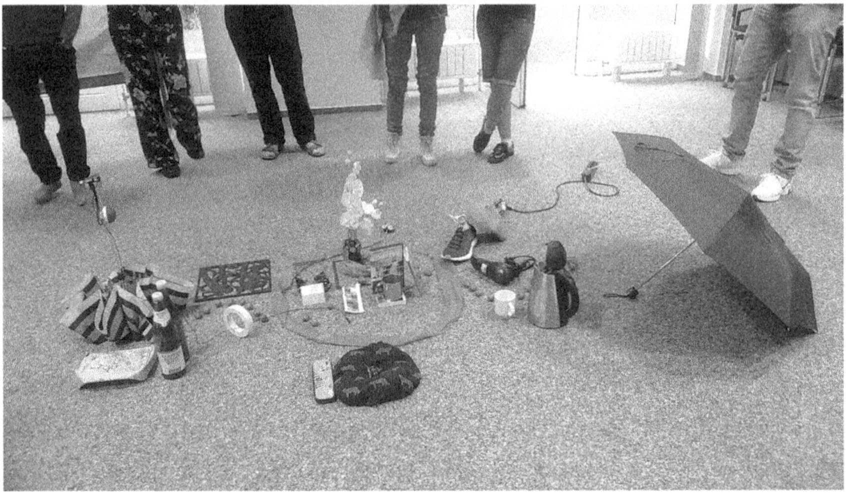

Photo by Pia Houni.

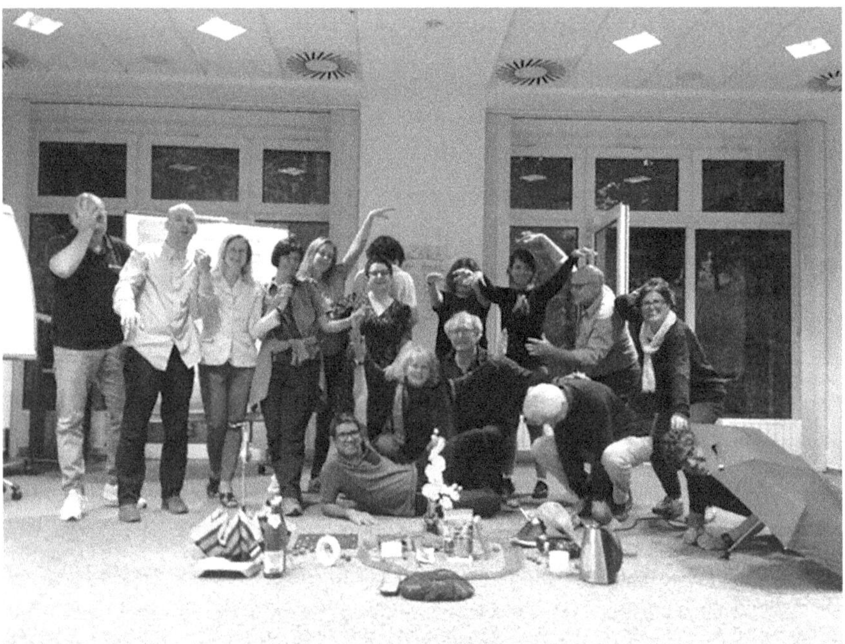

Photo by Pia Houni.

different elements connected with and enlightened each other. The other final action was to make a group statue. This was a nice and relaxing part, as the participants settled around the collage work and wanted to represent *Memorial* using their bodies. People who had done improvization before knew very well how to make a group statue. I must admit that we also laughed, as the statue reminded us of the Soviet Union from the era of sculptures—a famous statue like the Millennium of Russia. The final round of the workshop was a meta-dialogue, where participants shared their experiences without comments by others.

Second Case: Boundaries of Self-Portraits—Workshop

Eighth International Conference. Limits-Borders-Boundaries. August 2–8, 2019, Springe, Germany.

This international conference gathered philosophical practitioners together to offer lectures and workshops. The organizer of the conference was PPA.

The Theory

The idea for this workshop came from contemporary selfies. It is basically impossible to avoid seeing people take selfies everywhere. This led me to reflect on the history of portraits and the theoretical concept of identity. The first selfie was taken by Robert Cornelius in 1839. When he took this famous picture with the new technology of the lens, he wrote behind the photo: "The first light Picture ever taken, 1839."[9] Much later, in 2013, the word *selfie* was accepted into the *Oxford English Dictionary* as "a photograph that one has taken of oneself, typically one taken with a smartphone or webcam and uploaded to a social media website."[10] Before modern technology, selfies or portraits were paintings. For most artists, its target was to favor its subject, just like selfies do today. I am sure we are all aware of how deeply we are living inside a visually dominated world. In the 1970s, many theorists started paying attention to visual culture, like John Berger (1972) in his book *Ways of Seeing*. A number of other scholars followed suit, such as Jacques Lacan, Jackson Pollock, Stuart Hall, Roland Barthes, and Jean-François Lyotard. It is important to note that the interest in visual culture permeates several researches—for example, in the television and internet fields. Perhaps in philosophy, our example could be the phenomenology of Merleau-Ponty, who wrote about how we receive information through our senses.

The approach for this workshop also builds on the previous theoretical ideas combined with our daily passion to take selfies everywhere we go. It is shocking to discover how many people have died taking selfies. Dangerous places or situations directing people to find unique photos have resulted in these horrific deaths. Approximately over half a million animals suffer around the world due to tourism and selfies. In 2022, approximately 379 people around the world died while taking a selfie.[11]

The Practice

Before the workshop, I asked participants to send me selfies that they would be willing to share with the group. Everybody did, and some even sent several photos. People who could not participate in this workshop (but who were involved in the conference) asked permission to send selfies as well and gave me the right to use their photos as material. We made a collage of these selfies on the wall. People had the right to organize the selfies as they liked. People who had signed up for the workshop but were not present got a place on the wall under the headline: "Missing persons." The selfies were all very different. Some were up-and-close face photos, others more like an office profile, few were taken somewhere in nature, and there was even a nude photo.

After observing the photos together, we started talking about why selfies are so important to us and how selfies construct the identity and stories of our lives. An interesting aspect was to realize how much selfies offer people the option to play with and modify the photos and of course repeat the same photo with different layouts or filters to find the best image. We can create stories, visualize situations, look for compassion, and share daily life.

After this part of the workshop, people were divided into smaller groups. I gave them paper, colors, pens, and a short list of questions. Their task was to choose one or two questions and delve deeper into them. They were instructed to form a visual presentation of the group work and hang it on a clothesline that I had set up in the room earlier. Every group shared their presentation, and after a full round of presentations, we turned back to look at the original wall of selfies, where we started. The wall looked different now than when we started our workshop. There were empty spaces after people had removed selfies to use in their own group. It was a little surprise to participants how strongly these empty spaces on the wall impacted their imagination and feelings. They argued that take-off selfies—the empty places—represented our destiny, the point of life when we are not part of others anymore. We are like an empty space on the wall. It was meaningful for participants to share their definitions together and listen to others.

I collected some final comments and thoughts on how people described their own process in the workshop. Interesting questions were mentioned, like "How does a self-portrait help a person feel beautiful?" "Is there a difference between the modern selfie and self-portrait painted by a painter?" and "When does it make sense to take a selfie?" Participants described the process with short words, like artificial, self-presentation, a mask, and so on. "Photos can

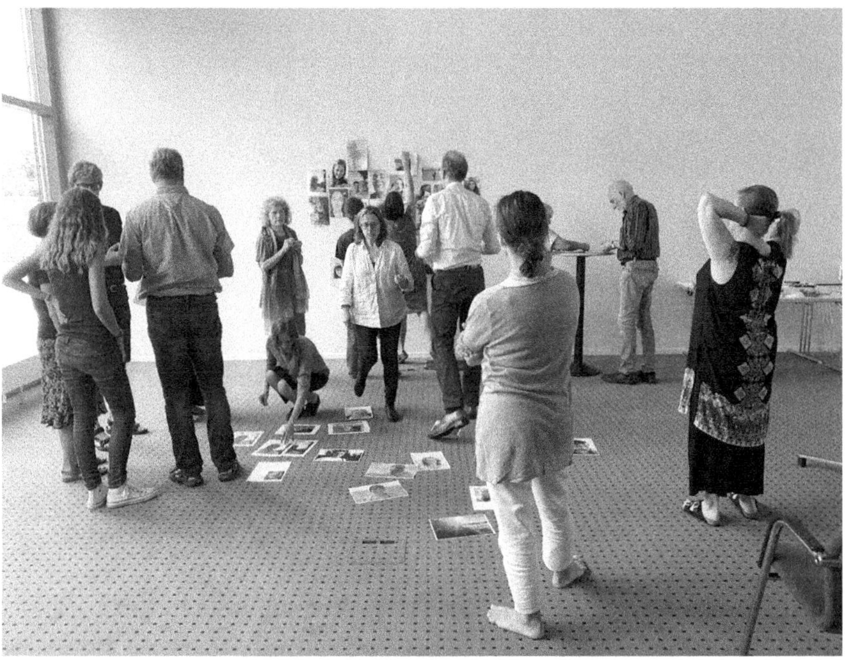

Photo by Katrin Blödorn.

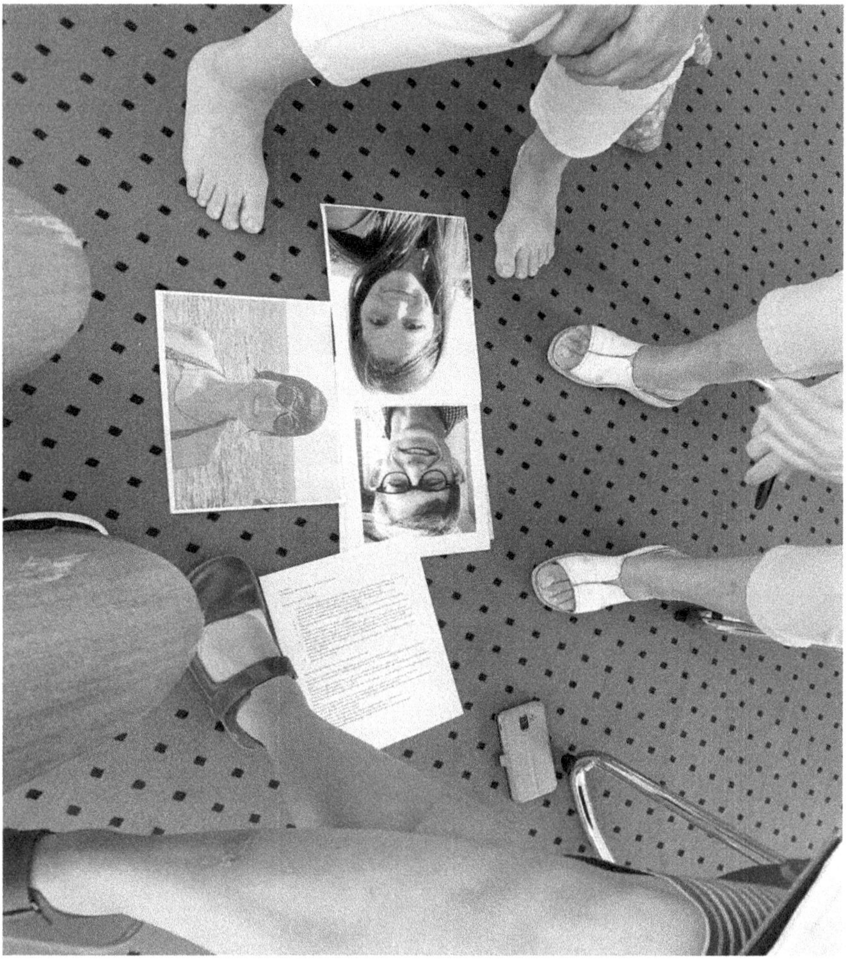

Photo by Pia Houni.

tell a story to yourself and others" was a common statement that participants shared after the workshop.

What Color Is the Sun?

Is the sun yellow? No, the sun is not yellow. The sun is essentially all colors mixed, and partly for this reason, the sun appears white to our eyes. The yellow sun is the phenomenon that we can observe. When we observe something, we usually use our senses to get information. Some of this information might be intellectual, but mostly, our first impression is experiential or based on emotions. In some cases, we connect this individual information to common knowledge and start to analyze and connect information about our previous experience. It is a subjective impression to think that the sun is yellow, but it is also interesting to connect this with knowledge and facts. I understand how this combination makes life meaningful. The ancient Greek word *dunamis* represents an aspect of the human good (Aristotle), usually being translated as *potentiality*, but which can be translated also as *capability of existing or action* (Sen 1993: 30). Some theorists, like Martha Nussbaum, have been interested in possibilities for a good life in democratic societies, and one perspective on this is talking about the capabilities that a person has. Nussbaum (2010: 78–80; 2013) has listed the following basic capabilities that are important to us: life; bodily health; bodily integrity; senses, imagination and thought, and emotions; practical reasoning; affiliation; other species; play; and control over one's environment.

We all are living in some society. We have dreams, hopes, and plans. There are many colors in society, sometimes like a rainbow, sometimes more scales of gray. We are always standing on the ground and look at things from this point. What we see around us and how we understand it are important for our life as individuals and as part of a community. When a society calls itself a democracy, it declares its responsibility for providing capabilities for all its members. A decent society cares about the dignity of its members, including the more vulnerable ones. Social justice means opportunities to participate and express oneself without punishment. Art is a "language," to which we have a right throughout life as a consumer, hobbyist, or as an educated artist. I believe that individuals and communities who participate in art activities get to know themselves better, gain stronger skills of empathy, through which we can live improved lives. The spirit of natural justice[12] cannot tolerate systematic humiliation by its basic governmental institutions. Without self-respect, there is no point in doing anything whatsoever. Without self-respect, one has no sense of value or any sense that life has meaning (Margalit 2016). This is important for both Nussbaum and Margalit, and for this chapter, because the idea of a democratic society means rights, duties, and capabilities for all members. Both Nussbaum and Margalit have also presented some critical arguments against the idealistic idea of a democratic society. In many societies, who understand themselves as democracies, rights and capabilities are not equal. If considered part of society, art and philosophy should be a privilege for all members. Art and philosophy, separately and together, imply possibilities for education, critical thinking, creativity, and other important indicators for a good life—nobody wants to deny this. Art and philosophy can support a democratic society, as both art and philosophy encourage reflection and dialogue. A person who considers and assesses arguments rather than following the crowd is a benefit for society (see Nussbaum 2010). So let us keep rethinking the yellow sun.

Notes

1 I would like to thank Jeanette Bresson Ladegaard Knox for the opportunity to write this chapter and for her patience with the timeline schedule. I also thank Julie Dyson for the language revisions. I take all the responsibility for the final version. My warm thanks to Ina Morsdal for her ideas and suggestions for this chapter.

2 I would like to make a note here and recommend further reading: Critchley (2019), Rorty (1992), and Halliwell (1998). Aristotle's idea of *mimesis* is important because his thinking has long prevailed in theoretical studies of art and philosophy. In the works referenced above, scholars explore what *mimesis* is and how differently, for example, Plato, Kant, and Hegel understand it. Of course, the ontological aspect is relevant: Do we repeat and represent life or not? This is a very interesting approach for philosophical practice as well.

3 I usually refer to my work as *art-based philosophizing*, but this is not engraved in stone. There are other suitable ways to refer to it as well. The fact is that I have not found a better expression that can include different types of art activities. I would also like to mention some colleagues who have been working in, thinking about, and developing this field with me, such as Adam Wallenberg (Sweden), Kati Kuula and Elise Liikala (Finland), Irena Boso (Russia–Netherlands), Kristin von Hirsch (Norway), and Mitsuru Mizutani (Japan). I also opened a Facebook group about seven years ago for philosophical practice and art.

4 Storytelling through oral tradition dates back to different points in history. These traditions use song, chant, and epic poetry to tell stories that have been handed

down from generation to generation. Myths were also first passed on through word of mouth, and this was the ground on which ancient Greek tragedies were born. The earliest surviving texts of plays are seven tragedies by Aeschylus, dating from the first half of the fifth century BCE. Why are these dramas so important here? They all represent our natural inclination to recycle stories and to learn about politics, family and city, passions, and morality. As Simon Critchley (2019: 34) has written, "Tragedy is the experience of moral ambiguity. The right is always on both sides and invariably also wrong. Justice is conflict . . . which means that the justice is divided."

5 Dialogue was a strong way to express the thoughts of characters and to develop dramatic action and plot. It is not surprising that Plato used the same "method" led by Socrates.

6 For theater scholars, the *Ion* dialogue is important. Perhaps for the first time in literature, we can read theoretical ideas about what creativity is and what the role of the performer is. At the end of the dialogue, we can read the word *enthusiasmos*, a kind of spiritual or divine power that permeates Ion throughout his performance. This means that Ion is not an individual artist; rather, his talent is alive by the grace of the gods. Historically, as far as I know, the next important instance of theatrical advice or theorizing appears in Shakespeare's *Hamlet*. There is a scene in which Hamlet directs the actors on how to play. We can take this text to be the first extant "acting manual."

7 It is important here to mention a few other names who have done philosophy in prisons: Marianne Walderhaug, Are Seljevold, and Anders Holt in Norway; Vaughana Feary and Maria da Venza Tillmanns in the United States; Kristof van Rossem in Belgium; and Olli Kaarakka and Pia Puolakka in Finland.

8 Available at: https://www.philosophisch-politische-akademie.de/ppa/ (accessed February 24, 2025).

9 Available at: https://blogs.loc.gov/loc/2022/07/robert-cornelius-and-the-first-selfie/ (accessed February 24, 2025).

10 Available at: https://global.oup.com/news-items/11001744/word-of-the-year-selfie-2013?cc=fi (accessed February 24, 2025).

11 You can read more about this topic, for example, in these news articles: Euronews Travel, available at: https://www.euronews.com/travel/2024/01/16/selfies-are-more-lethal-than-shark-attacks-should-more-tourist-destinations-ban-them and from BBC News, available at: https://www.bbc.com/travel/article/20240101-are-we-seeing-the-slow-decline-of-the-travel-selfie (accessed February 24, 2025).

12 In English law, natural justice is technical terminology for the rule against bias (*nemo iudex in causa sua*) and the right to a fair hearing (*audi alteram partem*).

References

Aristoteles (2000), Aristoteles IX, *Retoriikka, Runousoppi* (Rhetoric, Poetics), Gaudeamus.

Badiou, A. (2005), *Handbook of Inaesthetics*, Stanford University Press.

Barrientos-Rastrojo, J. (2023), *Experiential Philosophy and Prison: Training for Social Disintegration*, Philosophical Practitioners Association of India.

Berger, J. (1972), *Ways of Seeing*, British Broadcasting Corporation and Penguin Books.

Bolton, G. (2011), "Keep Taking the Words: Writing to Help with Anxiety, Depression and Mental Health," in G. Bolton (ed.), *Write Yourself: Creative Writing and Personal Development*, 99–114, Jessica Kingsley.

Brune, J. and H. Gronke (2010), "Ten Years of Socratic Dialogue in Prisons: Its Scope and Limits," *Philosophical Practice* 5 (3): 674–84.

Carel, H. H. (2013), "Illness, Phenomenology, and Philosophical Method," *Theoretical Medicine and Bioethics* 34 (4): 345–57.

Critchley, S. (2019), *Tragedy, the Greeks and Us*, Profile Books.

Davis, L. (2019), "Alkusanat 'Tärkeintä on hyvä tarina,'" in L. Berlin (ed.), *Siivoojan käsikirja 2. Tanssia ruusuilla (A Manual for Cleaning Women: Selected Stories by Lucia Berlin)*, Aula.

de Miranda, L. (ed.) (2024), *Philosophical Health. Thinking as a Way of Healing*, Bloomsbury Academic.

Eldridge, R. ([2003] 2009), *Johdatus taiteenfilosofiaan* (An Introduction to the Philosophy of Art), Gaudeamus.

Falagas, M. E., E. A. Zarkadoulia, I. A. Bliziotis, and G. Samonis (2006), "Science in Greece: From the Age of Hippocrates to the Age of the Genome," *FASEB Journal* 20 (12): 1946–50.

Fancourt, D. (2017), *Arts in Health: Designing and Researching Interventions*, Oxford University Press.

Fancourt, D., H. Aughterson, S. Finn, E. Walker, and A. Steptoe (2021), "How Leisure Activities Affect Health: A Narrative Review and Multi-Level Theoretical Framework of Mechanisms of Action," *Lancet Psychiatry* 8: 329–39.

Fancourt, D. and S. Finn (2019), *Health Evidence Network Synthesis Report 67: What Is the Evidence on the Role of the Arts in Improving Health and Well-Being?*, World Health Organization.

Feary, V. (2002), "Medicine for the Soul: Philosophical Counseling with Cancer Patients," in H. Herrestad, A. Holt, and H. Svare (eds), *Philosophy in Society*, Oslo Academic Press.

Feary, V. (2005), "Art and the Good Life. The Role of Literature and the Visual Arts in Philosophical Practice," *Philosophical Practice* 1 (2): 95–112.

Gaunt, B. and M. Kieran (eds) (2018a), *Creativity and Philosophy*, Routledge.

Gaunt, B. and M. Kieran (2018b), "Philosophising About Creativity," in B. Gaunt and M. Kieran (eds), *Creativity and Philosophy*, Routledge.

Guttensen, K. (2024), "The Philosophy of Emotions: Implementing Character Education Through Poetry," *Educational Philosophy and Theory* 56 (9): 910–25.

Hadot, P. (2002), *What Is Ancient Philosophy?*, trans. M. Chase, Belknap Press of Harvard University Press.

Halliwell, S. (1998), *Aristotle's Poetics*, University of Chicago Press.

Knox, J. B. L. (2020), "Stories of Despair: A Kierkegaardian Read of Suffering and Selfhood in Survivorship," *Medicine, Healthcare and Philosophy* 23 (1): 61–72.

Knox, J. B. L. (2023), "Impromptu Drama: Human Flourishing Among Children and Young Adults with Cerebral Palsy," *Nordic Journal of Arts, Culture and Health* 5 (1): 1–12.

Kokanovic, R. and M. Stone (2018), "Listening to What Cannot Be Said: Broken Narratives and Lived Body," in D. Bowman, R. Kokanovic, and J. Parker (eds), Special Medical Humanities Issue: *Representing Trauma; Honouring Broken Narratives, Arts and Humanities as Higher Education* 17 (1): 3–181.

Kronfeldner, M. (2018), "Explaining Creativity," in B. Gaunt and M. Kieran (eds), *Creativity and Philosophy*, Routledge.

Margalit, A. (2016), *The Decent Society*, Harvard University Press.

Morgan, G. and P. Nelligan (2018), *The Creativity Hoax. Precarious Work and the Gig Economy*, Anthem Press.

Nelson, L. (1949), *Socratic Method and Critical Philosophy: Selected Essays*, trans. B. Blanshard, Yale University Press.

Noë, A. (2015), *Strange Tools. Art and Human Nature*, Hill and Wang.

Nussbaum, M. C. (2010), *Not for Profit: Why Democracy Needs the Humanities*, Princeton University Press.

Nussbaum, M. C. (2013), *Creating Capabilities. The Human Development Approach*, Belknap Press of Harvard University Press.

Parker, J. (2018), "Stories, Narratives, Scenarios in Medicine," *Arts & Humanities in Higher Education* 17 (1): 3–9.

Rorty, A. (ed) (1992), *Essays on Aristotle's Poetics*, Princeton University Press.

Sen, A. (1993), "Capability and Well-Being," in M. C. Nussbaum and A. Sen (eds), *The Quality of Life*, Clarendon.

Young, J. (2001), *Heidegger's Philosophy of Art*, Cambridge University Press.

4

Cathartic Care

Otherness in Doctoring and Dialoguing

Jeanette Bresson Ladegaard Knox

Prologue

In Margaret Edson's Pulitzer Prize–winning play *W;t* ([1993] 1999), the audience follows the agonizing end of Dr. Vivian Bearing in a teaching hospital. Dr. Bearing is a prominent professor of seventeenth-century English poetry with a stellar academic career. We learn that she has dedicated her life to the study of John Donne's intricate *Holy Sonnets*, their poetic wit and mystery in particular. She knows about life and death, she claims at the outset of the play, thanks to Donne's poems that "explore mortality in greater depth than any other body of work in the English language" (Edson [1993] 1999: 12). The professor is now suffering from stage-four metastatic ovarian cancer for which she agrees to undergo an experimental chemotherapeutic treatment on the advice of Dr. Kelekian, a leading oncologist and researcher. As the aggressive and often painful treatment commences, she lives through the irony of becoming the subject of research as she subjected Donne to her literary analysis. Her moment of biographical disruption (Bury 1982), where life is turned inside out, is met by her defiance and toughness, convinced somehow that her intellectual brilliance will script a way out of her cancer narrative. Professor Bearing is a hard character with an uncompromising attitude toward her students. Terminally ill, she realizes through a series of revelatory flashbacks that she could have offered more "human kindness" to her students. In one scene, she replies when a student asks for an extension on a term paper due to the death of her grandmother, "Do what you will, but the paper is due when it is due" (Edson [1993] 1999: 63). Ironically, it is the same kind of human kindness that she comes to desperately crave from her doctors.

We follow how the patient addresses her illness with her professorial methodical rigor and rational command while she begins, scene by scene, to question her control of events and her self-absorbed values. Themes such as kindness or compassion over intellectualism or expertise are highlighted both in Professor Bearing's rather cold rapport with her students and in her doctor's distanced rapport with her. They both intellectualize human relationships, severing the bond between mind, body, and soul, and both of them use wit and sarcasm to keep people at bay. Her literary scholarship and the medical professionalism that she encounters express disciplines that use language to not only obfuscate but also reduce subjects to objects rather than to promote a human connection when it matters the most, either to optimize learning or to uphold dignity in intrusive examinations and grim life circumstances.

This chapter explores how Aristotle's notion of *catharsis*, Levinas's concept of *Other*, and Marcel's idea of the *mystery of being* can inform a humanistic and holistic approach to patients in health care. Using Edson's play *W;t* as a reference point throughout the chapter, I carve a compassionate and courageous rapport between patient and health care providers in contrast to the dehumanizing experience of the play's protagonist. Holding space for the alterity and vulnerability of a diseased person can support a cathartic process that facilitates emotional release, personal growth, and existential alignment and thereby add value to dark, chaotic, and incomprehensible conditions. Human interaction is a place for much misunderstanding and hurt regardless of the context (a hospital room, a classroom, a living room, a prison cell, etc.), and the challenge of building meaningful and wholesome relationships is key to enhancing philosophical dialogue. I argue that the conceptualization of attentive face-to-face encounters with the Other in the clinic is transferable to philosophical practice to strengthen not only its prime jewel of reflection but also empathy, presence, and courage and that simple acts of kindness can hold a healing value to patients and participants in philosophical practice alike.

The Notion of Catharsis

Catharsis is not an uncommon notion in ancient Greece (Nussbaum 1992). We find it both in the works of Plato and Aristotle, for example. As *W;t* masterfully shows, when serious illness strikes, tragedy often follows in its wake. To Aristotle (1987), it is only tragedy that can release *catharsis*. Though scholars agree that the notion is an essential part of his literary theory, Aristotle did not offer much attention to it. He mentions it only twice in *Poetics* to explain how tragedy can impact an audience through pity and fear.[1] Yet the notion has become foundational in dramaturgy and storytelling.

Shakespeare's *Macbeth* is a prime example of the purgation of pity and fear. The audience harbors pity for the tragic figure of Macbeth when his ambition and obsession with power are in full display, causing him to lose his integrity and eventually his life. As scenes of his spiritual ruin and the destruction of his virtues unfold, the fear of becoming morally corrupt, making bad choices, and being alone or disillusioned with life nests within us because we can imagine situations where our dreams and willpower steer us astray. However, I refrain from viewing the cathartic process in the narrow sense of the tragedy. The purging of emotions can equally be instigated by joyful scenes that transcend having a mere "feel good" impact. Just as the viewers live through anger and revolt at the wrongful imprisonment endured by Tim Robbins's character in *The Shawshank Redemption* (1994), a cleansing release of emotions of joy, freedom, and justice erupts when he crawls through a filthy tunnel that he has been painstakingly digging almost since being incarcerated nineteen years prior. The audience rejoices with him as he stands in a downpour with open arms facing the sky. Or upon seeing the space dance between EVE and Wall-E in the movie *Wall-E* (2008), we are taken back to uplifting and defining memories of the vitality in romantic affection and a basic appreciation of life. Correspondingly, a cathartic process can be expressed in scenes that are full of tragic and comedic elements, for example, when Jim Carrey's character in the movie *The Truman Show* (1998) walks up the stairs to escape the closed-in world that was created for the amusement of TV viewers to disappear into freedom and an existence he does not yet know.

In dramatic art, catharsis refers to scenes in a play that depict morally amplified and existentially relatable events where the audience can imagine themselves living through similar situations as the actors on the stage. As the professor in *W;t* becomes a student in the art of living, the harsh realities she faces about how she has conducted herself through life reverberate in the audience. Addressing the audience directly as she continually does, it is hard not to have multiple seeds of fundamental questions planted in the listeners: Am I living a good life? Am I a good person? Have I made the right choices? Have I found purpose? Her doubt, her anguish, and her regret transform the audience into participants in her transformative journey to a more refined awareness. In Shakespeare's *Romeo and Juliet,* we weep with Romeo as he commits suicide by drinking the poison he erroneously believes Juliet drank. We cry as we witness him slip into his demise because the scene transports us back to memories of love lost by either death or separation. It may have been the loss of a lover like Romeo or the loss of a friend, relative, or pet.

The notion of catharsis explains the impact of the performing arts (e.g., tragedy and comedy) on the audience. Whether it be on the stage or in the cinema, storytelling is, when it is well written and well delivered, compelling and holds the potential of shifting perspective in the listener. In the movie *Sophie's Choice* (1982), which was based on the 1979 novel by William Styron, our heart and everything we believe to be human and right are torn asunder when a soldier in a Nazi camp demands of Meryl Streep's character to choose between her two children, forcing her to decide who is to be saved and who is to be gassed. Scenes such as these represent an emotional upheaval that can set a series of cleansing contemplations in motion because the scenes resonate with some of our own experiences, though they may not be as dramatic as what we read or watch on stage or on the screen.

W;t portrays the drama, disruption, and discernment that unfold within an illness narrative. Through this narrative, a revealing story of the interactions between the ill person and her health care providers is depicted. Throughout, the play gestures toward the possibility of deeper interpersonal exchange between patient and provider; however, even moments that appear intimate—such as Professor Bearing sharing a Popsicle with nurse Susie—are quickly absorbed back into impersonal routines or abstract calculations of costs and benefits. The protagonist's change of heart in the latter part of the play illustrates how her situation—and the cathartic aspect of her illness narrative—is nested within a moral context. Life situations that bring out the raw nature of the human condition (e.g., uncertainty, vulnerability, and mortality) can destabilize a self (Frank 1995). The response to these life situations, and their philosophical puzzles, is what builds character and a moral self; it is also what can enlarge or diminish existence.

The Other's Otherness and Mystery of Being

What does *catharsis* look like in the patient–health care provider relationship? What could be the philosophical backdrop of *cathartic care*? How may we conceptualize it? Many philosophers in the French Continental tradition have reflected on the nature of subjectivity and interpersonal, caring relationships. Simone de Beauvoir, Jean-Paul Sartre, Emmanuel Mounier, Maurice Merleau-Ponty, Gabriel Marcel, Emmanuel Levinas, and Paul Ricœur are prominent examples. To ensure the clarity of my message in this chapter, I will lean on Levinas and Marcel, seeing that some of their central concepts particularly ground my vision. In different ways, these two philosophers underscore the significance of human relationships, embodiment, and the ethical–existential dimensions of human existence in a way that specifically serve a holistic and person-centered approach to care practices.

Dialoguing with Husserl and Heidegger, in particular, Levinas demonstrates in *Totality and Infinity* ([1961] 1979) how ethics must be conceived as first philosophy. Levinas's ethical phenomenology turns on the challenging relationship between self and other, making it exceedingly relevant for a discussion on the clinical encounter (Zaner 2003) between a physician and a person who is ill. According to Levinas ([1961] 1979), the face of the other person is a compelling symbol that conveys not only their uniqueness but also their vulnerability and mortality. It is through encountering the face of the other that we become aware of our moral obligation to respond to their needs and acknowledge their intrinsic worth. Recognizing that people in their human existence share this vulnerability and mortality, the face calls us to be compassionate and empathic while simultaneously making space for their unique alterity and the inherent asymmetry between people.

In describing the face further, I need to include Levinas's ([1961] 1979) concept of Other. When a middle-aged white male from the Midwest enters the streets of Harlem, can he fully understand what it is like to live as a Black single mom working three jobs? Can she put herself in his shoes? Or imagine a conversation between the CEO of a family-owned business such as Johnson and Johnson and a student enrolled at a city college? These individuals have little in common and will most likely harbor very different life views. However, instead of getting caught up in finding commonalities, Levinas encourages us to acknowledge oppositional differences between people, or (their) alterity in his terminology. In acknowledging differences, we must refrain from committing acts of othering—that is, converting others into abstract entities that we can distance ourselves from; we should celebrate difference. Othering should not be confused with Other or Otherness. There is a difference of attitude. Othering is a form of tribalism or tunnel vision that undergirds disputes and conflicts between people and, as a result, tends to propagate inequality, marginality, and stigmatization (Akbulut and Razum 2022), even violence and war. Othering is an objectifying and reductive process or a testament to dehumanization, whereas the Other is an intersubjective and inclusive notion that recognizes the suffering and mortality of others (Levinas [1961] 1979). However, society tends to teach people to think of the world in organizing, general categories that diminish the Other to the Same, difference to identity, and infinity to totality.

In other words, the Other is fundamentally different and irreducible to my own concepts and categories and, consequently, not to be perceived as "merely an analogue of myself" (Levinas [1961] 1979; in J. Wild's introduction: 13). In my encounter with the Other, an ethical responsibility is imposed upon me (Levinas [1961] 1979). With Levinas's concept of the Other, he challenges traditional ideas of subjectivity and self-centeredness. He argues that our encounter with the Other disrupts our self-perception, points out our blind spots, and calls us to acknowledge the presence, concerns, and demands of the Other. In facing the Other, we may learn valuable lessons that may also reconcile us with our own bias and fragility. To ground our moral concerns, states Levinas, we should recognize that the Other has a profound ethical meaning, as it situates the self in the irreducible presence of a mortal and vulnerable human being. This other human being is not subsumable to *my* concepts. In this way, the other person—that is, "you are you" (Levinas [1982] 1985)—is a whole universe of mystery that can leave us in awe and with an impulse to care.

Seeing the other person as a whole universe of mystery leads us to the philosophy of Gabriel Marcel. Central to Marcel's ([1935] 1965) philosophy is the distinction between problem and mystery. A problem is external to us. It is an obstacle that can be removed, or solved, with proper techniques and knowledge or objectively analyzed. A mystery, on the other hand, reaches the very depth of our being and beyond. A mystery *touches* me as an individual embodied, concrete self in that it cannot be separate from my lived experience of it. Thus, a mystery requires a personal immersion to be experienced. There are no final answers or solutions to mysteries, of which Marcel examines love, presence, hope, and death, to mention a few. In his work and defense of man's humanity, Marcel (1963) called out the tendency to reduce the mysteries of human existence to problems, which, in his view, degrades existence to a collection of mechanical or technical functions—something to be categorized, measured, and rationally fathomed. Mystery is a concept that defies understanding a person as the amalgamation of his or her functions that can be neatly tucked into a case file. Diminishing mysteries to orderly systems can make us less able to care and be truly present. In fact, Marcel ([1933] 1984: 11) worried that this form of reductive thinking can turn the hospital into "the inspection bench or the repair shop."

Marcel distinguishes between different levels of human interaction from the basic form of exchanging information, or communication, to a sense of community, or communion, that supports and builds presence, hope, and love, for example. Recognizing the other person as Other who carries within them an indemonstrable being and ineffable mystery can be a portal to a profound connection that moves far beyond a mere transmission of messages or simple communication. To Marcel, humans are innately relational, even insisting that "we are" is a better starting point for philosophy and life in general than a self-enclosed "I am." Such a perspective argues for a richer, deeper entanglement with being through continual attunement and communion with others. It is a perspective, a modality of being, that dissolves human disconnectedness and makes for a genuine healing dialogue.

Cathartic Care in Medical Practice

In recent years, Levinas's ethics has been applied in nursing science and practice (Nordtug 2015). Though far fewer in number, more and more studies apply his philosophy to medical practice and doctoring (Edgoose and Edgoose 2017; Benaroyo 2022). In the context of the clinical encounter, it is beneficial to study human suffering using Levinas's ethics given that his thoughts are grounded in a moral sensibility that transcends the subject's own perspective to encompass the encounter with the other person. It is, in fact, through a moral sensitivity that the subject discovers the Other. Through the Levinasian concept of the face, the ethical responsibility at the heart of the patient–health care provider relationship can be accentuated while simultaneously offering a metaphor for cathartic care.

Levinas's notions of alterity and responsibility for the Other add ethos to the human experience of illness on the one hand and doctoring on the other. As an alternative to perspectives that center on autonomy, Levinas wants us to seek the infinitely Other. Objective medical discourse can be transcended by the proximity of the face—the equal or the raw, naked, and embodied self—of the Other. The Other is not a notion or a cognitive other but the Other that I experience with all senses. The Other is revealed through alterity. This means that the Otherness of the other person is not based on my knowledge of myself. If I were to base this Otherness on myself, I risk transforming the Other into Sameness. The face serves as a gateway into the Other. Put differently, the face engenders a human connection. It is the face of the Other that calls you to responsibility despite the Other's Otherness or maybe even because of it.

In a hospital setting with its highly technological equipment and the daily execution of professional expertise, there is an ever-present risk of reducing the other to the same—alterity to identity—and replacing dialogue with monologue. Embracing the Other as totally Other leaves the self curiously wondering who this Other is. Presuming to know the Other based on generalizations is denying the appeal coming from this particular face. It is through the acknowledgment of the Other as alterity that peaceful coexistence can be established. It is natural to interpret the face as the patient with this or that illness, but this stance expresses a reductive, objectifying logic: "To be sure, most of the time the who is a what. We ask 'Who is Mr. X?' and we answer: 'He is the President of the State Council,' or 'He is Mr. So-and-so.' The answer presents itself as a quiddity" (Levinas [1961] 1979: 177). A doctor eclipses the primary ethical relation that defines Levinas's philosophy by resorting to a totalizing relation to his/her patient that results in quieting the Other's otherness and call for responsibility, transforming the who (the patient) into a what (the illness). Having "who" as the focal point of the relationship "envisages a face" (Levinas [1961] 1979: 177).

In summation, with Levinas, we can conceptualize critical distinctions in the clinical encounter that will help bring out its complexity and depth. The polarized opposition between subject (i.e., doctor) and object (i.e., patient) is valid from an epistemological point of view. The doctor knows more than the patient about his or her disease and its pathology and prognosis. However, when reading the relationship through the ethical lens of Levinasian philosophy, its asymmetry is leveled by way of the commitment to Other and his or her potentially transformative situation. Ethical responsibility is premised upon seeing the Other as a face or as a fellow human being sharing similar conditions of existence. Epistemologically, the relationship between a doctor and a patient hinges on the professional knowledge and excellence of the doctor, whereas the ethical perspective brings out the moral question of what constitutes a good doctor. Doctoring depends on both aspects of the relationship. In *W;t*, Vivian is addressed on the level of knowledge. Though the doctors' professionalism certainly stems from the impetus to help and learn about her disease, the attitude toward Vivian does not go beyond treatment and being a resource for research. Her spiritual restitution of selfhood is mirrored in her face, yet she and her doctors do not enter into a face-to-face relationship. As a result, the relationship remains ethically asymmetrical. The ethical relationality—or, in other words, the intimate intersubjective connection that is facilitated by an openness to vulnerable dialogue—is not established, as the doctors fail to *see* Vivian and respond with care for her cathartic process.

In health care, there is a natural pull toward solving the problem of illness symptoms by way of medical or surgical treatment. In fact, it is the whole point of medical practice. In cancer, this implies chemotherapy, radiation, or operation to remove a tumor or tumors. Vivian, we hear, has undergone several painful and experimental treatments. As she lies in her bed, Dr. Kelekian addresses the technical and functional aspects of Vivian's illness and disregards how she also carries a unique life story and humanity. In her treatment and gradual demise, she experiences how medicine becomes a technique of degradation

(Marcel [1951] 1962) and far from fostering any form of communion. Where a Marcelian problem is information driven (the collection of data on an illness with the purpose of a cure), a mystery transcends knowledge to encompass a coexistence, a sense of suffering with the patient or cowanderer, where one person (i.e., a physician) wanders alongside another (i.e., patient). In the case of illness and death, there is much more at play than biological dysfunctions. In contrast to acting solely as a diagnostic puzzle solver or skilled technician, adopting the wise gaze of mystery can help the physician navigate doctoring, making it more wholesome as he/she recognizes the inherent uncertainty in the human experience and the fundamental vulnerability embedded in illness. In health care, this perspective can encourage presence, humility, and human kindness while acknowledging each patient's experience as unique and multifaceted. Through this gaze, the physician is able to connect to and nurture human relationships that have as their point of departure a "we" that is defined by the word *with*, creating an alliance, rather than "I" (Marcel [1935] 1965, 1963) and, thus, transform the clinical encounter into a partnership, communion, or community of care. In acknowledging his patient's wounded humanity (Pellegrino et al. 2008), Dr. Kelekian can connect to his own.

The transformation of Vivian into a vulnerable human who has inner clarity and strength begs the question of how doctors are supported when they grapple with moral dilemmas, disillusion, and detachment in their profession. The mysterious, vulnerable face of patients turns medicine into more than a conversation of the risks and benefits of a treatment; it constitutes medicine fundamentally as a moral practice. But how exactly is moral reflection deepened, and what does it take to practice careful listening in the clinic?

Attending to Attention

Moving on from the philosophical foundation of cathartic care, I will unfold a specific skill or mindset that seems necessary for the exercise of my proposed Otherness-centered care that enables physicians and other health care providers to *see* the Other's otherness and mystery. In describing this skill, I draw on the pioneering work of MD and literary scholar Rita Charon.

Through decades of adamant advocacy and teaching, Charon (006) has demonstrated how attention to narrative is effective in achieving an empathic and engaged patient–physician relationship. Marcel conceptualizes a form of attention (availability or *disponibilité* in French) that can serve as a theoretical scaffolding for Charon's (2006, see chapter 7) notion of *narrative* attention. Marcel ([1933] 1984: 40) writes that "the person who is at my disposal is the one who is capable of being with me with the whole of himself when I am in need." This form of attention expresses the willingness to be present with the other and be attentive to his/her perceptions: "Presence is something which reveals itself immediately and unmistakably in a look, a smile, an intonation or a handshake" ([1933] 1984: 40). Compromising this presence risks fostering alienation and indifference.

Some foundational prerequisites are needed for cultivating a specific attention to *catharsis* in the care of ill people. To represent what the patient has expressed and to authentically participate in their suffering entails listening with care and awareness of the patient's perspective (i.e., *seeing* the patient's Levinasian face). It is to attend to attention or radical listening (Charon 2006; Charon et al. 2016). Radical listening is the act of mindful attentiveness that is sharply attuned to nuances in narratives we hear or read. In getting to know a patient, Charon et al. (2016: 166–7) encourage "letting what is being said—usually some form of account of illness—wash over me and wash into me. . . . (T)o simply absorb all that is being made manifest." This state of mind implies the temporary suspension of her clinical duties of "being a judging outsider who is being put to the test to know what to do about a problem and being a welcoming receiver of its mystery, willing to sit within all its doubts" (Charon et al. 2016: 167). The attentive reader will quickly notice how Charon's understanding of the patient–physician relationship echoes Marcel's thinking.

Only through radical listening can health care providers act on behalf of their patient and genuinely connect to their unique narrative and otherness. Radical listening is clearly not passive listening. Aside from being honed by the method of close reading (Charon 2006; Charon et al. 2016), I believe that it involves the art of dialogue where *Socratic curiosity* is adopted. Socratic curiosity is not intrusive. Rather, it resembles narrative humility (Charon et al. 2016: 148–9) and expresses a position of "not knowing" (Plato 2002). Naturally, this is not to glorify ignorance but, rather, to suspend the presumption of knowing the truth about something or someone. One's blind spots can be an invitation to a relentless intellectual and existential investigation. In adopting a Socratic curiosity, the interlocutor understands the impossibility of knowing the totality of another's story though he or she is dedicated to perpetually digging deeper into the story and experiences through probing questions and an open, tolerant mind. At the same time, there is a commitment to examine one's own perspectives and perceptions in the situation as a way to avoid reading subjective expectations into a patient's lived experience. This kind of curiosity is both rooted in the willingness to be moved by a story and the aspiration to help the Other's story emerge as they see it. Undertaking a neutral position on the emotional, existential, and moral aspects of a patient's story strengthens Socratic curiosity and a fuller understanding of the patient.

Being diagnosed with cancer as in the case of Vivian Bearing in *W;t,* we can conceive of her cathartic process as a "clearing away" by way of an emotional discharge that enables her to achieve a moral state of renewal. It is this profound narrative process that her doctors fail to recognize in their treatment of her. Studies show that patients get interrupted after less than twenty-three seconds on average (Phillips and Ospina 2017). Imagine if space was made for a patient to tell her story for three minutes uninterrupted? It would give the health care professional a chance to probe into what matters to this particular individual. In this way, the patient can emerge as a person with a unique story defined by memories, aspirations, values, and visions. Tuning into how the transformative event of illness marks a patient's distinctive history, social situation, and the moral decisions to be made will help the health care provider better grasp how the patient deliberates and his or her struggle and strife. It will position medicine within a humanistic frame that mandates both competence and compassion in the act of doctoring. The idea of doctoring as a moral activity is not new. It dates back to antiquity. This moral activity is illustrated through the Levinasian face, whose concept also shows us how narrative attention is the backbone of cathartic care.

How does the physician learn to see the Levinasian face of his or her patient? Starting from medical school, a commitment must be made to moral learning. Moral learning can be informed by "narrative attention" and by

Socratic dialogue, which will provide an apparatus for the alleviation of the human suffering of illness. It anchors medical practice in human questioning and humility. The doctor's and patient's moral learning are two different processes, yet they both hold cathartic elements. Physicians' moral learning concerns being acutely aware of the cathartic process that illness can cause in a patient, and thus, learning entails the ability to listen and see suffering. The patient responds to the call embedded in the illness experience as is beautifully and painfully portrayed in *W;t* and, as a consequence, can live through a transformative experience.

The health care provider who adopts a cathartic care approach in the clinic invites the ill person to manifest who he/she is as a person with a past, present, and future (however compromised), not merely as a patient in a situation of illness. It is an approach that defies the ethics of strangers (Toulmin 1981) by acknowledging the importance of knowing the person in one's care (Björk and Hirsch 2024). How do health care providers do that? By inquiring questions, by astute observations, and by attending to silence to listen better. At the basis of these features of presence lies a curiosity that doctors are quite familiar with and, in fact, trained in: a curiosity about the composition of the body, how it functions, and its symptoms of illness. Doctors, nurses, midwives, and other health care professionals have a perceptive clinical sense of the patient. I am advocating for a *philosophical* and *narrative* sense to be added to their perceptive skills.

Although the primary purpose of this chapter is to inspire a deeper understanding of patients' life stories when disrupted by serious illness rather than to describe concrete measures for a fast-paced, often resource-strained medical environment, it may be beneficial to at least propose a couple of easily adoptable actions and low-cost implementable strategies for effectively integrating cathartic care into everyday clinical practice. One obvious avenue is to organize workshops and seminars to educate health care professionals on existential transformations and the principles of cathartic care. These events can include role-playing exercises, case studies, and specialist talks. Another path to pursue is to encourage health care providers to engage in regular reflection sessions where they discuss their observations, challenges, and emotional responses to patient care. These sessions can help health care providers develop a deeper sense of patients' existential situations and clearly distinguish between whose views and values are in play, when, and why. Such an understanding can be reinforced by scheduling regular team meetings to discuss patients' existential suffering and collaborate on holistic care plans that address both medical and existential aspects. Additionally, forming multidisciplinary teams that include philosophical practitioners can offer diverse perspectives on patients' care. Facilitating reflective dialogues among staff can help foster strong, trusting relationships with patients, allowing them to feel acknowledged, comfortable, and safe in discussing their existential health.

Cathartic Care as a Practice of Existential Health

The enigma of health lies in its often-overlooked nature (Gadamer 2018), which can lead to existential complacency. When illness strikes, this complacency is shattered, prompting a profound reevaluation and reorientation of one's embodied life, where existential health (e.g., Sigurdson 2016; de Miranda 2024; see also Knox 2020 and chapter 5 in this anthology) can be promoted through cathartic care.

While it may seem evident that philosophy and the arts can contribute significantly to restoring existential health, this perspective is not widely recognized by the medical establishment. The fields of *medical humanities* or the broader term *health humanities* strive to integrate the arts and humanities into medical practice. Their goal is to counterbalance the technological, cost-effective, and objectifiable aspects of modern medicine. Within a health care system that is still largely governed by reductionist Cartesian dualism that separates somatic and mental processes (Toombs 1988), it becomes especially poignant to emphasize that patienthood is a role enacted by a person who steps into the hospital scene with an entire life story waiting to be told. When we are ill, we want to be taken care of. We want the pain to be alleviated, for treatment to be planned, and the state of illness to be monitored. As the disease is laid bare for us by health care professionals, so is our vulnerability and mortality—the individual narrative of our human condition. Certainly, informed consent and "do no harm" are at the basis of care practices for patients. But as *W;t* portrays, these grand old principles of medical ethics reveal but a fraction of the clinical encounter. Ethics do not cure diseases; neither does human kindness, but in the midst of great diagnostic and therapeutic advances, physicians will fail their patients by turning a blind eye to the humanity that defines their profession.

Usually the literature focuses on empathy as the key to acquiring insight into the subjective illness experience. Empathy is crucial for the clinical encounter to be a good one. Though I am not disputing the importance of empathy, my hypothesis is that it is only part of the whole picture. It is not only the illness story that needs to be inquired into, but also who the person is, what the values are, what matters, visions for life ahead, moral choices to be made, and direction in life. The health care provider will need to become an existential seismographer, attuned to the human vibrations present in each encounter and within the ill person before them. This involves monitoring the subtle underlying movements hidden from plain view to fully sense what lurks beneath the surface. This existential aspect links directly to the ill person's sense of being and fullness in life and nurturing connections with people, animals, places, and more while also paying attention to the "lesion in the self" caused by illness (Sacks 1984: 67).

A foundational principle in medical ethics is *act on behalf of your patient*—that is, beneficence—but it is difficult to act in such a way without knowing the ill person's story. Medical benefit targets the disease and expresses what science, technology, and know-how can do to treat an illness. It is addressing the patient from the medical point of view as a problem to be solved and follows the biomedical model. However, medical benefit may not always be in the best interest of the patient, as it depends on how the patient views well-being, the value of continued life, and overall purpose. When medical students and clinicians learn to perceive medicine as the practice of listening and healing as equal to treating and curing, we may see a reduction of apathy, cynicism, and moral injury as a wonderful by-product. Thus, implicit in cathartic care lies an educational appeal to learn how to interact with patients. With Levinas and Marcel, we have been able to better conceptualize how to understand and approach the *person* who is ill. A care that centers around otherness and mystery can address the whole person in all his or her uniqueness and vulnerability rather than as an isolated set of symptoms or something similar to oneself. This approach does so by integrating attentive and dialogically based care into medical practice.

Patient-centered, person-centered, family-centered, personalized, and individualized care are many terms that indicate the change in how health services are perceived and conducted. They all signpost a move away from the traditional practice of symptom or system-centered health care. Cathartic care belongs to the family of these care practices, yet it adds to them by providing a philosophical framework that emphasizes attention to the alterity and mystery embedded in the ill person that marks their unique healing process and sense of existential well-being.

Cathartic Care in Philosophical Practice

The crux of this chapter centers on describing an approach to patients in health care where true otherness is perceived, acknowledged, and respected. I have conceptualized this approach by borrowing from philosophers such as Aristotle, Levinas, and Marcel. However, in an anthology on philosophical practice, it seems appropriate to end with reflections on how these thoughts may translate into philosophical practice.

In philosophical practice, whether it involves just one individual or a group, the way to relate to people is significant if a sincere, truthful, and wondrous dialogue is to take place. In supportive philosophical dialogues, the practitioner ignites the courage of either individuals or groups to explore philosophical questions and moral and existential experiences. By encouraging individuals or groups to delve into the challenging aspects of their lives, moral clarity and greater self-awareness can emerge. In other words, a cathartic release of emotions and thoughts can manifest through this dialogical process. However, a cathartic release of this nature does not yet express the sort of care practice I am developing in this chapter. We need to draw on Levinas and Marcel once again because their concepts can underscore the embodied *and* metaphysical nature of existence as well as the significance of human relationships. By the same token, cathartic care can substantiate an ethical and ontological process within a subject(s)[2] rather than merely focusing on its well-known epistemological and conceptually clarifying approach in philosophical practice.

Levinas's notion of Other prompts philosophical practitioners to recognize the unique perspective and vulnerability of the individuals they engage with.

The notion calls for a commitment to understanding their particularities without imposing preconceived notions onto them. To put this in different terms, it is a moral commitment to pay attention to the voices and concerns of others, which can direct the practitioner toward concrete ethical challenges that individuals and communities face. Sitting face-to-face with the Other invites the practitioner to engage in a dialogue that essentially concerns the alleviation of their unease or suffering.

To achieve a dialogue that serves this alleviation, the involved parties join a partnership where they walk side by side. In *Ethics and Infinity*, Levinas ([1982] 1985: 95) declares that the human face "orders and ordains" us, underpinning the awesome responsibility in the meeting of two or more Others. Suspending personal ambitions, notions, and strategies on the part of the philosophical practitioner, the conversation is marked and led by the narrative of the Other(s). It holds all the uncertainties, ambiguities, and perplexities of lived experience that, at the same time, shape the vulnerability of the Other. The philosophical practitioner responds to this vulnerability as an appeal to his or her compassion and presence, creating a safe environment in which the visitor can freely engage in a critical and creative contemplation on the issues he/she wishes to examine. In this way, the ethical life of the practitioner becomes a key component in how to philosophize with others.

Within philosophical practice, Marcel's idea of mystery can highlight the importance of recognizing the limits of our knowledge and intellectual capability to analyze experiences and phenomena in that some aspects of human existence evade rational or logical comprehension. With the incorporation of mystery into philosophical practice, it is possible to explore the existential depth of human experiences and touch the metaphysical realm of our being. Mystery is inherent in the act of philosophizing, as philosophical questions do not provide any final answers. It is not the purpose of philosophical practice to deliver definitive explanations. By engaging in mystery, the practitioner can engage in the embodied experiences of the individual/group in front of him or her while simultaneously adopting an ethical stance that acknowledges the unique narratives of each individual. Moreover, through the notion of mystery, the practitioner understands how questions are inseparable from the one posing the questions. Each individual is inextricably engaged in his/her questions because they concern the essentials of his or her existence. In the dialogue, the practitioner and the individual/group try to maintain a creative openness toward the world. It is through this dialogue that they can bring to light the unverifiable aspect of life: the mystery of being. Without mystery, there is no cathartic care.

As Vivian scrambles to make sense of her way of living in the past and now, an unfathomable human urge for purpose, truth, and coherence roams within her. It is an urge that arises from the imperfection of life, the messiness of reality, and the finite character of existence—or, in sum, the broken world, in Marcel's words. This urge, therefore, is far more than a psychological urge to have one's wish or need (e.g., ambition, social status) satisfied before moving on to the next need. In contrast, it has deep-seated roots that lie both within us and that go far beyond our reach. In this way, this "urge" or ontological exigence (Marcel [1933] 1984) is connected to mystery. Toward the very end, Vivian begins to carefully listen to the ontological exigence as her North Star, leading her to a profound sense of meaning and authenticity even if she is at death's door. Within the context of philosophical practice, the ontological exigence helps shift the focus from conceptual and epistemological clarity to turning one's attention to an existential alignment with the world and others or creating resonant human relationships. It is a practice that supports the guest's pursuit of the mystery of being by appealing to this unfathomable exigence. Acknowledging the mystery in the Other is responding to the calling within the person to exist in a process of authentic becoming and tuning into the unique and fragile process of this becoming.

In essence, cathartic care in philosophical practice offers a specific attitude toward one's practice and attention toward the people involved in it that hinges on valuing and calling forth humility and courage.

Epilogue

It is appropriate to end this chapter the way it started with the play *W;t*. The personal journey of Vivian's moral self, or her *catharsis*, in the latter part of the play where John Donne's poems on life and death, doubt, faith, and divine judgment become embodied experiences and not cerebral studies, is not quite paralleled by the medical professionals treating her. *W;t* ends with a heart-wrenching scene that underscores the importance of narrative attention and care practices as a fundamental moral activity. Dr. Posner, who is in charge of the experimental chemotherapeutic treatment protocol and a former student of Professor Bearing, initiates cardiopulmonary resuscitation procedures when her heart stops despite hearing nurse Monahan screaming that the patient has opted not to be resuscitated. When he is informed of her wishes and the DNR by the nurse, he continues the resuscitation attempt because her survival serves his research, or as he utters "She's Research!" (Edson [1993] 1999: 82. The capitalized R is in the play). His reaction shows a weak and uncompassionate connection to his patient. Vivian's physician has clearly failed to practice narrative listening and Socratic curiosity, not to mention displaying a lack of attunement to her existential health. Dr. Posner does not know what his patient wants and even forgets that he was, in fact, present when the papers were signed. He seems guided more by ambition than compassion, yet upon pondering on his tragic decision-making immediately after the failed resuscitation attempt, the audience is left wondering if he glances at the beginning of a cathartic process when, in this climactic scene, he realizes his mistake. He will become yet another proponent of cerebral living if he does not take up the lesson embedded in his disastrous mistake.

At the moment of death, which her health care providers seem to interpret as a failure, Vivian is healed. However, Dr. Kelekian's and Dr. Posner's shortcomings lie not in their patient dying but in their inability to recognize the restoration of her inner truth. They have focused so intensely on restoring her body to ensure her survival—a noble goal in itself—that in their attempt to do so, they have neglected to connect with their patient and her transformative cathartic process.

By expanding the boundaries of awareness of someone's vulnerability and humanity and by connecting to their being or intrinsic worth, we are but conceptually strengthening elements that are already at work in medical practice and philosophical practice. Using probing questions, doctors search for the accurate diagnosis of patient symptoms. Health care professionals want to do good for patients, and patients want to be seen and heard as people who happen to be sick. By listening to patients' stories, health care providers can be reminded of why they are really in health care. Injecting a cathartic care approach can accentuate the healing environment in medical practice and support physicians in engaging in radical listening to patients' needs, abilities, concerns, and goals to help them fulfill their vision of a life worth (or not worth) living even if it means death. Through a reflective exposé of mortality, *W;t* becomes a play that examines what makes life worth living. Within this exposé lies perhaps the true cathartic calling of doctoring and dialoguing.

In the end, *W;t* harbors a subtle message that is not restricted to the medical profession or patienthood but to us all: the resolution to be fully human in human endeavors, the redemptive resources in human connections and biographical reassessment, and the reconciliation with the undeniable facts of life and death. By paying close attention to the critical moral question that is relevant for every human being "How do I best live a good life?" we can all become the *face* of human healing whether it be our own healing or that of others.

Notes

1 I should add that scholars do not agree on how to interpret the famous passage in *Poetics* where Aristotle explains *catharsis*.

2 This is not the place to discuss Levinas's philosophy of ethics—that is, opposition to ontology—or Marcel's focus on concrete ontology (i.e., his inclination not to explicitly incorporate ethics into his philosophy).

References

Akbulut, N. and O. Razum (2022), "Why Othering Should Be Considered in Research on Health Inequalities: Theoretical Perspectives and Research Needs," *SSM Population Health* 20: 101286.

Aristotle (1987), *Poetics*, R. Janko (trans.), Hackett.

Benaroyo, L. (2022), "The Significance of Emmanuel Levinas' Ethics of Responsibility for Medical Judgment." *Medicine, Health Care and Philosophy* 25 (3): 327–32.

Björk, J. and A. Hirsch (2024), "An 'Ethics of Strangers'? On Knowing the Patient in Clinical Ethics," *Medicine, Health Care and Philosophy* 27: 389–97.

Bury, M. (1982), "Chronic Illness as Biographical Disruption," *Sociology of Health and Illness* 4 (2): 167–82.

Charon, R. (2006), *Narrative Medicine: Honoring the Stories of Illness*, Oxford University Press.

Charon, R., S. DasGupta, N. Hermann, C. Irvine, E. R. Marcus, E. R. Colsn, D. Spencer and M. Spiegel (2016), *The Principles and Practice of Narrative Medicine*, Oxford University Press.

de Miranda, L., ed. (2024), *Philosophical Health. Thinking as a Way of Healing*, Bloomsbury Academic.

Edgoose, J. Y. C. and J. M. Edgoose (2017), "Finding Hope in the Face-to-Face," *Annals of Family Medicine* 15 (3): 272–4.

Edson, M. ([1993] 1999), *W;t*, Farrar, Straus and Giroux.

Frank, A. (1995), *The Wounded Storyteller: Body, Illness and Ethics*, University of Chicago Press.

Gadamer, H.-G. (2018), *The Enigma of Health: The Art of Healing in a Scientific Age*, John Wiley & Sons.

Knox, J. B. L. (2020), "Stories of Despair: A Kierkegaardian Read of Suffering and Selfhood in Survivorship," *Medicine, Healthcare and Philosophy* 23 (1): 61–72.

Levinas, E. ([1961] 1979), *Totality and Infinity*, Kluwer Academic Publishers.

Levinas, E. ([1982] 1985), *Ethics and Infinity*, Duquesne University Press.

Marcel, G. ([1933] 1984), *The Philosophy of Existentialism*, Citadel Press.

Marcel, G. ([1935] 1965), *Being and Having*, Harper & Row.

Marcel, G. ([1951] 1962), *Man Against Mass Society*, G. S. Fraser (trans.), Henry Regnery Company.

Marcel, G. (1963), *The Existential Background of Human Dignity*, The William James Lectures 1961–2, Harvard University Press.

Nordtug, B. (2015), "Levinas' Ethics as a Basis of Healthcare—Challenges and Dilemmas," *Nursing Philosophy* 16: 55–63.

Nussbaum, M. (1992), "Tragedy and Self-Sufficiency," in A. O. Rorty (ed.), *Essays on Aristotle's Poetics*, 261–90, Princeton University Press.

Pellegrino, E. D., H. T. Engelhardt and F. Jotterand (2008), *The Philosophy of Medicine Reborn: A Pellegrino Reader*, Notre Dame Studies in Medical Ethics, University of Notre Dame Press.

Phillips, K. A. and N. S. Ospina (2017), "Physicians Interrupting Patients," *JAMA* 318: 93–4.

Plato (2002), *Five Dialogues: Euthyphro, Apology, Crito, Meno, Phaedo*, Hackett.

Sacks, O. (1984), *A Leg to Stand On*, Summit Books.

Sigurdson, O. (2016), "Existential Health. Philosophical and Historic Perspectives," *LIR J* 6: 8–26.

Toombs, S. K. (1988), "Illness and the Paradigm of Lived Body," *Theoretical Medicine and Bioethics* 9 (2): 201–26.

Toulmin, S. (1981), "The Tyranny of Principles," *The Hastings Center Report* 11 (6): 31–9.

Zaner, R. (2003), *Ethics and the Clinical Encounter*, Academic Renewal Press.

5

A Theoretical and Creative Life

Luis de Miranda

Introduction: Writing, Thinking

At first glance, art and philosophy might appear to be at odds.[1] Art revels in the singular, if not the extraordinary. It is a poetic exploration of an artist's unique voice and vision. Philosophers, on the other hand, pursue something different: They search for true principles that can apply broadly to many situations, if not all.

Yet this seeming conflict was absent from my mind when, at sixteen, I embraced my life's calling: I wanted to deepen my (and our) understanding of existence. Writing fiction seemed like a good way to understand the world.

Throughout my twenties and thirties, I dedicated my artistic life—which unfortunately was not my full-time life—to fiction writing. I wrote stories and created characters, progressively publishing several novels in French that were later, in some cases, translated into other languages: English, Chinese, Turkish, Swedish, and so on. Critics labeled my works as "philosophical fiction"—a description I accepted even though it wasn't always meant as praise.

My interest in fiction declined over time: After turning thirty, I found myself writing philosophical essays. Theory became essential to me, and truth more important than storytelling. Beyond just writing, I always wanted to think deeply and in an embodied fashion—this was, and remains, my greatest joy.

In my thirties, still living in Paris, I hadn't yet entered academia as a profession. I was what people called an "independent thinker." My essays, partly phenomenological, combined philosophical, literary, and poetic elements with a natural flow that pure logic lacks. Through writing and self-reflection, I realized that well-crafted philosophy and literary art aren't radically different. Both must in fact balance the specific with the universal.

Philosophy at its best isn't purely abstract; it connects with the thinker's personal experiences and subjective world. It starts from individual experience before growing into a broader worldview. Similarly, fiction works best when it helps us think through metaphors and analogies that carry a worldview. The world of story and fiction writing and the larger world of philosophical writing can mirror each other's interpretations.

For the ancient Greeks, *theoria* wasn't just abstract thought either; it was a way of life, an embodied coherence, a form of felt contemplation (Aristotle 1995: 441–2). To theorize with passion means creating order from chaos but also letting creative chaos emerge from order—it's an endless creative dialectic. Truth partly changes and evolves through its continuous collective creation.

Art, in its many forms, tries to capture the phenomenological truth of what we find remarkable and sublime—think of Cézanne painting the same Provençal hillside again and again. Sometimes art shows us society's hidden side, revealing our mistakes and flaws, calling us to seek wisdom, justice, or peace. Sometimes beauty and meaning are right in front of us, clear and visible, if we just take time to look carefully beyond our routines and conventions. Other times, they hide in remote spaces, estranged by corruption or decay. As Deleuze and Guattari (1996: 163–90) explain, our feelings and perceptions help us make sense of things just as much as our concepts do. There's a continuous connection between art's storytelling and philosophy's ideas; bringing them together can become a way of life.

We know that our body moves in the world through proprioception, a sense for its own presence in space-time. I believe that our mind moves in the world through what I call "proprioconception," a sense of its own felt cogitation in the space-time of symbols. Such is life in its existential flow, a dance between proprioception and *proprioconception*.

Creative Real

At age eight, I developed an unusual belief: I imagined I wasn't really my parents' child but came from another planet. I saw myself as an observer from space, sent to the earth to study humans and write reports about them. This childhood fantasy became a preview of my future work of writing books and articles that sometimes feel like messages to a distant civilization.

My early writing often seemed strange, especially in first drafts, although I did not try to be different intentionally. Poetry—including philosophical poetry—isn't primarily about trying to be unusual; it's about expressing our natural uniqueness and desiring to be understood without being forced to fit standard rules. One publisher noted how often the word *normal* appears in one of my novels. Normal may indeed be the enemy of both art and philosophical practice.

Unlike physical or mental health, philosophical health shouldn't follow strict rules or offer the same solution for everyone. Instead, it's about expressing our unique form of life while helping create a shared world where diversity can unite (see de Miranda 2024).

I aim for my philosophical practice to be open rather than rigid, allowing some mystery, because it comes from lived experience rather than pure analysis. Embodied philosophy, like poetry, tries to understand how everything connects without destroying that connection. Theory shouldn't kill its subject through excessive analysis. The world isn't a puzzle of separate pieces but a flowing whole, a giant coral reef with parts moving together like fish.

In my books, I welcomed this idea of everything growing together in what I called "Creal," the Creative Real. I first introduced the term *Creal* in my novel *Paridaiza*. The story imagines a future where people leave behind a deteriorating earth to live in a sophisticated digital reality, similar to what we now call a metaverse. Through this fictional setting, I began exploring how humans create and inhabit new worlds, whether digital or physical. *Creal* is a portmanteau word combining *creation* and *real*: it means that our ultimate reality, the true Real, is a creative flux. This view is shared by most process philosophers, from Heraclitus to Deleuze, via Whitehead.

My exploration of the Creative Real or Creal didn't stop with fiction. I developed it into a philosophical framework called "crealectics"—literally, the study and practice of working and living with creative reality. Think of crealectics as a bridge between imagination and reality: it examines how we transform possibilities into compossible (compatible) worlds and experiences. For example, in my current action-research role at Vattenfall, a Swedish energy company, I'm in the process of establishing a "crealectic laboratory" in partnership with their research and development unit. Here, we use philosophical practice to spark innovation by helping people tap into their creative and critical potential, both individually and in groups. We're showing how philosophical thinking can have practical applications in the engineering world (de Miranda 2025).

This work demonstrates one of my core beliefs: The boundary between imagination and reality isn't as firm as we may think. When we create anything—whether it's a story, business strategy, or scientific theory—we're engaging in "compossibilizing." This term means the art of bringing different possibilities together in ways that work harmoniously. It's like being a composer who must ensure all instruments in an orchestra play together or an architect who must ensure all elements of a building support each other in a way where the whole is greater than the sum of the parts.

When we create, we're not generating something from nothing. Instead, we're more like filters or channels for the Creal, the endless creative potential that already exists in the universe. Just as a sculptor doesn't create the marble's capacity for adopting shapes but reveals a form within it, artists and philosophers don't create raw possibilities but help shape or structure them into meaningful forms.

To understand this better, consider how a novelist works. They don't invent language or human emotions; rather, they filter and arrange these existing elements into new patterns that tell a story. Similarly, when scientists or philosophers develop new ideas, they're not creating fundamental truths but discovering and articulating patterns that were virtually possible within reality itself. As philosopher Alfred North Whitehead (1978: 21) argued, creativity isn't something humans add to a static and passive universe; it's built into the very fabric of reality, the universe being deeply creative in itself. In other words, the universe is constantly generating possibilities and evolving, and human creativity is just one expression of this larger creative and perhaps unconscious force.

Art, in all its forms, shows that we can help build worlds, breathing creativity into everything we do. But we can only create effectively if we listen deeply to the creative flow that already exists in the cosmos. Creativity isn't just humans imposing their will on chaos or nothingness; it's a fundamental feature of the universe, and humans are one local, perhaps privileged, expression of it.

A central principle of crealectics is indeed that creativity forms the fundamental essence of the universe. Just as energy and matter are the basic building blocks of reality, creative processes are equally elemental. If we understand the cosmos as a "Creal"—a Creative Real in flux—then our intelligence must work in harmony with this creative nature. Crealectic intelligence means learning to work with these natural creative forces to bring about harmonious realities that align with both what is possible and what can exist together more or less harmoniously—that is "compossibly."

This idea of compossibilization builds on the work of the philosopher Leibniz (1991), who made a crucial observation in the seventeenth century: while many things might be possible in theory, not everything can exist together in the same world. Some realities can coexist peacefully, while others clash. When two or more possibilities can exist together without contradiction, we call them "compossible"; they are compatible rather than conflicting. Our laws of physics, for instance, define what can coexist in our physical world. You can't have an object that is both completely still and in motion at the same time; these states aren't compossible. Our reality emerges from these compatible possibilities working together, creating what we might call "worlded structures"—organized patterns of existence that arise from the interplay of creative forces.

Beyond traditional logical analysis and dialectical reasoning, though both remain important philosophically, crealectic consciousness—indeed, the consciousness of the thoughtful artist—recognizes that we are constantly immersed in a flow of creative possibilities. These possibilities exist before we even begin to think about them, given to us through our fundamental connection to the original creative force of the universe. This perspective matters deeply for practical philosophy: When we cultivate a relationship with possibility and compossibility, it changes how we act and think.

Crealectic intelligence helps us see the world not as a collection of separate parts but as an interconnected, living whole. In this view, living well means embracing our role as artists of reality, consciously shaping our world through thoughtful, careful, long-term action. This is where art and philosophy converge: Both seek to discover and create the most harmonious combination of possibilities—what we might call, echoing Leibniz, the best of all compossible worlds.

Philosophical Counseling

Born to Portuguese parents, I was brought to France as a toddler. This early migration left me in a kind of liminal space, often feeling out of place. I grew up in a Paris neighborhood dominated by brutalist architecture, living among gray structures that resembled Bentham's Panopticon—a prison designed so that inmates could be controlled from a central point of gaze while observing them continuously (Miller and Miller 1987). This was my territory, where horizons seemed limited and natural spaces were rare, making the vitality of freedom or nature seem like a distant promise.

During childhood, I struggled with a sense of disillusionment. Sitting at my desk, I would dream of colorful pyramids—perhaps a personal symbol for a better world. I felt fundamentally alienated, as if I couldn't fit into the complex puzzle of human society.

While it's common for children to use imagination to make sense of their world as part of normal development, some of us spend our first twenty years feeling profoundly out of place. The challenge isn't just that we feel misunderstood; more fundamentally, we struggle to understand other human beings, who are yet supposed to be "like us." Philosophy later taught me an important lesson: It's normal to feel abnormal and perhaps abnormal to be completely normal.

Undoubtedly, forming a shared world requires codes and structures. Without them, we would lack the patterns needed to create stable and common realities. These codes are like invisible threads that weave together our common existence. One may think of them as the grammar of reality; just as language needs rules to be meaningful, our shared world needs structures to be navigable.

However, in the crealectic view, these rules and codes play a secondary role compared to something more fundamental: what I call the "crealing emotion" within us. This is our living connection to the endless tide of creation that flows beyond all structured worlds since at least the Big Bang. This expanding force, the Creal, is not just the source of art's inspiration but the very essence of thought itself. In other words, in *proprioconception*, conception is not only conceptualization but also self-creation. We cocreate ourselves all the time.

As a philosophical counselor, my primary role isn't to force people into rigid logical frameworks but rather to help them reconnect with this fundamental creative sensation—their sense of what's possible and what should be compossible—before helping them elaborate and navigate their life's purpose or intersubjective worldview.

Since 2022, my preferred counseling method has been the SMILE_PH approach (sense-making interviews looking at elements of philosophical health), which I developed while working with individuals living with a tetraplegic condition and sitting most of the time in a wheelchair.

This structured dialogue process carefully explores six key dimensions of philosophical health: (1) the bodily sense; (2) the sense of self; (3) the sense of belonging; (4) the sense of the possible; (5) the sense of purpose; and (6) the philosophical sense. By methodically exploring these six aspects, starting from the most tangible—our physical experience of embodiment—counselees can gradually build a personal philosophy that authentically reflects their lived experience. The approach acknowledges that few, if any, individuals have ever achieved a perfectly consistent philosophical system, and this incompleteness is also what keeps philosophy alive and poetic. Even Hegel's *Phenomenology*, which is only roughly systematic, contains inherent ambiguities. This aligns with Merleau-Ponty's insight about the fundamental ambiguity of human existence (Sapontzis 1978). Subjects can never be as clear as objects.

This recognition of life's inherent complexity—a creative dialectic between order and chaos—is why I practice a semistructured approach like SMILE_PH. It provides a framework for meaningful dialogue while leaving room for personal interpretation and style. The method helps people discover their own philosophical voice without forcing them into rigid patterns of thought.

The etymology of *author* suggests something about our bodily nature: To author means to augment or grow, implying that a body engaged in creation naturally tends toward growth, especially in its most productive periods. This innate *joie de vivre* is a sentiment typically associated with artists, who are often described as "bon vivants" in French, or "enjoyers of life" in literal translation. As a young aspiring author, the theme of joy was so central to my existential and philosophical exploration that it became the simple title of my first novel, *Joie* (de Miranda 1998). Written during my time in New York, in my twenties, its narrative weaves together music, nature, and philosophy, suggesting that composing music, contemplating nature, and engaging in deep thinking aren't mere luxuries but essential nourishment for a soul seeking vivid engagement with the world.

These themes—belonging, creativity, and joy—aren't separate elements but interconnected aspects of philosophical health. They remind us that philosophy isn't just about abstract thinking but about finding our purpose and place in the world and engaging with it fully. The SMILE_PH method of dialogue helps people explore these connections, moving from their immediate bodily experience to broader questions of meaning and purpose.

Sense-Making and Philosophical Practice

The first element of the SMILE_PH method focuses on the bodily sense. In my previous writings, I've argued that the body's ideal state is one of "joie de vivre"—a profound joy that emerges not from external circumstances but from the simple fact of being alive and participating in creation. This joy expresses itself as a desire for unity within diversity or, conversely, diversity within unity. Being truly alive means more than just avoiding death; it means embracing life's natural tendency toward growth, abundance, and playful interconnection.

The second element of philosophical health in SMILE_PH concerns the sense of self. In my case, developing this sense was crucial for survival: My first decades were marked by a father whose verbal abuse and incoherent cynicism created what Augusto Boal would call a "policeman in the head" (Boal and Epstein 1990)—an internal critical voice that took years to quiet. No artist can thrive with such an arbitrary internal critic, and in my experience, the very act of philosophical thinking became a way to escape this destructive influence. In the meantime, my mother was the silent accomplice of the oppressor, offering no alternative refuge. In fact, my father represented not just an internal policeman but also acted as the "media in the head"—embodying a worldview that saw corruption, danger, and deviance everywhere while forgetting the capacity for wonder, gratefulness, and imagination.

Despite—or perhaps because of—this challenging beginning, I've spent years developing a healthier relationship with myself, remaining my own best friend. Through my writing and investigation, I've sought autonomy, not merely as a reaction against parental influence but as a quest for philosophical grounding—what artists might call finding one's unique style and overview.

Yet I must admit to a very slow pace in achieving a fixed sense of self, if any. My natural curiosity drives me to explore various styles and expressions. Moreover, I've come to understand that our existential selves, inspired by the Creal, are inherently fluid and ambiguous, more like wells of possibility than fixed essences. In my essay *Being and Neonness* (2019), I use neon lights as a metaphor to critique the self-help industry's tendency to push people toward constructing rigid identities—like neon signs that trap a free-flowing gas within inflexible glass structures.

The third element of philosophical health explores the sense of belonging. At age nine or ten, I encountered my first serious bout of existential questioning. My parents' constant arguments created a discordant backdrop to my life. I struggled to understand how these adults could be my guardians or how my schoolmates could be my friends. The communication patterns and mental habits of those around me, including at school, often felt mechanical, distant, or disconnected. Like many teenagers, I found myself in an emotional maze, where making sense of the world seemed like an overwhelming challenge.

Today, people often discuss "well-being" but rarely consider what I called "well-belonging" in my book *Ensemblance* (de Miranda 2020a: 240). In an open society, we should be able to find communities that share our worldview actively—groups where we can belong while maintaining our individual perspective. Sometimes the worldview we share with our chosen community might be another form of ideology, but ideally, it's one we've consciously chosen and can critically examine rather than one that's been imposed upon us. We can and should be the authors of our lives, even in a community of interest.

The Sense of the Possible

The fourth element of philosophical health in the SMILE_PH method addresses our relationship with possibility itself. My deep understanding of this dimension came through personal experience. At thirty, I fell into a strong depression. For months, human society appeared to me as nothing more than a flimsy facade, and the earth seemed like a lonely rock drifting meaninglessly through space. Getting out of bed became a monumental task, and each day felt empty. Nothing seemed possible.

What helped me find my way back was channeling creative energy into action. With determined effort, I gathered a team of volunteers and directed my first (and last) short film, *Double or Quits*. We built a set that symbolized the interior of a mind. The story centered on a depressed man playing the board game Risk against his doppelgänger—a playful reflection of himself wearing a multicolored Harlequin jacket, like a joker in a deck of cards who can represent all possible values. During production, something remarkable happened: A profound sense of connection flowed between everyone involved, from makeup artists to electricians. The experience of directing this collaborative effort filled me with love and pride, ultimately helping me emerge from my melancholy with a renewed sense of life's possibilities.[2]

We all know people who are physically healthy, mentally capable, and yet wake up feeling that the future is dull or hopeless, just as I once did. Every door seems painted on, an illusion not worth opening, and reality feels like a cardboard stage set. In medieval Europe, when religious thinking dominated, this state was sometimes called "The Dark Night of the Soul" (Barratt Brown 1923). This evocative term has come to represent a universal human experience: a profound spiritual and existential crisis where individuals feel completely disconnected from any sense of the divine or meaningful. They face overwhelming doubts about life's purpose. This desolation goes beyond mere absence of spiritual comfort; it's characterized by a deep sense of emptiness and spiritual drought.

However, connecting depression with spirituality doesn't mean every spiritual crisis indicates mental illness or that depression is always a spiritual journey. Yet the overlap is significant. Depression often triggers existential questions like "Who am I?" or "What is my purpose?" These are fundamentally philosophical questions that require philosophical engagement to be addressed meaningfully.

Depression's duration and intensity vary greatly. For some, like my experience at thirty, it's intense but relatively brief. For others, it stretches across years like a chronic metaphysical discomfort, demanding endurance. Whether viewed through spiritual, psychological, or philosophical lenses, traversing a desert of depleted possibility tests our capacity to endure, transform, and ultimately transcend even the deepest despair into creative and meaningful action. People can emerge from depression feeling renewed, with a deeper connection to what they find sacred or meaningful, and a more profound sense of inner peace. Since I finished editing this short movie more than twenty years ago, I have experienced almost every day a high sense of the possible.

Within what feels like pure emptiness, there exists potential for profound transformation, provided we recognize that the Creal's abundance is more fundamental than nothingness. A depressive period can serve as a rite of passage, a purification process where the soul sheds unnecessary attachments, destructive illusions, and excessive preoccupation with mundane concerns. By enduring and eventually transcending this desolation, we often develop a clearer, more profound relationship with future possibilities. This can lead to a deeper understanding of our creative role in the cosmos.

I proposed to call "eudynamia" a good sense of the possible and the compossible. It is a word derived from two Greek words: *eu*, meaning good or well, and *dynamis*, meaning potential, possibility, or empowerment. The term is of course inspired by Aristotle's concept of *eudaimonia*—often translated too reductively as "happiness" or "well-being"—which is the realization and fulfillment of one's human nature in a flourishing manner. It is not merely a transient emotion or a fleeting pleasure but a deep and enduring state that embodies the highest creative responsibility for a human being.

But what does "possible" mean exactly? As we have seen, Leibniz defined the possible as that which does not imply a contradiction within itself but also with the fundamental structure of the surrounding compossible world. The possible becomes dangerously limitless if it is not related to something else. Taken in isolation, in monadic bubbles of reality, there is an infinity of possibles, even if we never see most of them actualized. There are many possible facts or worlds, but very often, they are not compatible with each other.

If this event or state is compatible with another event or state in the same world, then it is compossible, possible together. Compossibles are simply realities that are compatible rather than contradictory. Many people tend to think of possibilities in isolation without considering the articulation or consequences of their possibilities in a given world, environment, or society.

In fact, one might say that it is the most common mistake of humanity in the last two hundred years: to have a blinkered view of the possible, a monotropic mindset that can achieve great innovations or feats in specific fields, often designed without considering the general social and natural environment and the long-term global consequences. The past three centuries of industrialization celebrated the realm of possibility. Yet, now, our damaged planet yearns for the triumph of the "compossible"—a holistic, harmonious vision of balance between persons, Earth, actions, and societies.

There again, art can teach us to live more meaningfully, because it is a tradition in which compossibility, as composition, has always been important. A work of art is a set of possibles that have been composed, *compossibilized,* to suggest a harmonious state in the piece or, by critical contrast, outside of it.

Similarly, for individuals, a true understanding of possibility must be an embrace of the compossible, wherein diverse realities converge and expand their potential through optimal consonance. Leibniz was often mocked for his idea of the best of possible worlds, but he did not mean that our world is perfect; rather, the world in which we live, although locally imperfect, is the one that maximizes the coexistence of as many beings as it is compossible for the whole to incorporate.

For Leibniz, the best of all possible worlds maximizes the existence of its multiplicity of entities—that is, the full expression of their collective eudynamia in the long term. Of course, this can imply a local trauma for such and such individual being, like the premature death of a loved one, for instance. Voltaire, in his famous *Candide* (2006), mocked Leibniz by pointing to the many infants dead in the Lisbon earthquake of 1755: How could this be the best of possible worlds? A good sense of the possible is not enough: We also need a purpose, a garden to cultivate.

Purpose and Worldview

The fifth element of philosophical health is the sense of purpose. I discovered my life's purpose at sixteen, following a transformative solo journey to Africa. As a teenager, I was an avid reader, particularly drawn to nineteenth-century and existentialist novels that questioned conventional reality. But I also craved direct experience and discovery. In the summer of 1987, I convinced my parents to let me travel alone, supported by a Zellidja scholarship that perhaps helped ease their concerns about the risks involved. I spent a month exploring Guinea-Bissau, then a politically unstable military nation with one of the world's poorest economies.

The country had gained independence from Portuguese colonization during my early childhood. In a curious twist of fate, my mother had taught there briefly while pregnant with me, making my journey a symbolic and perhaps somewhat Freudian return to my origins. I traveled the country with a backpack, interviewing people about their daily lives and writing an essay about postcolonial lived experience interwoven with my personal observations—sixteen years after my prenatal connection to the place.

Guinea-Bissau's culture and way of life profoundly challenged my European assumptions. I realized how much of what I took for granted was actually contingent—that is, not necessary but merely one possible way of living. Time itself moved differently there; I could walk for hours on a jungle path, trying to reach the next village, with apparently nothing happening except monkeys throwing stones at me. When I returned to Paris, I would stand bewildered in supermarkets, questioning why they offered ten different kinds of toothpastes. The elemental simplicity of African life left a lasting impression, revealing by contrast the meaningless superficiality of Western consumerism.

My life's purpose crystallized during this period, shaped by both writing my African report and my deep appreciation for the great novels I had read and their wandering protagonists: I wanted to write books that not only would help me navigate the world meaningfully but might also help others do the same.

Many individuals who seek philosophical counseling are on a similar quest for purpose regardless of whether they live in Dhaka (Bangladesh) or Stockholm

(Sweden). They deeply desire clarity about their fundamental life orientation. They want to be more than just a cog or a ghost in the machine. Beyond questioning their place in the world, they seek to understand their unique value and perspective.

Their search goes beyond mere existential contemplation; they want help defining a set of guiding principles or values that can serve as an ethical and metaphysical compass, directing them toward realizing their personal ideals in the best possible world. Many of my counselees are curious about aligning their actions with fundamental principles to create some kind of a legacy, fostering environments that enhance both their own experiences and contribute to harmonious existence. Like writing a long novel, philosophical practice trains us in long-term thinking, encouraging us to consider the distant future consequences of our present decisions.

The sixth and last element of philosophical health is the philosophical sense itself. In 2007, I found myself again in my childhood apartment in Paris, living alone this time. I was deeply engaged in writing my speculative fiction novel *Paridaiza*, now translated into English (de Miranda 2020b).

Clara and Nuno, the main characters, discover a unique dimension harmonizing the private depths of a person's inner core with the outer world as if external reality reflected the inner realm. I initially called this nexus "Real-Real" (*Réel-Réel* in French). However, this name felt inadequate, more like an engine's stutter or a Platonic outburst than the lyrical term I sought. The Real seemed too reactive, not epic enough. While writing, I recalled Nietzsche's (1974) insight about active creative transformation of the Real versus mere reactive adaptation. This resonated deeply, and a new word emerged: *Créel* in French, combining indeed *creation* and *real* to form *Creal*. Despite my publisher's doubts, flirting with censorship, about this neologism, I insisted; the term not only found its place in my narrative but, as mentioned earlier, began to shape my own worldview, making implicit understanding explicit.

Over time, the Creal transcended its fictional origins. It evolved philosophically and existentially, painting a broader epistemic canvas. This is how I still view the world: The Creal is the often invisible field of creative becoming present all around us, working to generate unified compossibilities from infinite disparate possibilities, mixing both actualized reality and unactualized potentials.

Eventually, crealectics became for me the art of compossibilizing, referring to how humans and nonhumans build worlds. This, briefly described, is my philosophical sense of life. I see all of us as potential crealecticians, philosopher-artists.

Why does a world exist as it does and not in some other way? Most philosophers throughout history have tried to develop their philosophical sense into a system, seeking an abstract truth capable of explaining everything through universal conceptualization. This was called cosmology—a poetic description of the whole, its origin and dynamics—or ontology, a discourse on being.

We might not have a fully developed worldview, but we often have some sense of it—a vague intuition underlying our everyday choices, actions, or avoidances. Discussing this with a philosophical counselor is crucial because, retrospectively, all elements of philosophical health—body, self, belonging, possibility, and purpose—are influenced by our worldview or the lack of it. Whether we're conscious of it or not, it significantly impacts our behavior, decision-making, and interactions with others. It shapes our perception of reality, informs our moral and ethical beliefs, and influences our attitudes toward social and political issues.

When practicing philosophy, it's essential to consider whether embracing a particular life philosophy and its associated beliefs brings genuine fulfillment or merely serves as a coping mechanism for deeper insecurities and fears. The philosophies and beliefs we adopt aren't just abstract concepts; they become the very fabric of our reality, influencing our steps and paths, and reflect more or less well the shape of our destiny.

Conclusion: Deep Listening

I remember a pivotal moment in Paris when I was twenty-seven.

I had temporarily stepped away from philosophical reading, focusing instead on novels and books about society. At the time, I was writing novels and working as a journalist. One day, during a solitary lunch, I was reading an article about Hegel's philosophy between bites of pizza when I was suddenly overwhelmed with emotion. Tears came to my eyes as I reconnected with philosophy as a way of life. "Philosophy is sublime," I recalled.

Philosophy had been my oxygen, but somehow, in recent months or years, I had forgotten to breathe deeply. Within weeks, I resigned from journalism and, while unemployed, wrote my first philosophical essay, *Ego Trip* (2004), which was published during my master of philosophy studies at the Sorbonne. The book critiqued contemporary egocentrism and how individual claims can undermine universal thinking. It called for a shared cosmology beyond self-assertion and anthropocentrism. Above all, it defended deep listening and, once again, the cosmic sacredness of creation.

A philosophical counseling session is fundamentally an open conversation where the philosophical practitioner practices deep listening. This goes beyond mere hearing; it's an intentional immersion in the present moment, absorbing not only spoken words but also emotions, nuances, gestures, and underlying meanings. Philosophy, at its core, examines existential questions that emerge through dialogue: questions about our nature, purpose, and place in the cosmos. Through such conversations, we validate or challenge others' existence and narratives, indirectly affirming our shared presence in existence. In a world often dominated by solipsistic noise and selfish hurry, deep listening becomes a path to connection, understanding, and common ground.

But listening isn't limited to human voices; artists understand that the cosmos itself is a symphony deserving as much attention—if not more—than our neighbor's story or complaint. Listening isn't passive: it regenerates agency by fostering intercreation.

Philosophical practice helps people become active and intercreative rather than merely reactive. A higher purpose ideally manifests through affirmation rather than reaction or negativity. Through purpose's transcendence, people can embrace their circumstances, affirm their life's reality without bad faith, and actively create a space for meaning and encouragement rather than simply reacting to external events or seeking refuge in traditional moral systems.

I eventually stopped writing novels when I realized my most important work of fiction was my life itself and my role as a real-world shaper. The world is our artwork. We are constantly worlding our realities, and this should be a thoughtful process. Our life is theoretical and creative in that an active, performative desire for contemplation and understanding shapes it. Every day I am—we are—worlding with the Creal.

The crealectic music of the mundane spheres is about trying to discern a symphony within apparent cacophony. In it, art and philosophical practice become one unified action: the process of composing our perceptions and thoughts into a shared world—perhaps, tomorrow, the best of all compossible worlds.

Notes

1 The time to write this chapter was possible through funding from the European Union's Horizon Europe research and innovation program under the Marie Skłodowska-Curie Actions grant agreement No. 101081293.
2 The short movie *Double or Quits* can be seen on YouTube: https://youtu.be/PlPL4amSVv0.

References

Aristotle (1995), *Nicomachean Ethics*, in *Aristotle: Selections*, T. Irwin and G. Fine (trans.), Hackett.
Barratt Brown, A. (1923), "The Dark Night of the Soul," *Journal of Religion* 3 (5): 476–88.
Boal, A. and S. Epstein (1990), "The Cop in the Head: Three Hypotheses," *TDR (1988–)* 34 (3): 35–42.
Deleuze, G. and F. Guattari (1996), *What Is Philosophy?* Columbia University Press.
de Miranda, L. (1998), *Joie*, Le Temps des Cerises.
de Miranda, L. (2004), *Ego Trip: La société des artistes-sans-oeuvre*, Max Milo.
de Miranda, L. (2019), *Being and Neonness*, MIT Press.
de Miranda, L. (2020a), *Ensemblance: The Transnational Genealogy of Esprit de Corps*, Edinburgh University Press.
de Miranda, L. (2020b), *Paridaiza*, Snuggly Press.
de Miranda, L. (2024), "Worlding with the Creal: Autonomous Intelligence and Philosophical Practice," *Religions* 15 (1): 26.
de Miranda, L. (2025), "The Crealectic Method: From Creativity to Compossibility," *Qualitative Inquiry* 31 (1): 37–44.
Leibniz, G. W. (1991), *Monadology*, Nicholas Rescher (trans.), University of Pittsburgh Press.
Miller, J.-A. and R. Miller (1987), "Jeremy Bentham's Panoptic Device," *October* 41: 3–29.

Nietzsche, F. (1974), *Thus Spoke Zarathustra*, H. J. Hollingdale (trans.), Penguin.
Sapontzis, S. F. (1978), "A Note on Merleau-Ponty's 'Ambiguity,'" *Philosophy and Phenomenological Research* 38 (4): 538–43.
Voltaire (2006), *Candide*, T. Cuffe (trans.), Penguin.
Whitehead, A. N. (1978), *Process and Reality*, Free Press.

6

The Use of Poetry Therapy in Philosophical Practice

A Case Study—Ivan Petrovich and His Crisis of Faith

Vaughana Feary

I have always argued that there is a dialectical interplay between theory and practice. Although I begin with a theoretical discussion of the general use of poetry therapy in philosophical practice, my original theoretical perspective was enriched and expanded by using poetry in the specific case discussed in this chapter.

The use of poems for healing has a long history. The revival of poetry therapy in the United States was initiated by a pharmacist, Eli Greifer, who started poetry therapy groups in two different hospitals with the support of two interested psychiatrists: Dr. Jack L. Leedy and Dr. Sam Spector (Leedy 1969). Psychology has now used art and poetry therapy for some time in both individual and group counseling.

As the National Association for Poetry Therapy (NAPT) conceives of poetry therapy, the practice involves the therapeutic use of poems, narratives, and other spoken or written media (e.g., films and magazine articles) in treatment and counseling to promote the well-being of clients. Poetry therapy is not regarded as a stand-alone type of therapy for clients with mental disorders. However, psychiatrists and psychotherapists trained in bibliotherapy have used it to treat borderline personality disorder, suicidal ideation, post-traumatic stress disorder, substance abuse, and schizophrenia.

The long-standing connections between philosophy, poetry, and therapy were articulated recently by the development of humanities therapy in Korea.

Korean philosopher Young E. Rhee argued that in technologically developed capitalistic industrial societies, material well-being improves, but human well-being is reduced; there are increased problems such as depression, suicide, and anxiety conjoined with numerous types of addictions. These problems are cultural artifacts rather than mental disorders. Hence, the recourse for this "paradox of material prosperity" is neither psychiatry nor psychotherapy—both are regarded as forms of cultural imperialism—but rather a return to what is specifically human: a return to the humanities (philosophy, art, music, poetry, etc.) (Rhee 2011). The Eleventh International Conference on Philosophical Practice, which was conjoined with the Fourth International Conference on Humanities Therapy, was held at Kangwon University in Korea in 2012. It led to a wider interest by many practitioners in the relationship between philosophy and other branches of the humanities, especially poetry and poetry therapy.

Even before the conference in Korea, I had a long-standing interest in the use of poetry therapy in philosophical practice. In an earlier article, I suggested that art and poetry therapy, as influenced by psychologists, offered a truncated view of what art therapy can be (Feary 2005). Much richer conceptions of art and poetry therapy, and their use in philosophical practice, are suggested by the extensive philosophical literature in aesthetics about the nature of art and what art can accomplish.

As I argued in my article, art in general can do the following: art can represent (Plato and Aristotle); it can express emotion (Leo Tolstoy, R. G. Collingwood, Martha Nussbaum); it can reveal and disclose what would otherwise be hidden (Edmund Husserl, Martin Heidegger); it can use narratives to educate us (Søren Kierkegaard, Alasdair MacIntyre, Martha Nussbaum, Paul Ricœur, Gerd Achenbach); it can transfigure our worldview (Friedrich Nietzsche); it can trigger moral development (Lawrence Kohlberg); and it can serve as an agent for social change (Karl Marx and Herbert Marcuse) (Feary 2005). All these different uses of art and literature can suggest new philosophical perspectives and enrich the existing worldviews of our clients in philosophical counseling sessions. They can also greatly expand and enrich our conceptions of art and poetry therapy, which have been narrowly conceived by psychologists largely as expressive therapies used to achieve treatment objectives. Even the expressive function of poetry is overly simplified in psychological accounts of poetry therapy, which accounts for common assumptions that the poetry used in poetry therapy must be simple and that dialogue must focus on feelings to avoid overintellectualization. By contrast, I will show that working through difficult poetry can provide sufficient aesthetic distance for the client to simultaneously work through his/her own thoughts and feelings and what it might feel like for him/her to think in these new philosophical ways.

This chapter cannot explore the multiple uses to which philosophers might put poetry therapy. Nicholas Mazza's (2017) *Poetry Therapy, Theory and Practice* and Arlene McCarty Hynes and Mary Hynes-Berry's (1993) *Biblio/Poetry Therapy—The Interactive Process: A Handbook* are full of useful approaches that might be adapted to philosophical practice. I most frequently use poetry therapy in philosophical counseling primarily to quickly introduce some philosophical topic clients need to explore, disarm potentially resistive clients by introducing some beautiful or appealing poem designed to strike some chord within them, and gently open up a discussion of some theme that may be painful for clients. For the most part, I use poetry therapy with offenders or medical patients. The philosophical problem of the client, as in the case to be discussed, always dictates the choice of poems.

Poetry therapy is not literary criticism. In the ensuing part of this chapter, I discuss how I used poetry in philosophical counseling in a specific case. Working through selected poems of Emily Dickinson with Ivan Petrovich, a client experiencing a crisis of faith—considering the thoughts and feelings expressed and what it might feel like to think in that way—was not intended to clarify the worldview of the poet, isolate the perspectives of personae, or provide some correct analysis of specific poems but rather to use the poetry to open up new philosophical perspectives for the client.

I first met Ivan Petrovich (a pseudonym) as a private client who sought philosophical counseling with me because he thought that I might be helpful to him in dealing with his recent diagnosis of lung cancer. I saw him intermittently for eight years. During the early years, our discussions were focused on critical reasoning and philosophical approaches to coping with the anxiety, fear, and depression resulting from his disease, its recurrence following surgery, and the inevitable side effects of the treatment that was prolonging his life. In his last two years, when it was apparent that his disease was progressing more rapidly, his interest in philosophical counseling centered on exploring with me philosophical approaches to spirituality that I use in crisis counseling (Feary 2014). Finally, however, Ivan called to again resume appointments to discuss what he regarded as a "crisis of faith" in the face of death. It was in this final phase of counseling that literature became the primary vehicle for exploring the spiritual alienation that Ivan claimed was preventing him from "dying in peace."

Ivan was a sixty-year-old Russian immigrant who had obtained a PhD in history and had taught both history and Russian literature at a nearby community college. He claimed that during his youth in the Soviet Union, he had been an atheist, but soon after immigrating to the United States, he began attending a Russian Orthodox church in New York, in part to overcome the cultural alienation he felt in America and, in part, to explore a part of his cultural heritage previously denied to him in Russia. He then converted to Christianity. His interest in spirituality was also influenced considerably by his reading of Leo Tolstoy, particularly *The Death of Ivan Ilyich* and *Confessions*. He hoped that further philosophical dialogue with me could help him resolve his "crisis of faith" and "inability" to fully believe in Christianity.

I was extremely reluctant to undertake this phase of counseling. Faith can be a source of strength for terminal patients, and I certainly did not wish to undermine it. Of course, I counsel clients who have views with which I do not agree, but this kind of procedural neutrality is very different from being asked by someone for help in sustaining beliefs I did not find credible. Consequently, I suggested that Ivan might want to discuss his crisis of faith with Russian Orthodox priests, or with some other philosophical counselors to whom I could refer him, who would be better suited to help him with this issue. He said that he preferred to work with me, that he was too sick to think about changing counselors, and that he had liked our discussions about Tolstoy and hoped that we could discuss other literature relevant to his current issues.

After some reflection, during our next session, I began by asking him if he thought his so-called crisis of faith could be viewed as a type of alienation, estrangement, or distance from a God in whom, at base, he usually believed. When he agreed, I replied that this sounded very much as if his alienation from God was like that expressed in the poetry of Emily Dickinson and that, like hers, his crisis seemed to involve different categories and modes of estrangement from God. Ivan wanted to know if reading her poetry would help him feel closer to God. I said we would have to see, but as I understood Dickinson, she seemed to think that the way to transcend alienation was through the power of the poetic imagination. Her poetry was largely concerned with gradations of alienation and transcendence, or shifts between the two, and these concerns were reflected in her imagery. I said that some of Dickinson's readers and critics did find that reading her poetry helped them better understand, and sometimes resolve, their own spiritual struggles. I suggested that before our next meeting, he might read some poems in *Final Harvest*—a selection of 576 poems from a complete edition of Emily Dickinson's poetry selected by Thomas Johnson (1961).

Ivan and I were unable to meet for several weeks. When we reconvened, he had read the entire collection in *Final Harvest*. He said he empathized with Dickinson's spiritual struggles and was enthralled by her poems, with which he had previously had only limited familiarity. He wanted to discuss many of them at length. I suggested it might be useful to talk a little about the philosophical background of Dickinson's poetry and her use of imagery before we looked at individual poems together. Given Ivan's background in the humanities, I was able to discuss the substance of the material outlined below, albeit with considerable simplification.

By way of introduction, I told Ivan that it was my understanding of Emily Dickinson's poetry that the focus on alienation in her work is based upon a kind of unsystematic Calvinistic Hegelian metaphysics where God functioned as the Absolute. The most basic category of alienation for Dickinson is ontological (metaphysical separation). Man and nature are objectified manifestations of the Absolute, alienated from God through their separation from him and engaged in a perpetual process of alienation and de-alienation. In Dickinson's poetry, transcendence of the category of ontological alienation is often signaled by a persona uniting with sun, sea, father, light, home, and so on. Often subtle erotic imagery, conjoined with ecstatic tone and mood, suggests a moment of spiritual union. This includes imagery suggesting penetration (ships mooring in harbors, blossoms with bees and hummingbirds); satin imagery (suggesting either the coffin of death or bride of Christ); spatial imagery (suggesting increased proximity, a new angle of vision, or vertical ascent), together with frequent use of synesthetic imagery, all of which reinforce these images of confluence and union or its approach. In sum, attention to Dickinson's imagery serves a heuristic function in mapping Dickinson's ontology.

Dickinson's poetry is also often concerned with alienation as an epistemological category (the problem of knowing God) frequently expressed as riddles. The ontological gap between God and man creates an epistemological gap that must be transcended. Man is alienated consciousness as it confronts the phenomenal world, attempting to bridge the gap and know the divine mysteries concerning God's rational plan for the universe and the promise of immortality. Transcendence of epistemological alienation is often signaled by puns (I and eye, see and sea, sight and site), often conjoined with changes in perspective. There are gradations of this category of alienation expressed by the verbs *hear*, *feel*, and finally *see*.

Finally, Dickinson's poems are also concerned with alienation as a psychological category. As alienated consciousness confronts its separation from God and its inability to know, it experiences a sense of estrangement, depersonalization, and loss. These emotions are particularly acute during periods of transition.

Transcending alienation of this kind also seems tied to specific imagery involving gradations that range from pain through ecstasy. Often, transcendence can produce fear and anxiety in the unprepared alienated consciousness. By contrast, the shift to alienated consciousness is signaled by negative imagery: personae flee, light fades, fires go out, the stem never flowers, colors are hidden or lose their brilliance, seas recede, fickle birds and bees depart, and so on. Sometimes there is an eroticism tinged with sadism: the satin of the bride encounters only the coldness of stone, eyes are put out, prurient seas violate rather than embrace, and encounters become painful and damaging.

Dickinson's poetry also demonstrates concern with modes of alienation. To be alienated from God is to be alienated from our essential nature as children of God as well as alienated from others (believers who have faith). Alienation from God is also alienation from nature and from God's design as manifested in nature. Alienation from God, therefore, results in fragmentation of self and isolation from one's fellow creatures.

I told Ivan that, as we read some of the poems together, I thought it would be useful for us to focus upon the gradations in alienation and skepticism represented in the poetry that lie within a range between two extremes. At one end of the spectrum are poems that express an almost total lack of alienation and a lack of skepticism about transcending it. At the other end of the spectrum lie poems that exhibit extreme alienation and extreme skepticism. I asked where he would like to start, with poems expressing confidence in a Christian God or poems expressing skepticism. He said he would like to start with poems expressing confidence, which, I suggested, we could regard as the first category of Dickinson's poems.

Category One: Poems with Minimal Alienation and Skepticism About Transcendence

When we reconvened, Ivan had read the entire collection again. One of the poems Ivan wanted to discuss was:

> At last, to be identified!
> At last, the lamps upon thy side
> The rest of Life to see!
>
> Past Midnight! Past the Morning Star!
> Past Sunrise!
> Ah, What leagues there were
> Between our feet, and Day![1]
>
> —30, 174, 18

We agreed that this poem was confident. After long struggles (symbolized by the reference to midnight and many leagues), the persona finally saw light. There was still some ontological alienation; she was not at noon (with God) yet, but she was close enough to God for him to see her and for her soon to be with him and see life from a divine perspective. I pointed out two other poems in this positive genre: The poem that begins "Exaltation is the Going" (14, 76, 8) suggests the initial phases of transcending an alienated consciousness.

Another poem, which begins "I taste a liquor never brewed" (46, 214, 25), is where skepticism and alienation are almost wholly absent insofar as the reader does not doubt the judgment of the euphoric persona.

The remainder of the session was devoted to discussing when Ivan had felt similar confidence in his faith or closeness to God. He said that his first experiences of this state had been when he first attended Russian Orthodox Mass in New York after coming to this country and later when he attended Mass again after becoming a citizen. He had felt happy, close to God, and as if he would be able to endure any future hardship, secure in the knowledge that some higher power was guiding and protecting him. I asked him whether he felt close to God only when he was happy or perhaps he was happy only when he felt close to God and secure in his beliefs. He said he had been happy enough without thinking deeply about religious belief before he had been diagnosed with cancer, but now he was so unhappy and ill that faith had become all-important to him; he could not be happy without it. He indicated that he thought that he would be satisfied and at peace only when he had more than a taste of the "liquor never brewed." This was what he hoped to achieve before he died.

Category Two: Poems Involving Brief Transcendence of Alienation and Continuing Resolve

In the next session, I suggested we look at a second category of Dickinson's poems, where the persona has only briefly transcended alienation but remained determined to try again. Resignation to some degree of alienation, conjoined with a rejection of skepticism about eventually overcoming it, is expressed in the last stanza of a poem, which begins "We grow accustomed to the Dark":

> Either the Darkness alters—
> Or something in the sight
> Adjusts itself to Midnight—
> And Life steps almost straight.
>
> —164, 419, 98

Ivan identified with the poem, which he said characterized some of his own experience. After obtaining citizenship, he had no longer attended Mass or felt so connected to God, but he had been busy with intellectual goals and had "put a spiritual life on the back burner." Now, he said, he could no longer "adjust ... to Midnight."

Ivan quickly added that he also could identify with Dickinson's poem "A loss of something ever felt I":

A loss of something ever felt I—
The first that I could recollect.
Bereft I was—of what I knew not.
Too young that any should expect.

A Mourner walked among the children
I not withstanding went about
As one bemoaning a Dominion
Itself the only Prince cast out—

Elder, Today, a session wiser
And fainter, too, as Wiseness is—
I find myself still softly searching
For my Delinquent Palaces—

And a Suspicion, like a Finger
Touches my Forehead now and then
That I am looking oppositely
For the site of the Kingdom of Heaven—

—348, 959, 224

In reading the poem together, we agreed that it is constructed as a kind of metaphysical and epistemological riddle about loss. What is the loss? What is missing? The absence of spiritual orientation? Older and wiser, the adult persona continues the search to recover what is lost or missing but feels as if she may have been searching in the wrong place. I asked Ivan what he thought would constitute the right place for the persona. He suggested faith, something outside the person rather than within, perhaps nature. The poem encapsulates a variety of related alienations. The persona is alienated from God, and the pun on "site" in the last line brings in epistemological aspects of alienation as well. The use of "bereft" in the third line and "itself" in the eighth line emphasizes the dehumanization and loss attendant upon alienation from God, while the reference to the "mourner among the children" emphasizes that skepticism alienates the persona from those who share a common and perhaps naive belief system.

Ivan said that the absence of exposure to any spiritual tradition in his youth in Russia and his later alienation from religion, expressed by his withdrawing from membership in the Russian Orthodox church in New York, did make him feel as if something was missing in his life and that Dickinson articulated feelings very similar to his own, which he had not been able to articulate himself. Now that he was terminally ill, the absence of deep religious faith made him feel "bereft," with little affinity for those in the congregation in the Russian Orthodox church he had last attended or in cancer support groups online, where many of the participants relied on faith for strength. He also said that he had looked at various arguments for the existence of God and found them unconvincing and felt as if his spiritual life was painful and hopeless. Ivan also said that feeling alienated from God made him lonely. Despite the support of people who loved him, he felt distanced even from them in his thinking and spiritual malaise. I responded that it seemed that, for Emily Dickinson, the way to transcend spiritual alienation in this world was through the poetic imagination rather than through rational argument and that, for her, transcending spiritual alienation did not require adopting any specific religion or practice. Emily Dickinson herself had stopped attending church. I suggested that he try meditating, writing his own prayers, and keeping a journal about his thoughts concerning his present spiritual struggles. I also suggested that he look at a third category of Dickinson's poems, which focused upon the pain of both alienation and its transcendence, and see that Dickinson—a poet we both much admired—fluctuated between almost total skepticism and renewed hope and confidence.

Category Three: Poems Expressing the Agony Involved in Alienation

In our next session, Ivan told me that journaling and attempting to formulate his own prayers had been helpful to him, because he was no longer trying to discuss his problems with people who simply could not identify with them. He said that there had been some occasions in writing his own prayers that he felt better, but always, later in the day, he became saddened again and sometimes even felt worse and more discouraged. As a consequence, we looked at some poems that stressed the pain of alienation and its transcendence. We both thought that some of her finest poems belonged to this category. In her magnificent poem that begins "After great pain a formal feeling comes" (122, 341, 73), the condition of the alienated consciousness confronting death is one of exhaustion and emotional depletion. The persona's pain in the march toward death becomes the agony of Christ bearing the cross to Calvary. There is motion in the poem and through time, but it goes nowhere. The tone is skeptical; death, too, may be a motion into timelessness, without meaning or progression. Transcendence may be a chimera. Ivan identified with the feelings expressed in the persona's "hour of lead." Another poem belonging to this category that we discussed is below:

Before I got my eye put out
I liked as well to see—
As other creatures, that have Eyes—
And know no other way—

But were it told to me, Today—
That I might have the Sky
For mine, I tell you that my Heart
Would split, for size of me—

The Meadows—mine—
The Mountains—mine—
All Forests—Stintless stars—
As much of Noon, as I could take—
Between my finite eyes—

The Motions of the Dipping Birds—
The Morning's Amber Road—
For mine—to look at when I liked,
The News would strike me dead—

So safer—guess—with just my soul
Upon the window pane

Where other creatures put their eyes—
Incautious—of the Sun—

—115, 327, 68

The subject of the poem is epistemological. Two types of vision are being contrasted—alienated vision and transcendent vision—with the focus of the poem centering on the sentiments of the persona before and after the loss of transcendent vision. The concluding stanza of the poem expresses two types of skepticism. First, there is skepticism about whether the joy of the transcendent vision of the world sub specie aeternitatis (expressed in the second stanza) is worth the pain of its inevitable loss. Second, there is skepticism about whether that vision is worth the loss of personal identity implicit in transcendent consciousness. There seems to be a withdrawal from an active quest for God to a posture of receptivity. Other creatures have eyes and know no other way. By contrast, the persona has a choice to make between two types of vision and, in the loneliness of this choice, the persona is alienated from creatures that are in harmony with a transcendent reality.

After we had worked through the poem together, I asked Ivan what it was like when he felt close to God and whether there were other occasions besides those he had mentioned when he felt the boundaries between himself and God diminish. He said that he loved the sea and that sailing, for him, was a kind of mystical activity where he felt wholly at peace and at one with something larger than himself, where he felt the presence of God. I also asked if he felt a loss of personal identity at such times and, if so, whether he felt threatened by such loss. He said that feeling a part of something larger than himself was joyous, but on return from such trips, he was often depressed because of the diminution of joy in his daily life. He also said that loss of personal identity was a source of fear when he thought about dying. He said he wanted to be with God, but added, semi-facetiously: "I want to be with God, but also with my dog, my books, and my sailboat in heaven, too." My response was to the effect that he did not have to focus solely on Emily Dickinson's Hegelian God or necessarily on struggles to achieve a transcendent vision. Perhaps the key was to locate himself in places where his receptivity to a transcendent vision was strengthened, as it was by being at sea.

Category Four: Poems About the Psychology of an Alienated Consciousness

As a result of what Ivan had said, we looked at a fourth category of Dickinson's poems, which deals with other aspects of the psychology of alienated consciousness as it confronts the approach of a highly personalized, transcendent reality. In some cases, alienated consciousness regards the approach as menacing, as in the poem beginning "I started early—Took, my Dog" (209, 520, 128) and in the poem that begins "He fumbles at your Soul" (105, 315, 61). In these poems and in her better-known poem that begins "Because I could not stop for Death" (290, 712, 177), alienated consciousness is skeptical of transcendence, seemingly regarding God as a possible seducer rather than a lover. In other poems belonging to this genre, God is represented as teasing, mocking, evasive, and cruel. The personae in these poems display varying degrees of skepticism about the benevolence of God, although none of them suggest that perhaps God might be a reification of alienated consciousness. The attitudes of the personae range from aggressive defiance to open fear.

I asked Ivan about his own conception of God. He said that it was more difficult for him to have faith that God was benevolent than to have faith that he existed. He said that priests had reminded him that human suffering was a test of faith and that he thought he was failing it. Given his knowledge of Russian literature, I was surprised that this kind of skepticism did not remind him of the outright metaphysical rebellion of Ivan Karamazov in Fyodor Dostoevsky's *The Brothers Karamazov*, who famously could not forgive the suffering of a single child, but neither Emily Dickinson nor my client moved in the direction of outright rejection of God. Hence, I reminded him that this was a part of his spiritual struggles, not a failure, and that he was not alone in his skepticism; cancer and human suffering make us all at some time question almost everything. I suggested that perhaps we should conclude our discussion of Emily Dickinson by looking at two final categories of her poems: those dealing with nature and those where she dealt directly with the issue of death.

Category Five: Poems About Alienation, Transcendence, and Nature

In the next session, we discussed Emily Dickinson's ambiguity with respect to alienation and nature. In some poems, nature is saturated with the presence of God. The poem that begins with the line "A Slash of Blue" (40, 204, 23) leaves little room for skepticism or alienation. In a longer poem, which begins "By my Window have I for Scenery," nature provides only clues to God's nature, for the persona says:

> Was the Pine at my Window a "Fellow
> Of the Royal" Infinity?
> Apprehensions—are God's introductions—
> To be hallowed—accordingly—
>
> —326, 797, 198

By further contrast, in a poem beginning "These are the Days when Birds come back," the persona is clearly alienated from nature, which may offer only "the old, old sophistries of June" (23, 130, 13). The last two poems provide a nice contrast between the faith in nature one finds in Romanticism and modern skepticism about the reliability of nature as a basis for overcoming skepticism about transcendence.

Ivan found the Romantics much closer to his own sensibility and his own "apprehensions" much stronger and more convincing than Dickinson had found hers. Still, although design in nature seemed evidence for God, he said, cancer made him question it. If Ivan's circumstances had been different, I might have suggested he read Robert Frost's poem "Design" for a much darker perspective.

Category Six: Poems About Death and Skepticism About Transcendence

Our last session was devoted to Dickinson's death poems. Like most of my clients with cancer, Ivan seldom wanted to talk about death. At first, I thought that this reluctance was a cultural artifact, but I've found that clients from a variety of cultures do not want to explore the topic until they became candidates for hospice, and even then, they prefer to talk about their lives before cancer. Pastoral counselors seem to find less reluctance, which I suspect is because they counsel patients who have fewer doubts about their faith in God and the resurrection.

In this sixth and last category of poetry that Ivan Petrovich and I explored together, as in the other categories, we found gradations of alienation and skepticism about its transcendence expressed by different personae. Perhaps the most optimistic is the poem that begins:

Tie the Strings to my Life, My Lord,
Then, I am ready to go!

And concludes with the stanza:

Goodbye to the Life I used to live—
And the World I used to know—
And kiss the Hills for me, just once—
Then—I am ready to go!

—77, 179, 42

By contrast, another poem, which begins "That after Horror—that 'twas Us" (83, 286, 46), represents death as having "a metallic grin" and the "face of steel"—imagery that suggests skepticism about receiving the "steadfast honey," which is presumably life after death.

For the first time, after reading the poems, Ivan talked about dying at some length. He talked about what he would be losing in this life and said that he realized that it was time for him to begin saying goodbye to people and things he cared about. Until now, he had refused to consider practical end-of-life decisions; he had been passionately focused on living. He told me that he and his partner had talked about every aspect of his treatment but never addressed the issue of dying.

Ivan also talked, finally, about his fear of the painful process of dying and said that his fear sometimes caused him to consider suicide even though he believed suicide to be a sin. I suggested that he talk to his oncologist and also to a representative of a hospice program about ways in which they might assuage his fear by explaining how they might reduce suffering at the end with palliative care. I also said that, if his fears did not diminish after these consultations, the state in which we lived did have a program called MAID, an acronym for "medical assistance in dying." To qualify for that help, he would need proof from his physician that he was terminally ill; there was then a six-month waiting period. I explained to him that our state had such a program, which actively assists people to successfully and safely terminate their own lives, because many people think the teachings of some organized religions are wrong and that, in fact, there is nothing morally wrong about terminally ill patients committing rational suicide and that, given rights to autonomy, people had the right to end their lives as they saw fit.

After further dialogue, I felt confident that Ivan's reference to suicide was suicidal ideation, not yet an expression of intent. However, I did ask him if he would feel comfortable promising me that he would not consider suicide until he had thoroughly examined the issue with his treatment team and further explored the philosophical issues about rational suicide with me. I reminded him that he had sought counseling so that he could "die in peace" and that to do so required practical as well as philosophical investigations to avoid suffering. He promised to further explore the options we had discussed before making any decisions.

Ivan said that our present session had given him a great deal to think about, but before we ended the session, he wanted to understand what Emily Dickinson thought about death and immortality. He asked which poem I thought was representative of Emily Dickinson's perspective on death. I responded that I thought that her poems, taken together, all seemed to reflect ambiguity about life after death. Did he agree? I suggested that we look at some lesser-known poems, one short and one long poem, devoted to death. For example, one poem confidently begins with the line "I know that He exists," but the poem seems to conclude that death is the ultimate riddle, literally the last chance for consciousness to transcend alienation. Dickinson's personae play for high stakes, all or nothing, and the game cannot be lost, for the poem concludes:

Would not the fun
Look too expensive!
Would not the jest—
Have crawled too far!

—120, 338, 71

if God's game only ends in "Death's—stiff—stare" (120, 338, 71). Alienated consciousness, despite belief in God, has no answer to riddles about immortality.

The last poem that Ivan and I puzzled over opens with the line "The Color of the Grave is Green":

The Color of the Grave is Green—
The Outer Grave—I mean—
You would not know it from the Field—
Except it own a Stone—

To help the fond—to find it—
Too infinite asleep
To stop and tell them where it is—
But just a Daisy—deep—

The Color of the Grave is white—
The outer Grave—I mean—
You would not know it from the Drifts—
In Winter—till the Sun—

Has furrowed out the Aisles—
Then—higher than the Land
The little Dwelling Houses rise
Where each—has left a friend—

The Color of the Grave within—
The Duplicate—I mean—
Not all the Snows could make it white—
Not all the Summers—Green—

You've seen the Color—maybe—
Upon a Bonnet bound—
When that you met it with before—
The Ferret—cannot find—

—160, 412, 95

We agreed that Dickinson was posing a riddle about death and that she was contrasting two different kinds of death: corporeal death (the outer death) and spiritual death (the duplicate) from what might be three different perspectives. The first two stanzas seem to suggest the perspective of nature or perhaps youth (the grave is green); the next two stanzas seem to suggest a human perspective, the perspective of organized religion or perhaps the perspective of old age (the grave is white). The last two stanzas perhaps suggest the realm of the persona's own consciousness or a temporal realm after death.

The color symbolism of "white" is ambivalent. The stanzas where the grave is white might suggest the view of organized religion, in which case white might symbolize the resurrection, innocence, or purity. However, white has other connotations. Herma Melville, roughly a contemporary of Dickinson, devoted a whole chapter in *Moby-Dick* to the meaning of "whiteness," which, according to the narrator, Ishmael, could symbolize the good but also its opposite: "the heartless voids and immensities of the universe" (Cooper 1978: 41–2).

The thrust of the poem and the puzzling last line telling us that we have met the color before seem to suggest that the riddle of death permeates every realm of the universe and every phase of the persona's existential condition, eternally confronting the alienated consciousness. If there is an answer to the riddle, the answer is ambiguous. The connection between the first line of the penultimate stanza and the final line of the final stanza seems to suggest that for the alienated consciousness, confidence in victory over death cannot be supplied through the agency of reason (the ferret). The final stanza, then, nullifies even the guarded hope that seems to be suggested by the "daisy"—often Dickinson's symbol for herself but also traditionally the flower depicted in pictures of both the birth and death of Christ—that the riddle can be solved "deep" within the confines of one's own consciousness.

I asked Ivan whether he could empathize with Dickinson's perspective and what, if anything, her spiritual struggle implied for his own. He said that his crisis of faith was in part the result of looking for enduring certainties about God and about life after death. Perhaps then, I asked, should he have sought counseling with a priest rather than philosophical counseling with me, if, at the end, he would have to rely on faith rather than on logic and reason? Ivan responded that his priest had only told him to pray but that perhaps Emily Dickinson's poems were prayers. He said that working through her spiritual struggles had enriched his own spirituality, clarified many dimensions of his own struggles, and shown him that no experience would ever fully satisfy his desire for proof in a benevolent God and life after death. He was able to accept this now because working through Dickinson's spiritual struggles had led him to conclude that faith and believing in Christianity is a continual struggle for all deeply spiritual people.

Having faith is having a commitment to an ongoing process rather than achieving a goal, then, isn't it? I suggested. Yes, exactly, he agreed. He also said that his desire to feel closer to God as he neared the end of his life was clearer and less painful because he now recognized that sometimes he would feel alienated from God, and sometimes he would feel as if he were close to him and that this was part of being a Christian rather than some failure on his part. He also said that while there may be some insoluble riddles about life after death, he now recognized that his previously unacknowledged fears about physical suffering at the end of his life could be addressed and perhaps overcome. Finally, he said that he thought his puzzles and spiritual unhappiness would have been dismissed by most people with whom he might have discussed them but that working through Emily Dickinson's poetry had made him feel as if his struggles were understood and validated by a great poet.[2]

Conclusion

Clearly, the use of Emily Dickinson's poetry in counseling Ivan served to provide medicine for the soul of a man experiencing a crisis of faith in the face of his rapidly approaching death. Her poems represent universal dimensions of spiritual struggles and the alienation from God sometimes experienced by religious people. They mirrored those of Ivan, allowing him to understand his own crisis of faith more deeply. Her poetry also served as a vehicle for the expression of shared emotions Ivan had difficulty understanding and articulating in his own life. In part, because his spiritual alienation was multidimensional, Dickinson's images, metaphors, and riddles revealed insights largely inaccessible through other means. Her poems educated Ivan by suggesting new philosophical perspectives about the nature of spirituality and what it might mean to be a Christian, thus transfiguring his idea of faith. By helping him better understand his emotions, the poems also helped him to master them and understand their ontological, epistemological, and psychological ramifications at a deeper level. In the end, like Emily Dickinson, Ivan became reconciled to being a "mourner among the children," whose skepticism sometimes left him feeling, like her, "bereft"—alienated from God and those believers with a simplistic childlike perspective on the relationship between a man and his God, characteristic of some organized religions. He now recognized that faith is, by its very nature, a struggle and that his own struggles were validated by a great poet.

Poetry therapy can be a philosophical form of counsel. The choice of philosophical poems, and their use in mirroring a client's issues in ways that suggest new perspectives, can light our clients along the way of many philosophical journeys. The choice of poetry must always be predicated upon the client's philosophical problem and on how the problem and its possible resolution appear to him.

In conclusion, Emily Dickinson served as "a vital light" for my client and perhaps provided a modern addendum to Shelley's *Defense of Poetry* when she wrote:

The Poets light but Lamps—
Themselves—go out—
The Wicks they stimulate.
If vital Light

Inhere as do the Suns—
Each Age a Lens
Disseminating their
Circumference—

—257, 833, 214

Notes

1 All Dickinson poems cited are from Johnson's works. The first number refers to the number of the poem selected in *Final Harvest*. The second number refers to the number of the same poem in *The Complete Poems of Emily Dickinson* (Thomas

H. Johnson (ed.), The Belnap Press of Harvard University Press. Copyright 1951, 1955, by the President and Fellows of Harvard College. Copyright renewed 1979, 1983, by the President and Fellows of Harvard College. Copyright 1914, 1918, 1919, 1924, 1929, 1930, 1932, 1935, 1937, 1942, by Martha L. Hampson. Used by Permission: License R-12930 All rights reserved). The last number is the page number of the poem in *Final Harvest*.

2 Ivan Petrovich suddenly became very ill two months after our last session. He died in the emergency room.

References

Cooper, J. C. (1978), *An Illustrated Encyclopedia of Traditional Symbols*, Thames and Hudson.

Feary, V. (2005), "Art and the Good Life: The Role of Literature and the Visual Arts in Philosophical Practice," *Philosophical Practice* 1 (2): 95–112.

Feary, V. (2014), "Spirituality and Philosophical Practice: Counseling with Clients in Crisis," *Philosophical Practice* 9 (3): 1413–25.

Hynes, A. M. and M. Hynes-Berry (1994), *Biblio/Poetry Therapy—The Interactive Process: A Handbook*, North Star Press of St. Cloud.

Leedy, J. J. (ed.) (1969), *Poetry Therapy*, J. B. Lippincott.

Mazza, N. (2017), *Poetry Therapy: Theory and Practice*, Routledge.

Rhee, Y. E. (2011), "Philosophical Practice and the Humanities in Korea," *Philosophical Practice* 6 (1): 734–43.

Additional Reading

Anderson, C. R. (1960), *Emily Dickinson's Poetry: Stairway of Surprise*, Rinehart & Winston.

Collingwood, R. E. (1993), "Expression in Art," in J. A. Fischer (ed.), *Reflecting on Art*, 186–93, Mayfield.

Ferber, M. (1999), *A Dictionary of Literary Symbols*, Cambridge University Press.

Ferlazzo, P. J. (1976), *Emily Dickinson*, G. K. Hall.

Gelpi, A. (1965), *Emily Dickinson, The Mind of a Poet*, Harvard University Press.

Hogan, S. (2016), *Art Therapy Theories*, Routledge.

Lucas, D. D. (1969), *Emily Dickinson and Riddle*, Northern Illinois University Press.
Murphy, C. M. (2019), *Mystical Prayer: The Poetic Example of Emily Dickinson*, Liturgical Press.
Rupp, R. H. (ed.) (1972), *Critics on Emily Dickinson*, University of Miami Press.
Sherwood, R. (1968), *Circumference and Circumstance: Stages in the Mind and Art of Emily Dickinson*, Columbia University Press.

7

Pursuing Wisdom in Riddles

Practicing Philosophy with Poetry on the Puzzle of Our Existence

Sebastian Rehnman

Introduction

Gloom fills me.[1] Once again, I am lying awake in my bed and fall prey to my dark frame of mind in the middle of the night. I feel invaded and beleaguered as I agonize over my whole life, my existence. My feelings are black, my memories are black, my thoughts are black, and my imaginations are black: There is not this, was not that, will not be this, and may not have been anything at all. I anguish over how I exist, I fret about how I could have existed, I dread how I will exist, and I regret how I once will not exist at all. I feel distress for how life is, could have been, will be, and should not be at all. My train of angst-driven thoughts follows their familiar angst-ridden tracks. Here I cannot stand the ache of being any longer, so I rise and stroll out into a kitchen as dark as my soul.

There I do as so many times before—I quietly recite a poem by R. S. Thomas:

> But the silence in the mind
> is when we live best, within
> listening distance of the silence
> we call God. This is the deep
> calling to deep of the psalm-
> writer, the bottomless ocean
> we launch the armada of
> our thoughts on, never arriving.

It is a presence, then,
whose margins are our margins;
that calls us out over our
own fathoms. What to do
but draw a little nearer to
such ubiquity by remaining still?

—1990, 118

I chew on the poem as I chew on my sandwich till I feel relief and wonder. I go from misery to musing, from contention to contentment, from gloom to glee. Quietly I walk back through the silent house and lie down in stillness of body and soul, not even pondering how this change came about.

In the sketch above, I believe I, in part, practice philosophy. I take it that I follow the Socratic tradition of seeking wisdom by knowing myself with others (cf. Plato Ap, 21a-d, 28e, 41e; Chrm, 158e–159a, 160d-e, 164d; 48c-d; Prt, 343b, 348a, 348e; Alc I, 124a-b, 127e, 129a, 131b–133c, 132c; Phd, 230a, 257b, 259d, 261a, 278d–279-b; Le, 923a). I long to live consciously with a comprehensive understanding of my life and living, reflecting on and disposing my feeling, perceiving, thinking, remembering, imagining, acting, and desiring wisely. I aim for this by several exercises such as dialogue, meditation, journaling, and reading (e.g., Rehnman 2023a,b). Applying literature to my life and living seems appropriate to pursuing wisdom, since writers of prose and poetry most fully elaborate on our human experience. Poetry may in particular have the potential apart from other exercises to form—inform, reform, and transform—us in particular ways. For the departures from ordinary usage in the styles of enunciation, figures of speech, and order of words constitute the intensity and beauty of the verses that can raise our feeling, imagining, and pondering. Musing on the riddles, we may become alert to the sound of syllables and rhythms we hear and the sensations in our stomachs, hearts, limbs, or throats that accompany our feelings so as to receive and possess what we know of ourselves. Poetry allows us to respond not only to the meanings we understand but also to the meanings we feel, hear, and see. What we undergo in reading poems may consequently make us realize what leading a philosophical life means. So I chase sagacity through the extended language of poetry.

Although philosophy as a way of life has been recaptured since the 1970s (e.g., Rabbow 1954; Hadot 1969, 1995; Nussbaum [1994] 2009; Cooper

2012; Sharpe and Ure 2021), how we practice such a living has been pretty prosaic. Commonly, the instructions have been very general, abstract, or even negative, and poetry has certainly not been one of the exercises described. For instance, Cohoe, Grimm, Hidalgo, and Jeng say that they practice philosophy but do not show how (Cohoe and Grimm 2020; Hidalgo 2020; Jeng 2020; Grimm and Cohoe 2021). The most relevant comparison of practicing philosophy with poetry may be Jeng, but his exegesis of Plato only yields the conclusion that "[t]he philosopher needs to study the lives portrayed in poetry to defend his own, despite the dangers that he is exposing himself to" (2020: 169). Harte (2023: 71) similarly suggests that there is "a fair amount of philosophy that takes poetry as an object of study, but philosophy has farther to go in seeing poetry as a form of philosophizing."[2] All this comes to general and negative statements that assume Plato's "quarrel between philosophers and poets" (Rep, 607b5–6) was all he wrote on the topic. This moreover sharply contrasts not only with how specifically, say, Musonius Rufus (1947: F), Plutarch (Dpv, Dta), Marcus Aurelius (1930: Md), and Seneca (1965: Em) practice philosophy but also with how Socrates both composes poetry (Phd 61b) and claims that a lover of wisdom must become a lover of poetry (Rep, 607d, cf. 614b; Phdr, 60d-e; Chrm, 156d). It differs further from the claim of Aristotle that both philosophy and poetry tend to express universal human experience (*P*, 1451b5); of Plotinus that poetry can lead us to contemplate the Good (En, 5.8); of Plutarch that poetry prepares the young for philosophy (Dap); of Boëthius that poetry and prose fuse in pursuit of wisdom (1957: Dcp); of Montaigne that philosophy refines and derives authority from poetry ([1588] 2002: 2.12, 537); of Kierkegaard that the combination of poetry and philosophy contributes to our individual existence ([1846] 2002, title and esp., 569–70); of Heidegger that both philosophy and poetry are related to the origin of thinking ([1943] 1965: 55, [1959] 1985); of Wittgenstein that philosophy should only be composed poetically (1998: 28); and of Strawson that had he been able to choose talents, he "would have chosen to be a poet" ([1998] 2011: 228). So a tradition aligns the practice of philosophy with poetry, and if we want to further philosophical living today, we need to show how we seek to live with comprehensive understanding. We need to be specific, concrete, and positive, for instance, in reading poetry, to represent philosophy as a way of life.

R. S. Thomas's exploration of existential issues with poetical measures led to his nomination for the Nobel Prize. He gave the gist somewhat ironically: "I engage with philosophy in the morning, with the garden in the afternoon" (1977: 325). Poetry, he writes, is the "imaginative presentation" of "embracing an experience of ultimate reality" (1963: 9), since its "scope" is to express truth "in a more intense and memorable way than any other literary form is able to" (1966a: 169). However, I know no scholarship on Thomas in relation to pursuing wisdom. Although scholars commonly acknowledge his references to, say, Kierkegaard, Heidegger, and Wittgenstein (Thomas [1988] 2004: 35,1 71, 1992, 182),[3] his repeated autobiographical attempts toward self-knowledge (Thomas [1988] 2004, 1997) as well as his exploration of our existence and ethos almost everywhere, no one has shown how the poems may apply to living in pursuit of wisdom. Some amass the existential agony in the poems without analysis and application (Pikoulis and Roberts 1993), while others seem oblivious to the existential and ethical issues expressed (Shepherd 1996). Oddly, D. Z. Phillips's "contemplative philosophy" engages rarely with these issues in his excellent monograph on Thomas (1986, 2006: 215–26). Although the poem quoted in this section seems to encapsulate very many of Thomas's characteristics, I have only come across one brief comment (Morgan 2013: 40–1). Yet Thomas has been called "the Socrates of Wales" because of his mastery in helping us through poetry to become conscious of our previously latent conceptions (M. W. Thomas 2013: 191, 188),[4] and so his poetry has recently been used to illustrate how it may expand our philosophical imagination from conventional presumption (Burley 2021). I believe Thomas's poems can be powerful occasions of becoming and remaining receptive and possessive of what we already half-heartedly know of ourselves in our unruly yearning for wisdom. We can, and ought therefore to, become apprentices of this master in pursuing wisdom through self-knowledge with one another.

In this chapter, I exemplify but do not exhaust how I practice philosophy with Thomas's poem "But the silence in the mind." In the first section, I try to make sense of how the poem affects me, and in the second section, I elucidate how the realization of my existential moods inclines me to pursue wisdom. I finally conclude that we need to go beyond the facile opposition between philosophy and poetry and instead explore how works of art help us express our longing for inexpressible wisdom. Thus, this chapter is significant for all who long to lead a life answering comprehensive understanding.

Changing My Mood Through Poetry

In this section I pursue self-knowledge toward wisdom by attempting to delineate my experience in reciting Thomas's poem. I seek in some detail to put my feeling, thinking, remembering, imagining, and desiring into words. I trace how the poem makes me recall the living I want, baffled by the apparently absurd, and gently come to myself through ease and awe in attuning from anxiety to tranquility. Here I attend to my broad experience of the poem to become and be more receptive to my existence and thereby show what (as far as I understand or misunderstand) the pursuit of wisdom through self-knowledge with poetry may mean. This self-reflection is itself an exercise in practicing philosophy.

The beginning of Thomas's poem reminds me of what I really want: "But the silence in the mind is when we live best." I know I desire to live in that way. Yet, since adolescence, I have for longer or briefer time spans repeatedly and recurrently suffered severe and deep distress in and of living. I then feel overall sad, perceive everything darkly, remember the past with dislike, ruminate resentfully on things, imagine the future with worry, and hardly do or desire anything. However, when the odd first lines of the poet strike me, I feel I do not want to live in such a frame of mind. The conjunction "but" comes out of nowhere and seems to introduce an exception to an earlier, though missing, statement or question concerning our usual rage at and alarm in life. I do not desire to live in uproar but in calmness, and it slowly dawns on me that I want to live well—in Socrates' words, that "the most important thing is not to live but to live well" (Plato Cr, 48). That means for me partly to exist in and with peace of mind, ready to respond in contented manners, and reflect on myself having achieved at least some worthy and worthwhile goals in life as a whole. So, in reciting the poem, I realize to some extent what I really want to be, do, or undergo, and I come to my senses.

I seem to come to my senses by non-senses. The poem continues with words that do not make sense in their usual use, but their unusual use makes me ponder the apparent absurdities of silences, listenings, callings, and armadas. I begin to appreciate the peculiar uses of silence and listening in the verse. Obviously "the silence of the mind" cannot literally mean absence of sounds, since the mind cannot be said to be a room with dampened vibration of air. Nor can we commonly be said to be within listening distance of silence, since only that which can be said to make sound can be said to be heard, and we cannot be said to be in the space to hear that which cannot be heard, and that which cannot be heard is "the silence we call God." I grasp moreover that the vague verb "to call" allows Thomas to move from our naming the silence "God" to the deep silence of God summoning the deep of us "out over our own fathoms."[5] This cannot mean to be within the space of hearing the biggest guy around but cryptically receiving the inaudible calling of "the bottomless" and boundless abyss ("never arriving") into our incomprehension of ourselves. I further recognize that "the armada of our thoughts" cannot refer to a fleet of warships but to our own contentions when we do not live best. So these three puzzles confound me into consideration. In their ordinary use, the meaning of these statements can only be denied, but in their extraordinary use, they can be both affirmed and denied. These expressions are brought out of their ordinary context into an extraordinary context that is no context at all. Being startled in my melancholy, the metaphors do not motivate me into action but move me into amazement. I am unsettled by seemingly sudden astonishment and wonder vaguely at the paradoxes of the poem.

I barely notice that something may be odd with my thinking, and I come to acknowledge that my contentions may miss their target just as the warships in the poem miss their target. This seems to begin with feeling my liking for the sea challenged by "the armada of our thoughts." The maritime expressions of the poem catch and hold my attention, because I admire and respect the sea. My esteem is not mere sentiment but has formed my character in growing up and choosing to live near the sea. However, the armada preparing for or engaging in military encounter challenges my attitude to the sea, since in contrast to the silence and stillness of the mind I desire, there is commotion and strife. I feel somewhat confused by the meaning of this threat and perhaps also the beginning of fear and anger toward the significance of the armada. Yet not only do the warships sail on my beloved ocean, but they also will never reach their butt. Armadas can arrive at targets that are part of or within the boundaries of the sea, but this armada cannot, since this ocean is bottomless and thus boundless.[6] All this makes me feel curious. Perhaps my thinking is as misconceived as this armada: The warships and I would not exist without but cannot wage war against that which is beyond bottom and boundary. I may be asking *how* I exist beyond the bounds of sense and the grounds of certainty but should perhaps instead be acquiescing *that* I exist. In reading the poem, I undergo my sentiment for the sea and, on reflection, realize weakly not only that I feel the reasons for my attitude of reverence but also that I may understand neither my thoughts nor myself in the summoning presence of the bottomless, boundless, insurmountable, and unfathomable.[7] The poem allows me to ponder and assess my thinking; to redescribe and redefine my anguish. It excites then a feeling of interest and inclines me to probe the strange but futile armada on the peculiar ocean that disagrees with the agreeable meaning of the sea. I open up to the unexpressed and to the inexpressible.

Confounded by conflict, I come to experience some comfort in these extended uses from their ordinary uses. The meaning of the armada threatens my maritime sentiment and sense of identity, but my realizations of pointless contentions pave the way for new emotions. My musings on the riddles make me feel ease and awe. On the one hand, the poem cuts through my darkness and diminishes the burden of melancholy. For I feel not to struggle over how I live, because I am conscious that my contentions are futile, so reciting the poem gives me relief from my contentions. For relief is the emotion we undergo when we are delivered from a given distress, and my reflection on the words of the poem provides release. This alleviation makes it even pleasant for me to ponder the poem. On the other hand, the relief turns into awe as I oddly fear and revere that I live. For I feel profoundly that it is somewhat scary to have contended about *how* I live rather than be contented *that* I live, and then I do not merely ask how I live but astonish that I live. Thus, my recital occasions deliverance from my woes of life and excites wonder as the deep meaning of living strikes me. Even if these emotions of relief and wonder may be brief, their emergence seems important for the change I undergo.

My relief and wonder may then pave the way for the stillness of my mind. These emotions grow into a calm stance that I exist. My questions of *how* I and everything else exist transform into wonder *that* I and everything else exist. My object is not a thing or topic that is most general, but my state of mind is general. What puts me into my quiet temper need not but may be something, such as poetry. It is me being attuned toward whatever exists, and I receive the puzzle that anything exists rather than not. I do not contend against *how* this or that is but am confident *that* there is something at all. Perhaps I silently exclaim with Nietzsche: "How could I not be grateful for my whole life?" ([1908] 1969: 263). My contention against how I exist dissolves (at least for the present), and my contentment that I exist evolves. I need not be tranquil of how I exist but may be tranquil that I exist. The ease from my pervasive anxiety toward my existence turns into pervasive tranquility toward my existence. In this way, I seem to be moved from contention to contentment.[8]

So the recital of Thomas's poem "But the silence in the mind" affects my change of mood. I have in this section attempted to delineate how the poem seems to touch me, namely, from the agitation of being startled—over the attitude of admiration as well as the emotions of curiosity, relief, and wonder—to the mood of tranquility. Here the poem's extraordinary use of words provides an extraordinary occasion for understanding myself. The metaphor of the armada on the ocean connects with the meaning of the sea for me and my attitude of reverence for the sea, and I become conscious of my reasons for my mood of angst being groundless and senseless. This results in the emotions of relief and wonder, which mediate or modulate my moods, so that existence is joyous though not pleasant, and my change ends in the mood of tranquility, equanimity, or gravity. These affections involve meanings so basic to myself that what I mean partly constitutes what I feel and think. Thus, my misty musings begin in a mood of anguish and change into luminous longings in a mood of calmness. And in delineating my experience, I practice philosophy with poetry.

Constituting Our Mood for Philosophy

In this section, I continue to show that my change of moods through Thomas's poem connects with the practice of philosophy. I argue that my individual experience exemplifies our fellow pursuit of wisdom. For therein the understanding we undertake and the feeling we undergo are comprehensive, but the comprehensive feeling we call *mood* may incline or disincline us to comprehensive understanding, so we need to be in the right mood for practicing philosophy. I move, in this part of the chapter, from the first-person singular to the first-person plural, where the "we" points to a tradition of wisdom seekers that manifest a mood for philosophy partly in inclinations toward being sensible and astute. I proceed with the pursuit of wisdom narrowly conceived as expressing the inexpressible, where metaphysics and poetry combine with their particular powers. In this way, we practice philosophy with poetry.

What it means to be in the frame for practicing philosophy, we can only learn by examples. We master first the meaning of words by the behavior of others, including their verbal behavior, and apply it then to ourselves, so we need to give heed to what those characterized as wisdom seekers do and undergo in expressing the temper of their practice (for a development of this, see Rehnman 2021: 223–6, 2022). In his study of the models of the ancient philosophers, Pierre Hadot (1995: 352) concludes that *angoisse existentielle* lies behind their exercises toward wisdom. We may note, for instance, how Plato commonly portrays Socrates' calm and composed manners in dialogues (e.g., Ap, Cr, and Phdr); Plutarch may sum up in his *Peri euthumias* an ancient tradition of being well disposed for philosophy (Dta; cf. Gill 1994); Seneca repeatedly interconnects philosophical exercises and moods (e.g., 1932a: DcH; 1932b: Dta; 1965: Em XLI); Boëthius (1957: Dcp) struggles for solace; Montaigne (1588: 2.19) fosters himself toward peace in the face of worry, agony, and fear over death; Wittgenstein (1998: 4) conceives philosophy as a cool temple that surrounds the passions; Heidegger ([1927] 2006, 138) receives the present in calm contemplation; and McGhee (2000: 74) meditates to make sense of life. All these thinkers (and others) can become our mentors as adepts in the pursuit of wisdom. We can and should of course assess their performance in terms of, say, history, logic, and wisdom (cf. Rehnman 2022), but we need paragons of what state of mind can guide us in seeking comprehensive understanding of our whole life and worthy living. We need as apprentices to attend to what masters of philosophy do and undergo in showing themselves attuned to their practice. They provide paradigms to the practice of philosophy.

To live in zest of wisdom, we have to be in a certain state of mind. We need not just a frame of mind that occurs for a little while but lasts for a long while, even a lifetime, as the understanding in question comprehends our entire life and living. Moods persist of course for a time and pervade our feeling, perceiving, thinking, remembering, and imagining, and although they do not in themselves give us behavioral reasons, they incline or disincline our acting and desiring. But some moods are more comprehensive than others. Moods for (or against), say, music or sex are narrower than for (or against) existence. Such states of mind that dispose our broad experience toward our existence, I call existential moods, and they connect with practicing philosophy, since wisdom comprehends the understanding of our whole life, and to pursue that while conscious, we need to be inclined to living in wise ways. "The attunement of the mood contains," writes Heidegger, "being as a whole" ([1943] 1965: 33, my translation).[9] Such frames of mind do not give us reasons for but bend us toward pursuing wisdom. So, to practice philosophy, we need to be in an existential mood.

Although existential moods may imply comprehensive understanding and feeling of our life and living, we need to be judicious. For these pensive moods can either capture, overwhelm, and even passivate us or liberate, empower, and activate us and thus either disincline or incline us over time to pursue understanding of our existence. We may be anxious of our existence so as both to pay little or no weight and great or too much weight to it. We may be given to all degrees, from being trifling and silly (considering existence not worthy of our serious attention) to trembling and sullen (considering existence no worry of our anguish suspension). So we need to discriminate. In the words of Kierkegaard, "each human being has to endure the adventure of learning to be anxious in order neither to be lost in never having been anxious nor to sink in anxiety. He who has there learnt to be rightly anxious has learnt the highest." But if we do not persevere in "the true mood" of gravity, the Danish sage continues, our "mood becomes either melancholy or frivolity" (Kierkegaard [1844] 2014: 454, 322, my translation; cf. Plutarch Dta, xv; Heidegger [1927] 2006: 138). And this grave anxiety in existing I take to be R. S. Thomas's continuous condition of "remaining still" as "the silence in the mind is when we live best." Hence, from these and other mentors of our guild, we can learn good sense and keen penetration to be rightly anxious of our unfathomable existence. We want an existential mood that contributes to the practice of philosophy, and the masters of philosophy manifest such a state of mind.

A first way in which an existential mood for philosophy expresses itself is in being sensible. We must be attuned to recognize and heed the most suitable way of life. To pursue wisdom, we need to be in a frame of mind that is bent on being receptive to and possessive of our personal lives and living. For we live as particular persons in the particular circumstances of our particular histories and need to attend to our particular reasons in living. This involves asking ourselves about what, at what time and place, in what manner, with what degree, for what reasons, and with whom we may exist well (cf. Aristotle *NE*, 1104b28, 1109b16, 1111a4–5, 1126a33–4). For example, how do we act and react well to our pleasures in eating, drinking, and coupling? How do we act and react well to our fears in challenges, illnesses, and deaths? How do we act and react well in our relations with and to others? "No matter where one lives one cannot escape these questions, so long as one is living a human life" (Nussbaum 1988: 36). To raise and attempt to answer all those thorny questions of how we may exist well supposes a state of mind that allows for good sense and sound judgment. Thus, one way in which this existential mood shows itself is in inclining us to deliberate and decide well of how we may, do, and can live best. Traditionally, masters of philosophy take this as part of the intellectual virtue of *phronesis* or *prudentia* (e.g., Aristotle *NE*, 1138b19–1145b12; Aquinas [1266–73] 1940: 2–2.47–56).

A second way in which an existential mood for philosophy expresses itself is in being astute. The paradigmatic philosophical frame of mind may manifest itself not only in the penchant to understand *how* we exist but also in the bent to grasp *that* we exist. In trying to deliberate and decide how we exist, we seek to achieve not merely existing but existing well, while in trying to consider and comprehend that we exist, we aim to understand our very existence itself. This is not deliberation of how we exist but contemplation that we exist. For instance, "Not *how* the world is but *that* it is, is the mystery" (Wittgenstein 1922: 6.44, my translation). We are "then inclined to use such phrases as 'how extraordinary that anything should exist' or 'how extraordinary that the world should exist'" (Wittgenstein 1965: 8). We are not like the mistaken "armada" (in Thomas's poem) taken up with how to wage war but taken in with that there is an ocean to sail at all. We pursue an understanding that comprehends not only our individual existence from birth to death but also the universal existence from bang to crunch. We are disposed, according to Aristotle, to supremely understand the supreme, to continuously contemplate truth, to enjoy wondrously pure and stable pleasures, to sustain ourselves in contemplation of truth, to treat it most affectionately for its own sake, and to rest in the goal of contemplation. This existential mood for pursuing wisdom expresses itself in excellence, persistence, pleasure, self-sufficiency, love, and quietude (*NE*, 1177a20–b25; cf. Aquinas [1271–2] 1969: 586–7). All these behavioral manifestations show that we are in the mood for philosophy and are tempered to reason about and realize our very existence itself. We tune in and attune to existing. Traditionally, masters of philosophy take this as part of the intellectual virtue of *sophia* or *sapientia* (e.g., Aristotle M, 982b29–983a11, 1141a9–1141b7; *NE*, 1177a13–1178a8; Aquinas [1271–2] 1965: 1ad4; Rehnman 2010).

It should not be surprising that the mood for philosophy implies virtues, since both signify tendencies or pronenesses, but moods are *to* activity, while virtues are *from* activity. And exercising the intellectual virtue of wisdom is practicing philosophy par excellence. It is not merely seeking to be wise about this or that way of existing but seeking to be wise about what, for example, Aristotle calls the ultimate "cause and principle" of existence (M, 983a8; *NE*, 1141b5–8) and Plotinus dubs "the One" (En, 6.9.3). Here, the words "cause," "principle," and "one" are taken out of the contexts of their ordinary use, and we attempt to use them in the extraordinary context of "everything" and "nothing." We use them of that whereof, whereby, and whereto whatever exists. We attempt to talk about that which would presuppose nothing at all and which would make the difference between nothing and everything. How everything emerged from nothing is and must be inexpressible if it is to be the emergence of everything from nothing rather than the emergence of something from something. We are not talking about how things might have been and are not talking about anything at all. We are seeking to answer "Why anything rather than not?" with words that are taken out of their ordinary context into the extraordinary context that is no context at all but would account for their existing contexts.

We literally maintain the first cause and principle of existence, but we do not understand what we maintain, and as seekers of wisdom, we understand that we do not understand what we maintain. "We do indeed say something about it, but we neither know nor understand what we are saying of it" (Plotinus En, 5.3.14, my translation). Here, our use of "cause," "principle," and "one" does not account for but express or point to mystery. We are called out over our own fathoms and margins.[10]

Seekers of wisdom have traditionally attended to the margins of their use of language to fathom the unfathomable.[11] To think and talk of the one cause and principle for there existing anything at all, they coined odd expressions.[12] This appears in parts of adjectives that signal either loss or asset. On the one hand, there are, for instance, attributes such as bottomless and boundless or (Latinized) immense and infinite, eternal or timeless, and immutable or unchangeable. Here "-less," "un-," and "im-," or "in-" do not, of course, indicate deficiency but denial of bottom, boundary, space, time, and change. Likewise, there are attributes such as ubiquity, or everywhereness, that seem positive but are negative—namely, they deny that space can be ascribed to the One. On the other hand, there are attributes such as all-knowing and all-powerful or (Latinized) omniscient and omnipotent. Here "all-" and "omni-" seem to suggest the highest degree of power and knowledge but really point to what would account for the existence of all powers and knowers ordered according to their degrees. These do not attribute utmost power or knowledge of one power and knower among the powers and knowers that exist but express that all powers and knowers would not exist without the uncaused cause of power and knowledge. So, whether the morpheme is a negative or a superlative prefix or suffix, these attributes are taken beyond physics (Gr. *ta meta ta physiká*) into metaphysics and maintain that whatever can be said of what exists cannot be said of the one cause and principle of that which exists. I call these "metaphysical attributes," as they are not proper adjectives on par with other adjectives but were coined to *show* rather than to *say* what a peculiar subject of predication this is (cf. Aristotle M, XII; with Wittgenstein 1922: 4.1212 and 6.522). By means of these metaphysical attributes, seekers of wisdom can and did take words such as "gods," "divine," "deity," and "God" out of their original anthropomorphic context into their sapiential context of expressing the inexpressible puzzle of existence. These peculiar predicates express that God is nothing, in the sense that there is nothing to which the term "God" answers as a name answers to the thing named. "He is the almost anonymous" (Thomas [1990] 2004: 83; cf. Thomas [1975] 2000: 291).

This pursuit of wisdom into the attributes of the one ultimate cause and principle of existence connects with poetry. These extraordinary uses out of their ordinary uses may make still other extended uses suitable for seekers of wisdom. Metaphors take words from their ordinary context into an extraordinary context to express new meaning, and in exercising the virtue of wisdom, metaphorical attributes may be used in the context that is no context at all to express the mystery of existence. Kenny suggests that "the poetry of the inexpressible" is a "certain kind of poetry" that "endeavors to express the literally inexpressible" (2004: 17). For instance, we seek wisdom in the context of existence where there are sounds and silences, spaces and distances, deeps and surfaces, but in expressing that God is silence, within distance or space, deep, ocean, and presence, we are using these expressions in the context of that whereof, whereby, and whereto there is the context of existence. These attributes have criteria for their use in their ordinary contexts but no criteria for their use in this extraordinary context, and thus, they express the inexpressible. They do not say but show the One transcending whatever we are saying. Although these metaphors come from only one of R. S. Thomas's poems, and we can easily elaborate not only on his other poems but also on poems in the many wisdom traditions of the world (e.g., Rūmī 1968; Stryk and Ikemoto 1977; Śaṅkarācārya 1979), poetry obviously flourishes on extended language uses, and lovers of wisdom put symbolic, emblematic, and allegorical uses in their service, since the cause of existence cannot be *said by* but can only be *shown in* language. God "is this great absence that is like a presence" (Thomas [1978] 2000: 361). Therefore, the pursuit of wisdom includes what I call the metaphorical attributes of divinity.

Yet the metaphysical attributes remain important in the pursuit of wisdom. Attributes such as bottomless and boundless and immense and infinite are important to endorse metaphorical attributes. For we cannot distinguish metaphorical from literal, extraordinary from ordinary, uses without mastery of the ordinary and literal use, and if all our talking and thinking of the one cause and principle of whatever exists is metaphorical, then we cannot grasp that it is metaphorical. All divine attributes would be used properly and ordinarily: God would then be within distance as the ocean, the silence, or the presence and may be taken for Poseidon, Njord, or the thick, bearded oldie in the ceiling of a church. To keep ourselves from the idols of popular religion, we need to attend to the meaning of our negations and come to our senses in the non-senses of our metaphorical ascriptions. Only with an account of language as not saying but showing, can we distinguish between literal and figurative uses as well as between metaphysical and metaphorical attributes. To call God "silence" and "bottomless ocean" will then hardly mislead us into thinking that God is one thing among other things. Thus, we can draw nearer to the GOD of the philosophers and escape the gods of the anthropomorphists, Islamicists, and Jesuits.

However, attending to the metaphysical attributes of divinity hardly touches us. Although they can give us "wondrous pure and permanent pleasures" by constant contemplation in leisurely loneliness (Aristotle *NE*, 1177a20–26), most of us may need sustenance in our everyday life, and poetry can affect and does produce various kinds of feelings to pursue wisdom. Poetical expressions for divinity may stir—perturb or even disturb—us, lead us to judge what we value or esteem, and move us toward or against that which we care, together with the bodily sensations that may come along with those feelings. For example, poetry may startle, strike, inspire, and amaze us that there is anything at all. These and other agitations we cannot (logically) undertake but can only undergo, and so we cannot act *out of* but *because* we are agitated by existence. Our behavior cannot be motivated by amazement, but we may behave *in* or *with* amazement in existing. So, when we are agitated, what we feel gets into the way of what we were up to, and in that way, agitations modify our behavior. Poetry may, moreover, make us feel what we esteem of there being anything. Our respect, admiration, and reverence that anything should exist involve our reasons for feeling so, and thus, such attitudes may motivate or modify our behavior, but respect, admiration, and reverence are not *actions of* but *feelings for* pursuing wisdom. Poetry may further make us feel relief, wonder, joy, humility, and gratitude that anything exists rather than not. These and other emotions involve reasons for action of the past, present, or future and therefore what we can want and choose. The reasons contained in our emotions either motivate or modify our actions of pursuing wisdom—for instance, by reading and listening to poetry, being sensible and astute. We may then seek wisdom not only *in* or *with* but also *out of* our emotions of relief, wonder, joy, humility, and gratitude. Together with our agitations, attitudes, and emotions, we may of course also sense changes in heartbeat, muscle tension, and so forth, but these do neither motivate nor modify our search for comprehensive understanding of anything existing. Yet our agitations may modify our behavior, and our emotions as well as our attitudes may motivate and modify our searching for wisdom. Here, metaphorical attributes of divinity move us to practice philosophy, because they extend the ordinary use of language that affects us in everyday activities to affect us in our extraordinary pursuit of the wisdom that anything should exist.

So, to become and remain in the existential mood for philosophy, we need the various kinds of feelings contained therein that modify and motivate our behavior toward comprehensive understanding. Such a state of mind disposes us to not only deliberate *how* we may exist but also contemplate *that* we do exist. In this frame of mind, our experience guides our thinking and talking anomalously of the one ultimate cause by both negations and metaphors. Negative attributes such as bottomless and boundless and immense and infinite allow us to realize and distinguish the metaphorical attributes, while metaphorical attributes such as silence, space, deep, ocean, and presence may move, touch, and motivate us. Both kinds of attributes allow us to pursue divinity out of the ordinary anthropomorphic context into the sapiential context that is no context at all. In the grave anxiety of our existence—in the silence of the mind when we live best—we are inspired to love wisdom and consciously search for the answer to the question why something exists rather than not in metaphysical and poetical terms and to express the inexpressible mystery of our existence. Then "[s]pirituality is a meta-emotion that transcends the merely personal" and "expands the self to superhuman if not cosmic proportions" (Solomon 2007: 268).

Conclusion

In this chapter, I have exemplified the practice of philosophy with poetry. I have shown that to practice philosophy is strenuously striving to live one's whole life worthily with thorough understanding and that poetry, with its departures from ordinary usages, allows us to respond not only to the meanings we understand but also to the meanings we feel, hear, and see. For the broad experience we undertake and undergo bends us not only to deliberate and decide *how* to exist but also to reflect and realize *that* we exist. We practice then philosophy par excellence by exercising the intellectual virtue of wisdom, in that whatever we can say of what exists, we cannot say of the one cause and principle of that which exists, recognizing that we are expressing the inexpressible. We use metaphysical and metaphorical attributes of this mystery of existence, and they may marvelously occasion the existential mood of a tranquil or grave anxiety in us, inclining us to pursue wisdom. For metaphorical attributes, grounded in metaphysical attributes, *show* but do not *say* that we cannot (logically) ask for justifications of how we have, do, or will exist but can acquiesce in fascinations that we exist. All these attributes do not say but show the one transcending whatever we are saying and reading in our poems, and we may come to our senses in our non-senses. Poetry can then powerfully occasion us to become and remain receptive as well as possessive of what we already half-heartedly know of ourselves in our unruly yearning for wisdom. Thus, we may realize what leading a philosophical life means.

This has significant implications for future inquiries. In closely connecting philosophy and poetry in conduct, I have overcome my colleagues' conventional contrast of them. The particulars I go through in reading riddles, together with my recognition that the right kind of anxiety and tranquility toward my existence, do incline me to pursue understanding why anything exists rather than not. In this chapter, I have shown particularly how I practice philosophy with poetry and have sought to know myself only in relation to one poem, as we need to engage with the devil in the details to encounter the deity in the dungeons. We need further specific studies of not only how other poems but also how prose, music, film, sculpture, and painting may inspire a love of wisdom. We need to explore concretely and elucidate positively how works of art help us express our longing for inexpressible wisdom. Only so can we seek to personify and promote philosophical living today. Future studies need to probe particular practices of philosophy.

Notes

1 I'm grateful to Bloodaxe Books for permission to reproduce R. S. Thomas's poem "But the silence in the mind." I thank Asbjørn Fretheim and Emil Faugli for reflections on a very early synopsis of this chapter; Jeanette Bresson Ladegaard Knox for comments on the antepenultimate version; and Mikel Burley, Alex Harisiadis, I-Kai Jeng, Jeanette Bresson Ladegaard Knox, Zach Kramer, Joshua Schendel, and M. Wynn Thomas for comments on the penultimate version. I thank an anonymous reviewer for comments on the ultimate version.

2 "Poetry, at its best, may be the most transformative of all written forms, and so it may also be a candidate for spiritual exercise: poetry as philosophy" (Harte 2023: 62). Unfortunately, he does not show *how* poetry may be a transformative philosophical exercise.

3 For instance, "Wittgenstein's signposts pointing/at the boundaries of language/into the obligatory void." "Kierkegaard hinted, Heidegger/agreed" (Thomas [1992] 2004: 171, 182). During his life, Thomas devoted three poems to Kierkegaard ([1966b] 2000: 162; [1968] 2000: 183; [1995] 2004: 219), mentioned him in others ([1978] 2000: 357; [1992] 2004: 182; [1995] 2004: 214), and used his themes persistently. One poem is a synopsis of the history of philosophy ([1978] 2000: 357).

4 "R. S. Thomas is a master of maieutic irony—indeed, I am tempted to say that that is not only how he writes his poetry but *why* he writes it. It is his very raison d'être as a poet; because poetry is for him the maieutic structure par excellence.... It is so because of the hidden concentrations of meaning that inhere in the actual formal patterning of a poem" (M. W. Thomas 2013: 188). M. W. Thomas further shows Kierkegaard's influence on R. S. Thomas's continuous conception that becoming oneself is consciously choosing to live for what one values without ever being able to fully understand oneself (77–80, 117, 144–5). Rowan Williams has argued similarly (2003).

5 Alternatively, I presume all three instances of "call" may be taken for the one use of crying or shouting, and then our deep calls on the deep silence of God. But that seems less plausible.

6 Perhaps there is also here a reminder of "the timeless sea" (Thomas [1990] 2004: 72).

7 Compare R. S. Thomas's lines "lost himself in the amazing/ And labyrinth paths of his own impenetrable mind" (quoted in M. W. Thomas 2013: 58). "We asked our questions and passed on" (R. S. Thomas 2013: 166).

8 In private correspondence, W. Wynn Thomas wrote that my phrasings here reminded him of "The calm existence that is mine when I/Am worthy of myself! Praise to the end!" in William Wordsworth's *The Prelude* (Wordsworth 2008: 384/360).

9 "Die Befindlichkeit der Stimmung enthällt … das Seiende im Ganzen" (On moods, see, for instance, further in Heidegger [1927] 2006: 134–42, 339–45; Ryle [1949] 1963: 95–100; Freeman 2014; Hacker 2018: 16–22).

10 "There is a being, they say,/ neither body nor spirit,/ that is more power than reason, more reason/ than love, whose origins/ are unknown, who is apart/ and with us, the silence/ to which we appeal, the architect/ of our failures" (Thomas [1990] 2004: 88).

11 Or they failed to attend to the margins of their use of language as I argue against the anthropomorphism of Jonathan Edwards (2021).

12 Perhaps the poetical philosophy of Xenophanes of Colophon was the first account, in censure of Hesiod's and Homer's conception of the divine in human bodies, thoughts, and vices rather than the inexpressible One (Fragments B11–17, 23–6 in Diels and Kranz 1951, 1:113–39; cf. Plato Sph, 242d; Rep, 379b; Aristotle *M*, 986b18, 1072b). This tradition seems to be continued in Plato's *Euthyphro, Republic, Timaeus, Laws* X, Aristotle's *Physics* VII–VIII, *Metaphysics* XII.vi–viii, and onward.

References

Aquinas, T. ([1266–73] 1940), *Summa theologica*, 22nd edn, 6 vols., Marietti.

Aquinas, T. ([1271–2] 1965), *Quaestiones disputatae de virtutibus cardinalibus*, ed. E. Odetto, 2 vols., *Vol. 2, Quaestiones disputatae*, Marietti.

Aquinas, T. ([1271–2] 1969), *Sententia libri Ethicorum*, 2 vols., *Vol. 2, Opera omnia*, Sanctae Sabinae.

Aristotle (1894), *Ne. Ethica Nicomachea*, ed. I. Bywater, *Oxford Classical Text*, Clarendon Press.

Aristotle (1924), *M. Metaphysics: A Revised Text, with Introduction and Commentary*, ed. W. D. Ross, 2 vols., *Vol. 2, Oxford Classical Text*, Clarendon Press.

Aristotle (1965), *P. De arte poetica liber*, ed. R. Kassel, *Scriptorum classicorum bibliotheca Oxoniensis*, Clarendon Press.

Aurelius, M. (1930), *Md. Meditations*, ed. C. R. Haines, *Loeb Classical Library*, Heinemann.

Boëthius (1957), *Dcp. De consolatione philosophiae*, *Vol. 94, Corpus Christianorum, Series Latina*, Brepols.

Burley, M. (2021), "Reproaching the Divine: Poetic Theologies of Protest as a Resource for Expanding the Philosophy of Religion," *Journal of the American Academy of Religion* 89 (4): 1229–55. https://doi.org/10.1093/jaarel/lfab101.

Burnet, J. (ed.) (1901–5), *Platonis Opera*, 5 vols., Clarendon Press.

Cohoe, C. M. and S. R. Grimm (2020), "What It Takes to Live Philosophically: Or, How to Progress in the Art of Living," in J. M. Ambury, T. Irani, and K. Wallace (eds), *Philosophy as a Way of Life: Historical, Contemporary, and Pedagogical Perspectives*, 229–47, Wiley-Blackwell.

Cooper, J. M. (2012), *Pursuits of Wisdom: Six Ways of Life in Ancient Philosophy from Socrates to Plotinus*, Princeton University Press.

Diels, H. and W. Kranz (1951), *Die Fragmente der Vorsokratiker, griechisch und deutsch*, 6th edn, 3 vols., Weidmann.

Freeman, L. (2014), "Toward a Phenomenology of Mood," *Southern Journal of Philosophy* 52 (4): 445–76. https://doi.org/10.1111/sjp.12089.

Gill, C. (1994), "Peace of Mind and Being Yourself: Panaetius to Plutarch," *Aufstieg und Neidergang der römischen Welt* 36 (7): 4599–640.

Grimm, S. R. and C. Cohoe (2021), "What Is Philosophy as a Way of Life? Why Philosophy as a Way of Life?," *European Journal of Philosophy* 29 (1): 236–51. https://doi.org/10.1111/ejop.12562.

Hacker, P. M. S. (2018), *The Passions: A Study of Human Nature*, Wiley-Blackwell.

Hadot, I. (1969), *Seneca und die griechisch-römische Tradition der Seelenleitung*, de Gruyter.

Hadot, P. (1995), *Qu'est-ce que la philosophie antique?*, Gallimard.

Harte, R. (2023), "Spiritual Exercises and Poetry: Pierre Hadot and Du Fu," *Metaphilosophy* 54 (1): 61–72. https://doi.org/10.1111/meta.12598.

Heidegger, M. ([1927] 2006), *Sein und Zeit*, Niemeyer.

Heidegger, M. ([1943] 1965), *Was ist Metaphysik?*, 4th edn, Klostermann.

Heidegger, M. ([1959] 1985), "Das Wesen der Sprache," in F.-H. von Herrmann (ed.), *Gesamtausgabe I: Abteilung, Veröffentlichte Schriften, 1910–1976: Unterwegs zur Sprache*, Klostermann.

Hidalgo, J. (2020), "Why Practice Philosophy as a Way of Life?," in J. M. Ambury, T. Irani, and K. Wallace (eds), *Philosophy as a Way of Life: Historical, Contemporary, and Pedagogical Perspectives*, 249–69, John Wiley & Sons.

Jeng, I. K. (2020), "Ways of Discourse and Ways of Life: Plato on the Conflict Between Poetry and Philosophy," in J. M. Ambury, T. Irani, and K. Wallace (eds), *Philosophy as a Way of Life: Historical, Contemporary, and Pedagogical Perspectives*, 155–71, Wiley-Blackwell.

Kenny, A. (2004), *The Unknown God: Agnostic Essays*, Continuum.

Kierkegaard, S. ([1844] 2014), *Begrebet Angest*, ed. N. J. Cappelørn, 15 vols., *Vol. 4.2, Søren Kierkegaards Værker: Philosophiske Smuler, Begrebet Angest og Forord*, Gyldendal.

Kierkegaard, S. ([1846] 2002), *Afsluttende uvidenskabelig Efterskrift*, ed. N. J. Cappelørn, J. Garff, J. Knudsen, J. Kondrup, and A. McKinnon, *Vol. 7, Søren Kierkegaards skrifter*, Gad.

McGhee, M. (2000), *Transformations of Mind: Philosophy as Spiritual Practice*, Cambridge University Press.

Montaigne, M., de. ([1588] 2002), "Les essais," eds. P. Villey, V.-L. Saulnier, and P. Desan, University Library of Chicago.

Morgan, C. (2013), *R.S. Thomas: Identity, Environment, Deity*, Manchester University Press.

Musonius Rufus, C. (1947), *F. "The Roman Socrates": The Text of the Fragments with a Translation and Introductory Essay*, trans. C. E. Lutz, Yale University Press.

Nietzsche, F. ([1908] 1969), *Ecce Homo: Wie Man Wird, Was Man Ist*, eds. G. Colli and M. Montinari, 3 vols., *Vol. 6, Werke: kritische Gesamtausgabe*, de Gruyter.

Nussbaum, M. C. (1988), "Non-Relative Virtues: An Aristotelian Approach," *Midwest Studies in Philosophy* 13:3 2–53.

Nussbaum, M. C. ([1994] 2009), *The Therapy of Desire: Theory and Practice in Hellenistic Ethics*, Princeton University Press.

Paton, W. R., P. Max, and W. Hans (eds) (1993–2001), *Moralia: Bibliotheca scriptorum Graecorum et Romanorum Teubneriana*, 3 vols., Teubner.

Phillips, D. Z. (1986), *R.S. Thomas: Poet of the Hidden God: Meaning and Mediation in the Poetry of R.S. Thomas*, Macmillan.

Phillips, D. Z. (2006), *From Fantasy to Faith: Morality, Religion and Twentieth-Century Literature*, 2nd edn, SCM Press.

Pikoulis, J. and M. Roberts (1993), "R.S. Thomas's Existential Agony," *Poetry Wales* 29 (3): 26–32.

Plato. *Alc I. Alcibiades I*, in Burnet.

Plato. *Ap. Apologia*, in Burnet.

Plato. *Chrm. Charmides*, in Burnet.

Plato. *Cr. Crito*, in Burnet.

Plato. *Le. Leges*, in Burnet.

Plato. *Phd. Phaedo*, in Burnet.

Plato. *Phdr. Phaedrus*, in Burnet.

Plato. *Phil. Philebus*, in Burnet.

Plato. *Prt. Protagoras*, in Burnet.

Plato. *Rep. Respublica*, in Burnet.

Plato. *Sph. Sophista*, in Burnet.

Plotinus (1966–88), *En. Enneades*, ed. and trans. A. H. Armstrong, 7 vols., *Loeb Classical Library*, Heinemann.

Plutarch. *Dap. De audiendis poetis*, in Paton.
Plutarch. *Dpv. De profectibus in virtute*, in Paton.
Plutarch. *Dta. De tranquillitate animi*, in Paton.
Rabbow, P. (1954), *Seelenführung: Metodik der Exerzitien in der Antike*, Kösel.
Rehnman, S. (2010), "Natural Theology and Epistemic Justification," *Heythrop Journal* 48:1 017–22.
Rehnman, S. (2021), *Edwards on God*, Routledge.
Rehnman, S. (2022), "Learning to Love Wisdom from Masters: The Value of Jonathan Edwards's Philosophical Theology," *Jonathan Edwards Studies* 12 (1/2): 28–35.
Rehnman, S. (2023a), "Conversing Confidentially on Our Challenges: Two Practitioners Reflect on Their Experiences of Confiding Themselves in Conversation," in M. Weiss and G. H. Helskog (eds), *Reflective Practice Research in Higher Education Pedagogies*, 223–47, LIT Verlag.
Rehnman, S. (2023b), "Writing Expressively for One's Well-Being: Partly Constituting Oneself Through Self-Reflection," in M. Weiss and G. H. Helskog (eds), *Reflective Practice Research in Higher Education Pedagogies*, 249–73, LIT Verlag.
Rūmī, J., al-Dīn (1968), *Mystical Poems of Rumi: First Selection: Poems 1–200*, ed. A. J. Arberry, vol. 3, University of Chicago Press.
Ryle, G. ([1949] 1963), *The Concept of Mind*, Penguin Books.
Śaṅkarācārya, A. (1979), *A Thousand Teachings: The Upadesasahasri of Sankara*, trans. S. Mayeda, University of Tokyo Press.
Seneca, L. A. (1932a), *DcH. De consolatione ad Helviam*, trans. and ed. J. W. Basore, 3 vols., *Vol. 2, Moral Essays*, Harvard University Press.
Seneca, L. A. (1932b), *Dta. De tranquillitate animi*, trans. and ed. J. W. Basore, 3 vols., *Vol. 2, Moral Essays*, Harvard University Press.
Seneca, L. A. (1965), *Em. Ad Lucilium epistulae morales*, ed. L. D. Reynolds, Clarendon Press.
Sharpe, M. and M. Ure (2021), *Philosophy as a Way of Life: History, Dimensions, Directions*, Bloomsbury Academic.
Shepherd, E. (1996), *R.S. Thomas: Conceding an Absence: Images of God Explored*, Macmillan.
Solomon, R. C. (2007), *True to Our Feelings: What Our Emotions Are Really Telling Us*, Oxford University Press.
Strawson, P. F. ([1998] 2011), "Intellectual Autobiography," in G. Strawson and M. Montague (eds), *Philosophical Writings*, 222–47, Oxford University Press.
Stryk, L. and T. Ikemoto (1977), *The Penguin Book of Zen Poetry*, Allen Lane.
Thomas, M. W. (2013), *R.S. Thomas: Serial Obsessive*, University of Wales Press.

Thomas, R. S. (1963), "Introduction," in R. S. Thomas (ed.), *The Penguin Book of Religious Verse*, Penguin Books.

Thomas, R. S. (1966a), "A Frame for Poetry," *The Times Literary Supplement* 3 (March): 169.

Thomas, R. S. ([1966b] 2000), *Pietà: Collected Poems, 1945–1990*, Phoenix.

Thomas, R. S. ([1968] 2000), *Not That He Brought Flowers: Collected Poems, 1945–1990*, Phoenix.

Thomas, R. S. ([1975] 2000), *Laboratories of the Spirit: Collected Poems, 1945–1990*, Phoenix.

Thomas, R. S. ([1977] 2000), *The Way of It: Collected Poems, 1945–1990*, Phoenix.

Thomas, R. S. ([1978] 2000), *Frequencies: Collected Poems, 1945–1990*, Phoenix.

Thomas, R. S. ([1988] 2004), *The Echoes Return Slow: Collected Later Poems, 1988–2000*, Bloodaxe Books.

Thomas, R. S. ([1990] 2004), *Counterpoint: Collected Later Poems, 1988–2000*, Bloodaxe Books.

Thomas, R. S. ([1992] 2004), *Mass for Hard Times: Collected Later Poems, 1988–2000*, Bloodaxe Books.

Thomas, R. S. ([1995] 2004), *No Truce with the Furies: Collected Later Poems, 1988–2000*, Bloodaxe Books.

Thomas, R. S. (1997), *Autobiographies* (ed. J. W. Davies), J. M. Dent.

Thomas, R. S. (2013), *Uncollected Poems* (ed. T. Brown and J. W. Davies), Bloodaxe Books.

Williams, R. (2003), "Suspending the Ethical: R.S. Thomas and Kierkegaard," in D. W. Davies (ed.), *Echoes to the Amen: Essays After R.S. Thomas*, 206–19, University of Wales Press.

Wittgenstein, L. (1922), *Tractatus Logico-Philosophicus* (trans. and ed. C. K. Ogden), Routledge.

Wittgenstein, L. (1965), "A Lecture on Ethics," *Philosophical Review* 74:3–11.

Wittgenstein, L. (1998), *Vermischte Bemerkungen: Eine Auswahl aus dem Nachlass*, eds, G. H. von Wright, H. Nyman, and A. Pichler, 2nd edn, Wiley-Blackwell.

Wordsworth, W. (2008), *The Major Works*, in S. Gill (ed.), *Oxford World's Classics*, Oxford University Press.

8

Fiction in Philosophical Practice

Detlef Staude

Introductory Reflections on Philosophical Practice

Whoever speaks of philosophical practice has a wide variety of fields of activity in mind: counseling, education, clarification of concepts, discussion groups, philosophy in companies, philosophizing with children, and so on. The whole field is much broader than these few typical examples show. Moreover, it borders on other disciplines such as psychology, psychotherapy, sociology, and also art, each of which has its own objectives, orientations, and methods, so it is often not easy to relate them to philosophical practice or even to incorporate them to some extent.

In my philosophical practice, therefore, discussions occasionally touch on the content of psychology or sociology, and sometimes even art, though that is usually on the periphery of my practice. The focus is on philosophical questioning, philosophical concepts, and thought processes as well as dialogue. Those who study philosophy learn much about the great figures of philosophy and their questions, concepts, and answers. Sometimes, however, this leads to a jungle of names and ideas, and it remains unclear how they inspired each other's questions, concepts, and trains of thought and how formative ideas of philosophy emerged from the times, biographies, and traditions.

Narrated History and My Philosophical Novels

What we philosophers sometimes lack in our studies is the history of philosophy as a narrative history of historical backgrounds, ideas, inventions, and people, but this is where philosophy transcends its boundaries. Plato's dialogues are fiction, in which different figures of his time take different positions, ask questions, and give answers. This is how philosophy may become a story, and the dialogues have a beginning and an end, are set somewhere, and have characters and a central theme.

There is of course a basic problem with such stories: Should they primarily have a literary—that is, artistic—quality and thus fulfill the requirements of literature, or should they primarily have a philosophical quality and fulfill the requirements of philosophy? Both can be reconciled to a certain extent, but there remains a tension, because the two genres make different demands, and they often fail as stories if the philosophical element is too great. Or conversely, they may be satisfying in literary terms, but the narrative framework is more of a hindrance to the philosophical substance.

The history of philosophy often plays a major role in my philosophical practice, so I had the idea to write philosophical novels myself, one about the sophist Protagoras and the other about the philosopher Axiotheia. The latter is partly a fictional character, but her daughter is presented as Plato's historical student of the same name. Although both novels contain facts about the philosophers they portray, many of these contexts are hardly known to any philosopher as they were to me before my subsequent research. My two novels are narratively linked and cover the period from the Sophists up to Plato's Academy. In this way, the major philosophers of the time and the context become more memorable and imaginable.

Imaginability brings knowledge to life unlike abstract statements and names. This is an important part of philosophical novels like mine. It's the same for me as a writer, because I have to build a work of art in which historical facts are an important part or inspiration. Beyond that, I am the first reader of the stories, and I am often impressed by the world that has been created. When I read it a while later, I wonder myself what was historical and what was invented, because this new version of antiquity is so convincing. These are all important indicators of a work of art.

I can immediately use parts of my novels in my philosophical practice, but more importantly, this part of antiquity and its philosophical contexts has become more vivid for me. I can better imagine what I want to teach in my seminars, and the participants' questions become more vivid as a result. So art combines knowledge with feelings. I have been inspired by my novels to a series of seminars called "Tales of the History of Philosophy." Philosophical or historical movements or phenomena can sometimes be portrayed very well through stories or narratives that reveal the background to them. This series of seminars is therefore a consequence of my writing philosophical novels and shows that well-told stories can be exciting and reveal connections of thought or historical events.

Requirements, Effects, and Dangers of Narrated History

A story generally has a common thread. On the basis of this common thread in the main character's life story, one learns much about the historic period of the time that often involves serious danger for everyone, especially for wise women and men. Athens was not only the philosophical center of the Greek world but also a slaughterhouse for male and female philosophers. New ideas and clear thoughts can be dangerous at any time but especially in ancient times. Thus, in the end, more than a century of philosophical history stands before one's inner eye a little more clearly. One understands the intellectual development of the time as a network of mutual influence.

Together with the many other nonphilosophical elements of the novels, which nevertheless have historical significance, a panorama of a time is created that could previously only be imagined in fragments. Of course, the narrative thread and the characters in the novel are also an interpretation of the historical events, which is debatable, but the result is a great help in philosophical practice because it helps to imagine a time and a mental development that seems to be so far away from ours, yet our present time has so many things in common with it. Moreover, something else arises, which is especially important for philosophical practice: attraction.

Plato already called astonishment the beginning of philosophizing, as did Aristotle after him. For Plato, astonishment is also the end of the process of cognition in the insight-saturated view (théoria; θεωρία); for Aristotle, it is the impetus of the cognitive process. In modern times, wonder plays a significant role in aesthetics. In his forthcoming book *Works of Wonder*, the American philosopher Jesse Prinz (forthcoming: 46) argues that art is defined by the evocation of wonder: "The unity of art … is found in the fact that artworks, when successful, evoke wonder. In that sense, artworks can be called works of wonder."

Thus, we can understand how the abovementioned attraction comes about through the use of art in philosophy and in philosophical practice. If something is aesthetically successful, it causes amazement. The term "aesthetic success" is used to describe a phenomenon whereby an object or creation evokes a sense of wonder and amazement. As the importance of wonder in philosophy shows, this wonder also leads to knowledge. This line of thought shows that works of wonder—that is, successful works of art—can be successfully used in philosophical practice.[1]

The Liveliness of the Plot and the Characters

However, it is a high aspiration for a philosophical practitioner to be a gifted artist as well, and so I probably have to make some compromises in terms of how aesthetically felicitous the two works of art, the novels about Protagoras and Axiotheia, are. How effective and attractive they are to an audience I do not know, since I have not yet been able to publish them. But their effect on me is quite consistent with Jesse Prinz's claim that successful works of art are works of wonder. The effect that I observe is that they stimulate the imagination and the realization with the help of appropriate reading and research. It is remarkable how the world emerges in this way, resembling to the historical context of philosophy. This amazement, which my own work causes in me, turns me into a reader who marvels at the details and the world of Greek antiquity that emerges from them. It has become comprehensible to me in its historical and intellectual dynamics through the connections illustrated in these novels, both historically and intellectually.

Based on the questions that emerged, I continued to research the thread of the story, connecting the information and interpretations thus obtained with the needs of the story, with its plot, characters, and places. The difficulty lies in the fact that the subject matter is based on a multitude of historical and philosophical sources, which have been corroborated by various other sources. This made it challenging to form a work of art out of it—that is, to truly create a novel. But the tradition from the Greek antiquity is sparse despite many interesting evidences, and so one remains dependent on one's own creativity to create a lively world out of this. Furthermore, some sources are uncertain, and thus, it is reasonable to diverge from them to some extent.

The vividness of the characters and the plot is important, because

> cognition that is not alive occupies only half the soul, the power of cognition; a living one, however, at the same time occupies the power of desire, the other half of the soul, and it thus fills the whole mind.... [A] living [cognition] heats the vital spirits and takes possession of the heart, and I consider the aesthetic life of cognition to be the greatest beauty of thoughts.[2]
>
> —Meier (1748: 60)

It is possible to create a living artwork from available sources, historical requirements, and one's own ideas. However, the resulting world is also susceptible to the lure of superficiality and inaccuracy when it comes to facts. I try to avoid this, as the aim is not to create a fantastical, imaginary version of the past but one that can be relived through extensive factual fidelity. If you no longer stick to the facts, the story seems to become more vivid, but its content runs the risk of becoming fantastic and hollow—and, ultimately, less vivid.

The Philosophical Novel as Representation of the History of Ideas in the World Theater

Philosophical novels are representations of philosophical questions, ideas, and debates from the history of ideas. They follow the interpretation of the world as a *theatrum mundi*, a concept that has been prevalent since the ancient era and revived especially in the baroque[3] and Romantic periods. In the theater metaphor, the spectator or reader is immediately engaged, and the performance serves not only to entertain but also to instruct.[4]

And they also follow the theatrum metaphor—especially as philosophical-historical novels—insofar as the characters in the story should be brought to life as much as possible to grab the reader and thus make the history of philosophy more accessible. However, the action takes place within the context of the historical narrative and philosophical knowledge. The presentation of one's own knowledge of another time period with philosophically significant figures, whose questions and answers thus become comprehensible in a larger network of intellectual development, is one thing; the bringing to life of this time and the figures of the history of ideas through presentation is another. In accordance with the theater metaphor, they become actors of philosophers but, not in their entirety, rather as representatives of their roles in the history of philosophy.[5]

Therefore, passages selected from these novels can also be used for dramatic performances and used in this way in philosophical practice. Performing scenes and plays is something that some philosophical practitioners already do, such as Mike Roth with his concept of PhiloDrama.[6] But here another challenge becomes apparent that a practitioner in philosophical practice must address: Read or watched dialogues are presented only, not conducted. To exploit the potential of the dialogues presented, we as philosophical practitioners must focus on the subsequent conversation between the participants present.

Philosophy and Narrative

A quotation from Aristotle (1994: 29) clearly illustrates why a novel, or its components, can be effectively utilized in philosophical practice:

> From what has been said it also follows that it is not the task of the poet to communicate what really happened, but rather what might happen, i. e. what is possible according to the rules of probability or necessity. For the historian and the poet do not differ from each other in that the one communicates in verse and the other in prose – one could also clothe the work of Herodotus in verse, and it would be no less a work of history in verse than without verse –; they differ rather in that the one communicates

> what really happened, the other what could happen. Therefore, poetry is something more philosophical and serious than historiography; for poetry communicates more the general, while historiography communicates the particular.

If we agree with Aristotle, and I think there is much to be said for doing so, the vicinity of philosophy and poetry, as Aristotle understands it, is also an encouragement to write philosophical novels on the one hand and, on the other hand, philosophical novels that illustrate how things might have been should especially be philosophical in their effect insofar as they stimulate questions.

To understand from a perspective other than Aristotle's why literary fiction is well suited to empathizing with and understanding times, thoughts, and people, it is helpful to consider Paul Ricœur's concept of identity.[7] Ricœur distinguishes between a person's idem-identity and an ipse-identity. The idem-identity is identity in the sense of identifiability; the ipse-identity understands identity in the sense of self-concepts in time. In a real person, both are intertwined in the history of our life. In the history of philosophy, the idem-identity of a philosopher is in the foreground: Usually, some facts are offered here, important teachers, important students, and dates of life as well as explanations of one's main philosophical ideas. From a scholarly point of view, this is quite understandable. However, the person of the philosopher remains flat and difficult to understand. Not only that, the questions and ideas also remain pale data with sometimes more, sometimes less coherence, not held together by an ipse-identity.

Since individual identity always includes the history of other persons and social contexts, retracing these identities through a narrative is an excellent way of making people aware of them. Ricœur also points out that individuality is dependent on articulation. This describes the events from the perspective of acting subjects and thus constitutes narratable history. Identity grows out of the story that the subject tells himself, corrects, and revises in the light of new experiences. According to Ricœur, identity is thus narrative identity, and narrative identity contains not only descriptive elements but also normative ones (Haker 2000: 179–87).

Accordingly, narrative identities can also be fictionalized literarily. These fictions thus supplement the data known from philosophical history with the notion of an appropriate ipse-identity, and the corresponding philosopher becomes imaginable as a person and can be understood to some extent in the self-relation of time, relationships, encounters, and discussions and also with regard to his/her philosophy.

We are therefore better able to empathize with characters in narrative stories because we are accustomed to understand ourselves, our life, and our time from narratives and reflections.

The Work of Art and Dialogue

But does this imply that a philosophical novel is suitable for promoting dialogue in philosophical practice? Alternatively, can a literary work, or parts thereof, be employed in a comparable manner to philosophical texts? It is conceivable that this is a higher form of entertainment, but it may not be particularly stimulating for philosophical discourse. For example, it can be argued that the film adaptation of Umberto Eco's novel *The Name of the Rose*, while undoubtedly providing good entertainment for many, has not prompted a significant number of philosophical questions. This is in contrast to the novel itself, which may have prompted a more profound engagement with philosophical themes (Eco 1994).

But the work of art offers numerous possibilities, such as surprise and alienation, through which questions and reflections are stimulated. It is evident that artistic creations are based on a multitude of reflections in addition to creativity and expertise. These reflections are the essence of artwork and evoke ideas and questions in the recipients.

Seen in this light, the use of art in philosophical practice is an obvious possibility not only if it is taken for its entertainment value but also if the questions it raises are taken seriously and included in a dialogue. The dialogue should avoid focusing too much on factual issues because, despite its proximity to history and intellectual history, it is, after all, fiction.

As far as my novels are concerned, this becomes clear again and again. Of course, there are also entirely fictitious characters and storylines but also changes of narrative perspectives, with the result that, through their alienating effect, the reader is made aware of the interpretative nature of history and stories.

However, alienation is an important way to bring a refraction into a fictional text that stimulates questions. Nicola Gess (2019: 130–1) writes on this in *Staunen. Eine Poetik* (*Wonder. A Poetics*):

> The procedure of defamiliarization aims at making something known, familiar, suddenly appear new or strange, thereby triggering a sense of wonder that … is often connected with the claim to make a new experience possible or to set a new insight on its way. A large number of literary artifices are available for the procedure of defamiliarization; I limit myself here to a single one, namely the adoption of an unusual descriptive or narrative perspective. In his essay *The Art as Procedure*, Šklovskij proposes the procedure of "inadequate perspective" to achieve an alienation of the narrated.… Defamiliarization aims at the strangeness of the known, the familiar, and thus at an irritated astonishment that triggers a new perception and, if necessary, a striving for knowledge.

Nevertheless, do these reflections and questions have a degree of philosophical value that make them suitable for dialogue in the context of philosophical practice? For this purpose, I would like to use the example of Jostein Gaarder's (1993) novel *Sofie's World*. The revival of interest in philosophy among the general public in the 1990s can be attributed, at least in part, to this novel. It proved that philosophical novels can prompt questions that initiate a dialogue within the context of philosophical practice. Of course, not every philosophical novel is such a global bestseller. But it was certainly this success that inspired so many other authors to attempt similar projects. For example, Janne Teller's (2010) novel *Nothing That Matters in Life*, which is not necessarily regarded as philosophical at all, nevertheless appears to be an excellent candidate for the philosophical practice.

It should be noted that the philosophical novel is not a new phenomenon. Thomas More's novel *Utopia*, in particular, which draws upon the Platonic

Atlantis myth in the "Critias" and "Timaios" and uses them to criticize contemporary society, was undoubtedly influential in both the Renaissance and the modern era. It is evident that there exist philosophical narratives and novels that can stimulate philosophical dialogue, often transcending the boundaries of their own era.

Clearly, fiction can play a multifaceted role in philosophical practice. Not only does it provide entertainment, but it also encourages dialogue. Moreover, it can make a meaningful contribution to philosophical discourse.

Fictions with Clear Philosophical Relevance: Thought Experiments

It is obvious that short narratives, which are explicitly designed to illustrate a philosophical or ethical question—that is, thought experiments, are an ideal medium for philosophical discourse. This technique is used to explore a concept or idea through a hypothetical scenario. The earliest examples of this kind of narrative are those attributed to Zeno of Elea (490–445 BCE), with Achilles, the fastest runner in ancient Greece, and the tortoise perhaps the most well known (Aristotle 1991: 239b). If the tortoise is given a slight lead in a race, so the thought experiment recounts, Achilles would no longer be able to catch up with it, let alone overtake it. If Achilles has run ten meters, the turtle is already one meter farther; if Achilles has now run this meter, the turtle is ten centimeters further and so on. While the distance between them would decrease, Achilles would never reach the turtle. This paradox has engaged generations of philosophers. Therefore, it cannot be denied that it stimulates the questioning of assumptions and encourages dialogue. This is what thought experiments like Zeno's paradoxes are meant for, but—this is the clou—not by Zeno himself. He only wanted to illustrate and defend the teaching of his teacher Parmenides. Parmenides' central tenet was that all motion is an illusion.

Thus, it can be said that well-constructed, concise short narratives that illustrate a philosophical or ethical issue depend on three key elements: a clearly defined question, a clear position on that question, and a counterpoint to it. Now creativity is essential, as exemplified by the paradoxical argument put forth by Zeno. The problem alone would hardly retain its appeal if it were not for the imaginative narrative of Achilles and the tortoise, which provides a compelling illustration of the paradox in question.

The thought experiment serves to illustrate the potential of fiction in philosophy: It allows for the representation of philosophical questions, issues, and concepts. In contrast to philosophical narratives and novels, which are more expansive in their approach, the fictional element in a thought experiment is minimal. But if thought experiments are widely accepted in philosophy, why should similar acceptance not be extended to philosophical literature? Philosophy serves to represent the possible like fiction. Bertrand Russell ([1912] 1967: 20) clearly points out: "Whoever wants to become a philosopher must not be afraid of absurdities" and "It [philosophy] diminishes our certainty of what things are, but it increases our knowledge of what things might be" ([1912] 1967: 138).

The importance of fiction in philosophy lies in its ability to provide arguments in support of its propositions. Thought experiments provide arguments for certain positions or present conflicts with them. In philosophical narratives and novels, sometimes only passages in conversations present such arguments. However, they are less abstract and incorporate philosophical ideas more deeply and vividly.

The Significance of Narrative Texts in Philosophical Practice

The concentration of thought[8] that is characteristic of thought experiments can also be problematic, particularly when they are employed as a means of achieving a specific objective. In such instances, a dialogue or debate should be guided by the teachings of Parmenides rather than fixating on the paradoxes of Zeno. It is crucial to stimulate the imagination and encourage a broader range of thinking than simply focusing on a single problem.

It seems important to me that through a text, the imagination is also stimulated and thinking is not just fixed on a problem. Fixation on a single issue is appropriate in texts that are intended to illustrate precisely that, a problem. It also works well in most thought experiments in ethics. However, this approach does not facilitate an open dialogue,[9] which is a fundamental aspect of philosophical practice. Such an open dialogue is much more feasible through a fictional text, which expands perception and imagination, than through a construction that focuses on a particular problem.

Open dialogue is more effectively achieved through narrative fiction: It facilitates the creation of new imaginary worlds that are informed by our knowledge, experience, and the teachings of specific philosophers. This not only expands our understanding and imagination but also encourages us to reflect on our knowledge and imagination.

The narrative philosophical texts with their different characters present us with one or many different issues but, moreover, encourage us to adopt varying perspectives. That is particularly challenging, especially in historical novels, because—in my novels, for example—the reader is required to imagine themselves back in ancient Greece. Immediately we are confronted with the question of whether people like the characters in the novel are similar to us today or lived and thought differently. Furthermore, the novels facilitate the reader's imagination, thereby enhancing the ability to empathize with and understand the motivations of other individuals.[10]

Readers gain a personal understanding of philosophical ideas and problems while also recognizing that these ideas have always been embedded in cultural and discursive contexts. The questions and ideas may be universal and relevant today. Nevertheless, some of the answers or reasons why the questions seemed to be important are culturally rooted. Introduced by a historical-philosophical novel into our time period, the ideas and questions no longer remain abstract and distant objects of reflection. This approach can enable a deeper understanding of these ideas. For many, the historical and philosophical context of Greek antiquity is distant and often perceived through a narrow lens of preconceived ideas.

The narrative texts, which present the subjective perspectives of individual characters, may possess a manipulative potential that diverts attention from their philosophical content. In philosophical narratives, such as novels, the use of multiple perspectives and an emphasis on accurate representation are therefore crucial.[11] In my novels, I have used a variety of techniques to engage the reader: The passages in which the action is foregrounded stimulate the imagination more than those in which the dialogue and reflection are the primary focus. Thus, it is possible to engage the readers alternately in the world unfolding before and within them on one hand and with the philosophical questions, concepts, and positions on the other.

Another advantage of using such texts in philosophical practice is that the participants' questions and the following dialogues become more focused. This is due to the better understanding and coherent presentation of the historical context and its challenges. As a result, the dialogue can be more open ended while still remaining on topic.

Fiction in Philosophy

Furthermore, the distinction between philosophy and fiction is not as sharp as one might think, given Plato's reservations. In particular, he warned of the dangers of poetry (except when it praises the gods), which he considered as a form of subversive rhetoric and incompatible with the ideal state:

> [W]e must know the truth, that we can admit no poetry into our city save only hymns to the gods and the praises of good men. For if you grant admission to the honeyed muse in lyric or epic, pleasure and pain will be lords of your city instead of law and that which shall from time to time have approved itself to the general reason as the best.
>
> —Plato (*The Republic*, Book X 607a)[12]

It is evident that all poets/writers have never accepted this verdict. However, in Horkheimer and Adorno's (1969) *Dialektik der Aufklärung (Dialectic of Enlightenment)*,[13] a new verdict is issued that is no longer directed against the poets but against the "culture industry," which is described as "mass deception"—a clear similarity to Plato's criticism of poets. Thus, the criticism of fiction as untruthful, imitative, and promoting the inferior in people has been a constant theme through history, with Plato being one of the earliest exponents of this view. Regarding this tradition, it is unclear how fiction can be used in philosophy.

But fiction occupies a central place in philosophy, for example, with Descartes ([1986] 1996: I.12), who justifies his methodical doubt with a fiction:

> I will therefore assume that … a mischievous spirit, who is at the same time most powerful and cunning, uses all his cleverness to deceive me; I will assume that the sky, the air, the earth, the colors, the shapes, the sounds and everything external is only the play of dreams, whereby he sets traps for my credulity; I will assume of myself that I have no hands, no eyes, no flesh, no blood, no senses, but that I only falsely imagine the possession of them; I will obstinately persist in this opinion.

Here, of course, we are dealing with a thought experiment, as central to Western philosophy as, for example, the various fictions of a state of nature: "This, however, hinders not, but that philosophers may, if they please, extend their reasoning to the suppos'd state of nature; provided they allow it to be a mere philosophical fiction, which never had, and never cou'd have any reality" (Hume 1739: 3.2.2.14).

Obviously, fiction, within a defined framework, is quite capable of contributing to knowledge. The challenge in philosophical practice is to provide such a framework that allows the meaningful use of a fictional text. In the case of thought experiments, this use is evident if the dialogue is intended to address a specific problem or question. In the case of more narrative texts, the problem is usually not so clearly defined, and so dealing with them tends to trigger an open dialogue. But what kind of framework should they have to preserve their philosophical content?

At first sight, the answer seems to be more straightforward if we limit ourselves to the discussion of philosophical dialogues. After all, they are—starting with Plato's dialogues—as a matter of fact, fiction, not mere transcripts of conversations that Socrates is said to have had. Even though such philosophical dialogues represent conversations, they themselves are not conversations but fiction (Hösle 2011: 40).

Hösle (2011: 41) argues that a philosophical dialogue is only truly philosophical if it contains a statement about the matter under discussion. I agree with this view and wish to apply it to our question of what kind of framework is needed to ensure that the philosophical content of a dialogue is preserved. The first step is to identify the subject matter of the dialogue to be conducted. This can be done dialogically in the philosophical practice itself, although the dialogue must have a defined outcome. Then the topic is discussed. Now a framework for an open dialogue is created that is consistent with the principles of philosophical practice and in which fictional texts can play a role as a source of inspiration. Without this clear framework (the subject matter or topic as a reference point for the text), the conversation can easily lose its philosophical focus.

Another possibility is that the factual question (the topic) is predetermined. In such a case, additional questions from the participants can deepen further aspects of the topic and expand the dialogue. The aspect mentioned is of great importance to me. As I hold a relatively large number of seminars, there is usually a second part that is reserved for questions and joint discussion on the topic.

A closer look reveals that fiction is more prevalent in philosophy than initially assumed. It is therefore somewhat ironic that Plato uses a poetic fiction to condemn poets as untruthful and unsuitable for the ideal state. Furthermore, it is of great importance in philosophical practice that when using fictional texts, especially those of a narrative nature, a clear framework for the conversation is provided or, alternatively, created by the participants. This framework should be based on a guiding factual question to enable a dialogue with a philosophical focus.

Narrative Fiction and Cognition

Markus Wild posits that fictions possess an irreplaceable cognitive function for philosophy, namely that they facilitate the acquisition of knowledge.[14] We have already enumerated many examples that substantiate this thesis. Nevertheless, texts on fiction in philosophy typically concentrate on thought experiments in their narrower or broader sense, which focus on a specific philosophical or ethical problem and are intended to illustrate it. However, I am not concerned with such fiction but rather with narrative texts such as the philosophical novels I have authored.

The novels do not immediately address a specific philosophical issue but rather present several of them. In my case, they are integrated into a concise and narrative account of the history of philosophy in ancient Greece. The novels of the existentialists like Sartre or Camus serve to illustrate their teachings, and this is also true of other novels. The teachings of philosophers depicted in fictional texts also play a role in philosophical-historical novels such as mine. However, the overarching theme is the representation of the historical period in question, with all its possibilities and limitations.

In this respect, the term "literary representation" refers to the depiction of atmospheres and situations, as described by Hermann Schmitz. Schmitz defines these situations as a wholeness characterized by a high degree of complexity and diversity with a diffuse center of meaning.[15] This wholeness, according to Schmitz, contains a number of different elements, including facts, programs, and problems. Schmitz suggests that it is the arts that are best suited to representing and understanding such complex situations. Schmitz (2007: 2.5) defines poetry as a gentle explication of situations. While facts, programs (desires, intentions), and problems can be elucidated as individuals through discourse ("explicative speech"), the diffuse significance remains in the background. This is where poetry and literature can use a variety of methods to reveal the full meaning of a situation.

Although poetry and literature are capable of evoking meaningful impressions (Schmitz 2007: 9.5), our inquiry concerns their capacity to facilitate cognition. If we consider the gentle elucidation of situations in terms of their significance and the subsequent reflection and interpretation by the reader as a form of cognition, then literature and poetry can be counted as such. However, if we restrict the concepts of cognition and knowledge to the recognition of discrete phenomena and individual facts, programs, and issues, then the answer is negative. In this respect, it is clear why the overwhelming number of fictions in philosophy and ethics serve as thought experiments: They illustrate facts, programs, and problems, nothing more. They can be explained, but no further significance can be derived from this.

However, human beings are bodily wholes, and what is significant for them includes not only clearly identifiable facts, programs, and problems but also wholes with their internally diffuse significance. Therefore, one should not shy away from using different art forms in philosophical practice while reflecting the meaningfulness of the representations and situations contained in them in the corresponding dialogues or novels.

My novels help the reader to immerse themselves in a crucial period of Western philosophy. This is achieved through the portrayal and nuanced explanation of the circumstances in which the philosophers of the time found themselves. It is unlikely that I will always succeed in creating the kind of art described by Hermann Schmitz, namely, the kind of art that produces meaningful impressions over the course of a novel. However, when I do succeed, I am aware of it, as I am also my own first reader.

It is therefore necessary to consider that the concept of knowledge or cognition should not be limited to the cognitive, in the sense of explicable individual phenomena, facts, programs, and problems. Rather, the bodily level, including atmospheres, situations, and meaningful impressions, should be considered as a source relevant to cognition. This allows for a theoretical justification of the use of art in philosophical practice and in philosophy more generally.

Notes

1 Finn Thorbjørn Hansen argues in the same direction in his text: Hansen (Weiss 2015: 217–44).

2 "[e]ine Erkentnis, die nicht lebendig ist, nimt nur die halbe Seele, die Erkentniskraft, ein; eine lebendige beschäftiget aber zugleich die Begehrungskraft, die andere Helfte der Seele, und sie erfüllt demnach das ganze Gemüth. [...] [E]ine lebendige [Erkenntnis] erhitzt die Lebensgeister und bemächtigt sich der Herzen, und ich halte das ästhetische Leben der Erkentnis für die allergrößte Schönheit der Gedanken."

3 Shakespeare (2006: II. 7, V. 140–1): *As you like it* (1600): "All the world's a stage, / And all the men and women merely players."

4 See also Weber (2008).

5 For another interpretation of the theatrical metaphor in philosophical practice, see Bresson Ladegaard Knox (2015: 137).

6 See also the performance script Staude (2010: 67 pp.), Das Gastmahl des Euripides.

7 Hsiao Hui Huang of Soochow University in the Republic of China (Taiwan) uses Ricœur's approach in philosophical practice to facilitate, in a therapeutic way, a retelling of grief-provoking experiences that shape my identity, see Hsiao (2017: 49–64).

8 Two books that contain collections of thought experiments and fantastically appearing ideas from philosophy are Hauskeller (2003, 2006).

9 Bakhtin's conception, which is very well summarized in the following Wikipedia article, comes closest to my idea of an open dialogue: https://en.wikipedia.org/wiki/Dialogue_(Bakhtin).

10 Martha Nussbaum (1997) addressed this in the chapter "Imagination" in her book, Nussbaum.

11 On the use of narrative texts in philosophy classes, see also Merkel (2019).

12 εἰδέναι δὲ ὅτι μόνον ὕμνους θεοῖς καὶ ἐγκώμια τοῖς ἀγαθοῖς ποιήσεωςπαραδεκτέον εἰς πόλιν: εἰ δὲ τὴν ἡδυσμένην Μοῦσαν παραδέξῃ ἐν μέλεσιν ἢ ἔπεσιν, ἡδονή σοι καὶ λύπη ἐν τῇ πόλει βασιλεύσετον ἀντὶ νόμου τε καὶ τοῦ κοινῇ ἀεὶ δόξαντος εἶναι βελτίστου λόγου.

13 See also *The Culture Industry: Enlightenment as Mass Deception* (an excerpt); https://www.marxists.org/reference/archive/adorno/1944/culture-industry.htm.

14 Wild (2013: 1).

15 Schmitz (2007: 2.5). The German term is: *chaotisch-mannigfaltige Ganzheit mit einem binnendiffusen Hof an Bedeutsamkeit.*

References

Aristotle (1991), "Physics," in D. J. Barnes (ed.), *The Complete Works of Aristotle*, vol. 1, 315–446. The Revised Oxford Translation.

Aristotle (1994), *Poetics* (Greek/German), trans. and ed. M. Fuhrmann, bibliographically supplemented edn, Reclam.

Descartes, R. ([1986] 1996), *Meditations on First Philosophy*, trans. J. Cottingham, rev. edn, Cambridge University Press.

Eco, U. (1994), *The Name of the Rose*, Harvest Books.

Gaarder, J. (1993), *Sofies Welt—Roman über die Geschichte der Philosophie*, Hanser Verlag.

Gess, N. (2019), *Staunen: Eine Poetik*, Wallstein Verlag.

Haker, H. (2000), "Narrative und moralische Identität bei Paul Ricœur," *Concilium* 36 (2): 179–87.

Hansen, F. T. (2015), "The Call and Practices of Wonder: How to Evoke a Socratic Community of Wonder in Professional Settings," in M. N. Weiss (ed.), *The Socratic Handbook: Dialogue Methods for Philosophical Practice*, 217–44, LIT Verlag.

Hauskeller, M. (2003), *Ich denke, aber bin ich? Phantastische Reisen durch die Philosophie*, C. H. Beck Verlag.

Hauskeller, M. (2006), *Mögliche Welten: Neue phantastische Reisen durch die Philosophie*, C. H. Beck Verlag.

Horkheimer, M. and T. W. Adorno (1969), *Dialektik der Aufklärung*, Fischer Verlag.
Hösle, V. (2011), *Der philosophische Dialog*, C. H. Beck Verlag.
Hsiao, H. H. (2017), "Poetic Emplotment and the Power of Healing: On the Re-transformation of Happiness," in *Philosophical Practice and Counselling*, vol. 7, 49–64, The Korean Society of Philosophical Practice.
Hume, D. (1739–40), *Treatise of Human Nature*, Amyas Merivale and Peter Millican. Available at: https://davidhume.org/texts/t/3/2/2 (accessed November 22, 2025).
Knox, J. B. L. (2015), "Staging and Performing Dialogue: Employing the Theatre Metaphor as a Methodological Strategy for Facilitating a Socratic Dialogue Group," *Journal of Humanities Therapy* 6 (2): 137.
Meier, G. F. (1748), *Anfangsgründe aller schönen Wissenschaften*, Carl Hermann Hemmerde.
Merkel, L. (2019), "Der Beitrag narrativer Texte zur philosophischen Reflexion" [Online], Georg-August Universität. Available at: http://www.philovernetzt.de/index.php/konstruktionsprinzipien (accessed November 23, 2025).
Nussbaum, M. C. (1997), *Cultivating Humanity: Classical Defense of Reform in Liberal Education*, Harvard University Press.
Prinz, J. (forthcoming), *Works of Wonder*, Oxford University Press.
Russell, B. ([1912] 1967), *Probleme der Philosophie*, Suhrkamp Verlag.
Schmitz, H. (2007), *Der unerschöpfliche Gegenstand: Grundzüge der Philosophie*, Bouvier Verlag.
Shakespeare, W. (2006), *The Library Shakespeare*, Midpoint Press.
Staude, D. (2010), "Das Gastmahl des Euripides," in V. M. Roth and D. Staude (eds), *Das OrientungsLos: Philosophische Praxis unterwegs*, 67–81. Hartung-Gorre Verlag.
Teller, J. (2010), *Nichts was im Leben wichtig ist*, Hanser Verlag.
Weber, C. (2008), "Theatrum Mundi. Zur Konjunktur der Theatrum-Metapher im 16. und 17. Jahrhundert als Ort der Wissenskompilation und zu ihrer literarischen Umsetzung im *Großen Welttheater*," metaphorik.de. Available at: https://duepublico2.uni-due.de/receive/duepublico_mods_00083690 (accessed November 23, 2025).
Weiss, M. N. (ed.) (2015), *The Socratic Handbook: Dialogue Methods for Philosophical Practice*, LIT Verlag.
Wild, M. (2013), "Methodische Überlegungen zur Rolle von Fiktionen." Academia. Available at: https://www.academia.edu/2764392/Philosophie_und_Fiktion_2013 (accessed November 23, 2025).

9

Philosophers of Music

Imaginary Counselors for Musicians?

Manos Perrakis

Introduction

In the vast literature on philosophy and music, the relation between the philosophy of music and philosophical practice still remains an unexamined topic. Surely, the complex disciplinary nature of both is a grave reason. A propos of philosophical practice: Despite its ancient roots, philosophical practice as such is a new paradigm that emerged in the last decades of the twentieth century and, therefore, has not yet fully established itself. Then there is the question of a definition: *Philosophical practice* is very broadly defined as an umbrella term embracing all "philosophy in dialogue with non-philosophers outside of the academy" (Network for Nordic Philosophical Practitioners [NORDICCP], n.d.) or as a paradigm of practical philosophy under the denominators of life conduct and practical wisdom (cf. Achenbach 2010: 442). Concerning the philosophy of music, for some (e.g., and Martinelli 2019; Young 2023), the philosophy of music is a very old discipline with antique origins; for others (e.g., Klein 2019), we can hardly speak of the philosophy of music in antiquity. The notion of music in ancient cultures and the early notion of music in the Western world, known as *mousiké*—a unity of words, sound, and movement—have very little to do with music as an autonomous art, the prevailing notion from the nineteenth century until our days. According to the latter, the philosophy of music starts with the paradigm shift from vocal to purely instrumental music, music without words, music alone, so-called absolute music, that emerged at the end of the eighteenth century and established itself throughout the nineteenth century.

The aforementioned unique nature of both branches makes the relation between them hard to examine. However, the most significant reason is another: the nondiscursive nature of music. Music lives from the tension of being, on one hand, a very technical language, a kind of mathematics in sound, and, on the other, a language possessing the quality of ineffability we ascribe to the whole spectrum of the affective area, including emotions, feelings, affects, passions, sentiments, and moods—taking also into account their elusive character since they unfold within the inner sense of time in a manner similar to music. This fundamental contradiction is best suggested by G. W. Leibniz's (1734: 241) famous sentence "musica est exercitium arithmeticae occultum nescientis se numerare animi" (Music is the pleasure the human mind experiences from counting without being aware that it is counting) and its equally well-known paraphrase by Arthur Schopenhauer as "Musica est exercitium metaphysica occultum nescientis se philosophari animi" (Music is an occult exercise in metaphysics, in which the soul does not know that it is philosophizing) (Zöller 2010: 129). Or to consider this contradiction in the poetic language of mystic theology, we could remember the fifteenth-century music theologian Jean Gerson, who defines music as "numerosa vox amoris" (numerical voice of love), "amor numerōsus" (numerical love), and "numerus amorōsus" (loving number) (quoted in Anttila 2013: 44), delivering definitions that involve both the mathematical and the affective element.

Contrary to literature, which is considered to complement philosophy by demonstrating the particular while philosophy demonstrates the universal, music cannot demonstrate by means of narration issues of concern for philosophical practice. It is no coincidence that while the importance of literature for philosophical practice has been abundantly highlighted and the intersection between philosophical practice and literature has consequently been established as a field of inquiry, the same does not apply to music. We can discuss an issue from the perspective of philosophical practice by engaging with the plot of a Henry James novel, a theatrical character by William Shakespeare, or the lyrical of a poem by Stephane Mallarmé, but we cannot discuss similar issues by engaging with a phrase of a string quartet by César Franck or a symphony by Anton Bruckner despite their expressive potential and tremendous suggestive power. Sounds, no matter how elaborate and profound a composition may be, do not provide a solid ground since, as Eduard Hanslick (2018: 98) once remarked, "What in every art is still description, in music is already metaphor," and in this context, we might also want to consider Theodor W. Adorno (1998: 3) reminding us that "to interpret music means: to make music." So philosophical practice and music cannot be thought of in the manner of engaging with music to discuss existential matters through close readings of musical works. Even if that could be done in a song or an opera, it would be more like discussing ways a literary or dramatic content is being enhanced by musical means. So it remains to be asked whether the philosophy of music can be engaged within the context of philosophical practice as professional—in terms of addressing professional and career issues—rather than existential help.

This chapter sketches a map of possible implications of the philosophy of music for philosophical practice. Its core interest lies in the use of the philosophy of music not only for musicians but also for all who partake in the musical ecosystem. Among others, the following key questions are being addressed:

- How can we read the philosophy of music from the perspective of philosophical practice?
- How can we use the philosophy of music for musicians and music-related professionals?
- How can philosophers of music be seen as imaginary counselors for musicians?

To achieve these goals, I will try to cover the wide spectrum of the philosophy of music from antiquity till today by examining several exemplary cases, considering as well the paradigm shift from the antique concept of *mousiké* to the modern paradigm of purely instrumental music and music as an autonomous art.

How Can We Read Philosophy of Music from the Perspective of Philosophical Practice?

How can the philosophy of music be seen from the perspective of philosophical practice? The answer depends on the notion of philosophical practice we operate with. If we take the most elementary notion of philosophical practice as philosophy for nonacademic philosophers, then we may claim that philosophy of music from the perspective of philosophical practice is not aimed at academic scholars of music or philosophy. It concerns primarily musicians, listeners, and other parties involved. And should we apply an even more pragmatic notion of philosophical practice as professional help by means of philosophy, then the main target group in our case would be musicians.

Now, should we imagine a musician who attends the practice of a philosopher to get help with issues that concern their professional activity? Since local, national, and international music institutions offer counseling services on topics such as marketing, rights, networking, health, and well-being, we could easily imagine an extra one. The complexity of the professional world of a musician increases day by day, and grave new challenges have made their appearance in the last years: The economic impact of the pandemics in the creative sector, in general, and in the performing arts, in particular; the emergence of artificial intelligence in the arts, meaning that a new musical work in every possible style can be created with a few commands in a laptop; the establishment of artistic research at universities of music and performing arts that, for the sake of a transdisciplinarity phantasm, demands the musicians to become scholars of their own work; and the ongoing transformation of a great majority of musicians to full-time freelancers in times in which public ensembles have to fight hard for their survival are some of them. One could easily reach the conclusion that every new counseling offer that might provide some kind of assistance in a radically changing landscape should be welcomed.

The image of a musician visiting a philosophical practitioner can be a useful starting point, and the next step would be to ask which issues are of concern for musicians. No one would deny that two issues are especially at stake here: repertoire and musical interpretation. Undoubtedly, both issues are crucial for every musician whose permanent goal is to develop a personal style within a certain repertoire. Especially, the issue of repertoire needs special attention since we live in an era in which access to repertoire for both listeners and musicians is unlimited through a multitude of digital channels, and as a consequence, every musician is confronted with an infinite sea of possibilities as far as their repertoire is concerned. So how can the philosophy of music be of help here?

Philosophy of music could help musicians address questions of repertoire and interpretation. In the context of philosophical practice, musicians would be invited to ask themselves questions such as:

- ➢ Why do I choose what I choose to perform?
- ➢ How do I relate personally to the works I perform?
- ➢ How do I create an attractive program for my audience?
- ➢ How do I get new ideas for my musical practice?

Here, the philosophy of music could offer inspiration and impulses. So the task of philosophical practice using philosophy of music, or *music philosophical practice*, as one might call it, would be to unfold such a potential.

But apart from addressing the aforementioned and similar issues for musicians, music philosophical practice can be of relevance for other music-related professions. For example, the publicist of an ensemble may seek inspiring texts from philosophy to use in promoting material to offer an intellectual portrait of the artists or build some form of connection with the public and ask a philosophical practitioner to make suggestions or perform some ghostwriting task; a video jockey, who creates video content and curates video playlists for concert performances, DJ nights, and live events, can profit by descriptions of "translating" music into words and images; an album cover designer might want to get better acquainted by means of philosophy with metaphors we associate music with, such as the arabesque, the kaleidoscope, or the wave, to create a new powerful cover. Or they might want to discuss alternatives to a familiar metaphor found in previous covers of the same work in his/her struggle to create something new and unique. I put forward these examples to show that it is all about offering impulses and stimulating creativity. But philosophy of music mediated through philosophical practice can also help address more everyday concerns as well. A cultural manager trying to get funds for a new concert hall in the community or save an existing one may get help from philosophical insights on the value of music in the preparation of their arguments for the necessity of a communal music hall.

Philosophy of Music for Musicians: Performance and Repertoire

We have mentioned that the most important issues for musicians are repertoire and performance. Let us now see how the philosophy of music can be of help by considering a few examples.

Musicians strive for an authentic performance, whether authentic refers to the objective qualities of accuracy, precision, and faithfulness to the work—taking into account that the ontological status of musical works, at least in classical music, is not given but always made—or the subjective qualities of maximal self-expressivity. In both cases, authenticity is seen as the key to a successful performance. So, it can help to see how the philosophy of music addresses authenticity. Let us recall what one of the most influential philosophers of music in the last few years, Peter Kivy, has contributed to the subject. Kivy distinguishes four kinds of authenticities: (1) composer authenticity: the respect for a composer's original conception; (2) sonic authenticity: the quest to restore the sound materials with which a composer worked; (3) personal authenticity: the esteem accorded the performer's individual expression, which may at times deviate from what a composer indicated; and (4) sensible authenticity: the meaning attached to a performance by its audience (cf. Jackson 1997: 2–3).

This distinction between different kinds of authenticities could help a musician reflect on their performance and increase their self-awareness under the denominator of authenticity. It might lead to a change of attitude toward authenticity. Musicians could see the plural "authenticities" as an alternative to one "authenticity," in case they have not already done so, and try something new. Let us take the example of a musician who has always operated within the framework of sonic authenticity and has been negative to deviations of any kind. To reframe deviations under the label of personal authenticity could open up a new perspective. That is how the wonder of language operates: To rename a deviation or relabel it as personal authenticity means a shift of perspective.

Or, to consider another case, a musician who wants to defend their right to personal authenticity may find some support in Nietzsche (2003: 60):

> Causing the master to be forgotten.—The pianist who performs the work of a master will have played best when he makes his listeners forget the master, when it seems as though he is relating a tale from his own life or is experiencing something at that very moment. To be sure, if he himself is nothing of consequence his listeners will execrate the loquacity with which he tells us about himself. He thus has to know how to engage the imagination of his listeners on his own behalf. Conversely, it is this which accounts for all the weaknesses and follies of "the virtuoso."

Let us now go on with the repertoire. In the history of the philosophy of music, we find several typologies of musical works, since philosophers of music do not consider music alone but inside their own systems. In other words, typologies reveal how philosophers hear music through their own systematic premises. The acknowledgment of such typologies might help musicians reflect on their repertoire and make repertoire choices. Therefore, I will discuss a few typologies of musical works and ask how musicians could profit from them. I will take one example from antiquity, one from the nineteenth century, and one from the twentieth: Aristotle, Edmund Gurney, and Günther Anders.

In the eighth book of *Politics* (1341b: 32–5), Aristotle distinguishes between cathartic or enthusiastic, practical, and ethical melodies. This tripartite distinction is based on the effect of music on listeners. Cathartic melodies have a cleansing effect, practical melodies make listeners forget the struggles of everyday life, and ethical ones educate the soul. This typology comes from a society and era far away from ours. Nevertheless, it can help musicians think about the effects of their repertoire. There are three possible questions to engage with:

- ➢ Can all music be thought through such a tripartite distinction?
- ➢ What dimensions does the tripartite distinction make us aware of?
- ➢ Does an "ideal" program include cathartic, practical, and ethical melodies?

In chapter IV of *The Power of Sound*, Edmund Gurney distinguishes between impressive and expressive music. Impressive music leaves strong impressions of musical movement, of an ideal motion; expressive music leaves impressions of expressive nature; for example, it suggests emotions like joy or sadness. This distinction seems vague, given that the one element does not exclude the other, meaning that music can be both impressive and expressive at the same time. Gurney does not deny that; on the contrary, he just emphasizes that in most works, one element overwhelms the other. Musicians could use this distinction to reflect on their repertoire choices from a new point of view. Again, three questions to engage with:

- ➢ Are the works I perform rather impressive or expressive?
- ➢ Do I need to include more of one or of the other, and why?
- ➢ How is such a distinction important for relating to the audience?

In his *Philosophical Investigations on Musical Situations*, Anders distinguishes three modi of being inside music: a modus of "aufgelöst sein" (melted, dispersed), a modus of "gelöst sein" (released, be free), and a modus of "abgelöst sein" (detached). Anders's musical examples are for the first, Richard Wagner's *Tristan und Isolde*; for the second, Wolfgang Amadeus Mozart and the music of Viennese classicism in general; and for the third, a fugue by Johann Sebastian Bach, a mass by Josquin des Prez, and Arnold Schönberg's dodecaphony. Three exemplary questions to ask could be:

- ➢ Can a great part of the music repertoire be thought in this distinction?
- ➢ Could this distinction be helpful for my repertoire choices?
- ➢ How could I operate with it?

Formats of Philosophical Practice for Musicians

Philosophy of music could be embedded in the casual formats of philosophical practice (consultations, workshops, and philosophical cafés), as is the case with most issues of concern in philosophical practice. A musician could make use of an individual consultation, and members or representatives of ensembles could opt for a workshop or a philosophical café as well.

The most important thing is that musicians identify a need and bring an issue to discussion, and philosophical practitioners respond to it as best they can. The dialogue could be structured or improvised. An improvisation in the manner of jazz music (Pollastri 2007) or perhaps an atmosphere of pensive intimacy encountered in chamber music would be most welcome. One could start by discussing an idea, an intuition, or a quote. An important issue here is whether the client is familiar with philosophy or not. If they are, then the philosophical practitioner may refer to the philosophy of music explicitly by using terms, theories, schools, and names. The practitioner may even suggest lectures for further discussion. If not, then the reference to the philosophy of music may be implicit by just addressing thoughts and ideas without using references. Of course, these ways do not signify an "either-or" but an "also-as well." One could shift between an implicit or an explicit modus according to the case. The implicit-explicit modus applies to other formats as well, such as workshops or philosophical cafés.

How Can Philosophers of Music Be Seen as Imaginary Counselors for Musicians?

This chapter shifts the focus from areas and topics to the individual figures of music philosophy, which means asking how an issue could be seen from the perspective of a certain philosopher of music. What advice would they offer to a musician who wants to improve their repertoire? To address similar questions is fascinating due to its experimental character, and it could also be done in the context of academic knowledge transfer for musicological or philosophical projects (e.g., Perrakis 2019). Let me offer an example: to ask how an ancient philosopher would consider a contemporary development, the crossover of musical genres under the label of crossover music (e.g., when Renée Fleming sings Björk in an operatic style or a Jacques Brel's chanson is being performed by a mezzo-soprano and a theorbe), is nothing less than a thought experiment. It can be very inspiring and quite successful as well. That is exactly what Wagner did when he considered the music of his age, the purely instrumental music of Ludwig van Beethoven, as an ancient philosopher would do and then created the total artwork [Gesamtkunstwerk] that would establish him as one of the greatest innovators in music history.

To assess the potential of the individual figures that constitute the philosophy of music and its history, it would be helpful to make some distinctions and build typologies of music philosophers. The following section makes suggestions for music philosophical practice concerning typologies.

Typologies of Music Philosophers

First, we could categorize philosophers of music according to the schools of thought to which they belong. For example, we could put together thinkers such as Wilhelm Dilthey, Friedrich Nietzsche, Henri Bergson, José Ortega y Gasset, Ludwig Klages, Oswald Spengler, and Arthur Schopenhauer under the label of life philosophy and speak of the music aesthetics of life philosophy (see Perrakis 2020) or put together Hans Georg Nägeli, Johann Friedrich Herbart, Robert Zimmermann, and Eduard Hanslick under the label of nineteenth-century formalism (see Rothfarb 2011). Another option would be to establish general directions in the history of philosophy and see who fits where. That is the case of Martinelli, who highlights three lines of thought in antiquity (Pythagoreanism, Aristotelianism, and Skepticism) and carries this tripartition further in a de-historicized manner under naturalism, phenomenology, and empiricism (cf. 2019: VI–VII). That would initially provide a helpful picture, to create some initial strands, and then move to the individual character of each philosopher.

Second, we could distinguish between philosophers who have written on music, such as Aristotle, Immanuel Kant, G. W. F. Hegel, and Søren Kierkegaard, without being musicians themselves and philosophers who have written on music and who have been musicians themselves, such as Friedrich Nietzsche, Jean-Jacques Rousseau, Theodor W. Adorno, Vladimir Jánkelevitch, or Gabriel Marcel, just to mention the most known ones. However, this should not mean that those who have been musicians themselves have a bigger significance for philosophical practice for musicians. That would lead to a prejudiced reading under a false premise. Rather, to the contrary, this distinction is important to make clear that the predominant perspective in the philosophy of music is the listener's.

Third, we could distinguish between philosophers who operate within the ancient paradigm of *mousiké*, music as unity of word, sound, and movement, and those who engage with the modern paradigm of purely instrumental music, music without words, or absolute music. One may ask here: Why not simply draw a line and distinguish between ancient and modern philosophy of music? Because there are those who challenge the logic of both paradigms, philosophers such as Nietzsche, by showing their genealogical interdependence (Nietzsche 2005: 99) and those who combine it creating something new—the aforementioned case of Wagner.

Fourth, another typology might involve philosophers of music who were musicologists as well and vice versa, such as the Energetics August Halm and Ernst Kurth and, most prominently, Theodor W. Adorno. Here, it could be very intriguing to ask what is distinctly musicological and what is distinctly music philosophical, and above all, in what ways such a question makes sense. Is there any conflict to trace, and if so, how could such a conflict become productive? A philosophically informed musicologist is not identical with a musicologically informed philosopher. The focus of the former might be very different from the focus of the latter.

Fifth, it would be meaningful to also consider artists who have left traces of the philosophy of music by reflecting on it. I have here Rainer Maria Rilke in mind, who engaged with music in his poetics and wrote poems about his concert experiences, where he describes the movement of music in a quasi-phenomenological manner.

Sixth and last, philosophers who have written very little or nothing about music could also be of importance for philosophical practice for musicians because they were influential—often by engaging with musical metaphors—in the philosophy of music. This is the case with Henri Bergson and his concept of inner time (*durée*) (cf. Corbier 2012: 292) and Martin Heidegger ([1927] 1962) due to his concerns with hearing as an existential modus standing metaphorically for the way we are receptive to the world.

Identifying Key Texts

Next to the typology of music philosophers, we could search for key texts for music philosophical practice: key texts for the preparation of the music philosophical practitioner but also key texts for consultation. These should not only be necessarily discursive texts but also include other narrative and experimental forms such as autobiographies, notes, diaries, or aphorisms—of musicians as well. It is especially so if we consider that there are thinkers important for music who have delivered a significant part of their work in aphorisms, such as the early German romantics (Friedrich Schlegel and Friedrich von Hardenberg alias Novalis, above all) or E. M. Cioran. The hidden potential of alternative narrative forms can be immense. For example, an aphorism, which is a short sentence containing nothing more than a few words, can stimulate thoughts in various directions. Aphorisms are very important in philosophical practice (see Staude 2017), above all due to their ability to transmit a sense of wonder, which is, in my opinion, the starting point and the end of philosophical practice.

Identifying key texts would mean imagining a canon of music philosophical works for philosophical practitioners. Canons may not enjoy a good reputation nowadays; nevertheless, in one way or another, we still operate within canonical frames since canons, explicitly or implicitly, provide a minimal structure of orientation. Last but not least, we can put aside the weight of the word and embrace the latent musicality of a canon by thinking about musical canons.

Ideally, this canon would cover the whole extent of the history of the philosophy of music for the sake of plurality and the tracking of interesting strands. To be stimulating, the canon should follow the dialectics of the known and unknown, the familiar and unfamiliar, the timely and untimely—as defined by Nietzsche (2003: 60): "that is to say acting counter to our time and thereby acting on our time, and, let us hope, for the benefit of a time to come." A canon that constitutes one strand does not serve its purpose at all. In the following, I put some suggestions in a chronological order, selecting not only books and treatises but also articles, essays, and shorter texts.

I concentrate on Western philosophy and works mainly concerning the paradigm of classical music, although I believe that the inclusion of Eastern philosophies of music and philosophies that address other musical paradigms is indispensable.

Such an inclusion could also function as a corrective against long-established prejudices. To give an example, in the West, there is a tendency to discredit listening to music while doing other things as a disrespectful, if not illegitimate, modus of musical listening since it deprives music of the attention it deserves. From the perspective of the yin-yang scheme, the judgment is suspended, and such a modus of listening would just mean low "yin" energy (cf. Fung 2018: 88).

The vast majority of the fifty works listed below concerns primary works, but I also include a few secondary works. Next to established classics, this list includes forgotten works that deserve to be (re-)discovered and some unknown gems.

1. Plato, *Πολιτεία* (*Politeia*) (estimated between 390 and 370 BCE) and *Νόμοι* (*Nomoi*) (360–1 BCE)—for the ethical element of music.
2. Aristotle, *Πολιτικά* (*Politics*) (ca. 400 BCE)—for its tripartite typology of musical works (enthusiastic, educatory, practical).
3. Boëthius, *De Institutione Musica* (*Fundamentals of Music*) (between 510 and 523) (1492)—for its distinction between *musica mundana*, *musica humana*, and *musica instrumentalis*.
4. Jean-Jacques Rousseau, *Essai sur l'origine des langues* (*Essay on the Origin of Languages)* (1781)—for its notion of music as a primeval language and its introduction of a Northern and a Southern perspective in music and language.
5. Immanuel Kant, *Kritik der Urteilskraft* (*Critique of the Power of Judgment*) (1790)—for linking music to the form of the aesthetic idea.
6. Arthur Schopenhauer, *Die Welt als Wille und Vorstellung* (*The World as Will and Representation*) (1819)—for the will-expressivity of music and for being the first philosophy of music that inverts the place of music in the hierarchy of the arts.
7. Hans Georg Nägeli, *Vorlesungen* (*Lectures*) (1826)—for his distinction between two different directions (play of forms versus cantability) in the history of instrumental music.
8. Georg Wilhelm Friedrich Hegel, *Vorlesungen über die Aesthetik* (*Lectures on Aesthetics*) (1835–8)—for its notion of music as an art of inwardness.
9. Søren Kierkegaard, *Enten—Eller. Et Livs-Fragment udgivet af Victor Eremita* (*Either-or. A life-fragment edited by Victor Eremita*) (1843)—for the idea of "sensual geniality" and the notion of the erotic in music.

10. Eduard Hanslick, *Vom Musikalisch-Schönen* (*On the Musically Beautiful*) (1854)—for its polemics against the aesthetics of feeling by means of musical formalism.
11. Friedrich Nietzsche, *Die Geburt der Tragodie aus dem Geiste der Musik* (*The Birth of Tragedy from the Spirit of Music*) (1872)—for linking music to the Dionysian and highlighting the excessive character of music.
12. Friedrich Nietzsche, *Richard Wagner in Bayreuth* (1876)—the fourth and last of the *Untimely Meditations* (*Unzeitgemäße Betrachtungen*) by Nietzsche, highlighting the unhistorical effect of music.
13. Edmund Gurney, *The Power of Sound* (1880)—for its notion of an ideal motion in music and its distinction between impressive and expressive music.
14. Arthur Seidl, *Vom Musikalisch-Erhabenen* (*On the Musically Sublime*) (1887)—for defending music as the art of the sublime par excellence, opposing Hanslick's treatise on the musically beautiful.
15. Eduard von Hartmann, *Philosophie des Schönen. Zweiter systematischer Theil der Aesthetik* (*Philosophy of the Beautiful. Second Systematic Part of Aesthetics*) (1887)—for the idea of music as art that makes the unconscious conscious.
16. Rainer Maria Rilke, *Notizen zur Melodie der Dinge* (*Notes on the Melody of Things*) (written 1898)—for its notion of a unifying "melody of the background."
17. Wilhelm Dilthey, *Das musikalisches Verstehen* (*On Musical Understanding*) (written c. 1906)—for discussing how music expresses the abundance of life.
18. Oskar Bie, *Die Oper* (*The Opera*) (1913)—for a view on opera as the discursive place of unification of all art and life.
19. Ernst Bloch, *Geist der Utopie* (*Spirit of Utopia*) (1918)—for discussing the utopian moment in music.
20. Oswald Spengler, *Der Untergang des Abendlandes* (*The Decline of the West*) (1923)—for the notion of Western instrumental music as a Faustian art.
21. Ludwig Klages, *Vom Wesen des Rhythmus* (*On the Essence of Rhythm*) (1923)—for the philosophical implications of the distinction between rhythm and tact.

22. Heinrich Besseler, *Grundfragen des musikalischen Hörens* (*Fundamental Questions of Musical Listening*) (1926) and *Grundfragen der Musikästhetik* (*Fundamental Questions of Music Aesthetics*) (1927)—for applying Heidegger's phenomenology in music.
23. Günther Anders, *Philosophische Untersuchungen über musikalische Situationen* (*Philosophical Investigations on Musical Situations*) (written 1930/31, published 2017)—for linking certain types of music to ways of being in the world.
24. Gisèle Brelet, *Le temps musical* (*Musical Time*) (1949)—for a Bergsonian take on music as the art of time.
25. Evanghélos Moutsopoulos, *La musique dans l' oeuvre de Platon* (*Music in Plato's Work*) (1959)—for being one of the best studies on Plato's philosophy of music.
26. Joseph Kerman, *Opera as Drama* (1956)—for a strong take on opera as "dramma per musica."
27. Vladimir Jánkelevitch, *La Musique et l' Ineffable* (*Music and the Ineffable*) (1961)—for discussing ineffability in music.
28. Leo Spitzer, *Classical and Christian Ideas of World Harmony. Prolegomena to an Interpretation of the Word "Stimmung"* (1963)—a meticulous genealogy of a key aesthetic idea of music.
29. Harald Kaufmann, *Thesen über Wertungsforschung* (*Theses on Judgment Research*) (1968)—for its attempt to establish a science of aesthetic judgment in music.
30. Roland Barthes, *Le grain de la voix* (*The Grain of the Voice*) (1972)—for discussing the corporeality of voice.
31. Jean-François Lyotard, *Dieu et la marionette* (*God and the Marionette*) (1988)—for thinking musical time through Leibniz's monad.
32. Hans Blumenberg, *Matthäuspassion* (*Matthew Passion*) (1988)—for discussing the ability of music to keep a sense of the religious feeling alive.
33. Peter Kivy, *The Profundity of Music* (1990)—for introducing a new subfield in the philosophy of music: musical profundity.
34. Barbara Naumann, *Das Musikalische in Poetik und Sprachtheorie der Frühromantik* (*Musical Ideas-Instrument. The Musical in Poetics and

Language Theory of the Early Romanticism) (1990)—the standard reference work for the music philosophy of the early German romanticism.

35. Lydia Goehr, *The Imaginary Museum of Musical Works* (1992)—for discussing the origins of the notion of musical work.
36. Jerrold Levinson, *Music in the Moment* (1997)—for introducing the notion of concatenationism in understanding music, in contrast to the casual architectonic model.
37. Daniel K. L. Chua, *Absolute Music and the Construction of Meaning* (1999)—the most intriguing and thought-provoking work on the many dimensions hidden behind the notion of absolute music.
38. Jean-Luc Nancy, *À l'écoute* (*On Listening*) (2000)—for mediating on listening as distinct from hearing.
39. Mladen Dolar and Slavoj Žižek, *Opera's Second Death* (2002)—for the thought-provoking idea of opera as a dead-born genre and for discussing opera from a psychoanalytic point of view.
40. Corina Caduff, *Die Literarisierung von Musik und bildender Kunst um 1800* (The Literarization of Music and Plastic Arts around 1800) (2003)—for the literary topos of music as language that had a great impact on the philosophy of music.
41. Carolyn Abbate, *Music—Drastic or Gnostic?* (2004)—for elaborating on Jánkelevitch's latent distinction between a drastic and a gnostic attitude toward music.
42. Michael Spitzer, *Music and Metaphorical Thought* (2004)—an indispensable work for music and metaphor in the history of music philosophy.
43. Bernard Williams, *On Opera* (2006)—for discussing the tendance of opera to exceed its function as a music drama.
44. Hermann Danuser, *Weltanschauungsmusik* (*Worldview Music*) (2009)—for applying the Kantian aesthetic idea to historical musicology.
45. Kiene Brillenburg Wurth, *Musically Sublime: Indeterminacy, Infinity, Irresolvability* (2009)—a very thorough and comprehensive survey on the Musically Sublime.
46. Alain Badiou, *Cinq leçons sur le cas Wagner* (*Five Lessons on Wagner*) (2010)—for discussing the actuality of Wagner's total artwork.

47. Holly Watkins, *Metaphors of Depth in German Musical Thought. From E.T.A. Hoffmann to Arnold Schönberg* (2011)—for addressing one of the most important categories of musical metaphors.
48. Kathleen Higgins, *The Music of Our Lives* (2011)—for highlighting the ethical significance of the affective moment in music.
49. Nanette Nielsen and Marcel Cobussen, *Music and Ethics* (2012)—a comprehensive survey on a topic marginalized in contemporary music philosophy.
50. Daniel Martin Feige, *Philosophie des Jazz* (Philosophy of Jazz) (2014)—for discussing jazz from the perspective of European art music and music ontology.

These texts cover a wide spectrum of issues in the history of the philosophy of music. I write history of the philosophy of music to emphasize that the philosophy of music is also its history and should not be separated from it. That should not mean merely seeking and finding forerunners in the philosophical tradition or establishing continuities or raptures but, first and foremost, in accordance with the spirit of philosophical practice, the awareness of the weight of the philosophical tradition as an inextinguishable source of wonderment. Furthermore, I think it is important for such a canon to include works on opera as well since opera is the field of an agonistic interaction between music and the other arts, and in this sense, it makes aware of the antinomies a philosophy of music has to live with. At the same time, putting music close to opera keeps the notion of *mousiké* open. Therefore, the issue of opera is of great importance for the philosophy of music and should be relevant for music philosophical practice as well.

Epilogue

Philosophical practice can make the philosophy of music fruitful for musicians and other music professions from many perspectives. Seeking ways in which the philosophy of music can respond to the needs of musicians, the typologies of music philosophers together with canonical considerations might provide a helpful orientation for the preparation of the philosophical practitioner who wants to engage in music philosophical practice. The work toward the establishment of a *music philosophical practice* could thus become an important instrument for facing the challenges today's musicians have to deal with and also enrich the constantly widening field of philosophical practice under the denominator of the arts.

References

Abbate, C. (2004), "Music—Drastic or Gnostic?," *Critical Enquiry* 20: 505–36.

Achenbach, G. B. (2010), *Zur Einführung der Philosophischen Praxis: Vorträge, Aufsätze, Gespräche und Essays, mit denen sich die Philosophische Praxis in den Jahren 1981 bis 2009 vorstellte: Eine Dokumentation*, Jürgen Dinter.

Adorno, T. W. (1998), "Music and Language: A Fragment," in *Quasi Una Fantasia: Essays on Modern Music*, trans. R. Livingstone, 1–6, Verso Books.

Anders, G. (2017), "Philosophische Untersuchungen über musikalische Situationen" (Philosophical Investigations on Musical Situations), in R. Ellensohn (ed.), *Musikphilosophische Schriften*, 13–140, C. H. Beck Verlag.

Anttila, M. E. (2013), *Luther's Theology of Music: Spiritual Beauty and Pleasure*, Walter de Gruyter.

Badiou, A. (2010), *Cinq leçons sur le cas Wagner* (Five Lessons on Wagner), Nous.

Barthes, R. (1972), "Le grain de la voix" (The Grain of the Voice), *Musique en jeu* 9:57–63.

Besseler, H. (1926), "Grundfragen des musikalischen Hörens" (Fundamental Questions of Musical Listening), *Jahrbuch der Musikbibliothek Peters* 25:35–52.

Besseler, H. (1927), "Grundfragen der Musikästhetik" (Fundamental Questions of Music Aesthetics), *Jahrbuch der Musikbibliothek Peters* 26:63–80.

Bie, O. (1913), *Die Oper* (The Opera), S. Fischer.

Bloch, E. (1918), *Geist der Utopie* (Spirit of Utopia), Duncker & Humblot.

Blumenberg, H. (1988), *Matthäuspassion* (Matthew Passion), Suhrkamp Verlag.

Boëthius (1492), *De Institutione Musica* (Fundamentals of Music), Forlivo et Gregorium Fratres.

Brelet, G. (1949), *Le temps musical* (Musical Time), 2 vols., Presses Universitaires de France.

Caduff, C. (2003), *Die Literarisierung von Musik und bildender Kunst um 1800* (*The Literarisation of Music and Plastic Arts Around 1800*), Fink.

Chua, D. K. L. (1999), *Absolute Music and the Construction of Meaning*, Cambridge University Press.

Corbier, C. (2012), "Bachelard, Bergson, Emmanuel. Mélodie: Rythme et durée," *Archives de Philosophie* 75:291–310.

Danuser, H. (2009), *Weltanschauungsmusik* (Worldview Music), Argus.

Dolar, M. and S. Žižek (2002), *Opera's Second Death*, Routledge.

Feige, D. M. (2014), *Philosophie des Jazz* (Philosophy of Jazz), Suhrkamp Verlag.

Fung, C. V. (2018), *A Way of Music Education: Classic Chinese Wisdoms*, Oxford University Press.

Goehr, L. (1992), *The Imaginary Museum of Musical Works*, Oxford University Press.

Gurney, E. (1880), *The Power of Sound*, Smith, Elder.

Hanslick, E. (1854), *Vom Musikalisch-Schönen* (On the Musically Beautiful), Rudolph Weigel.

Hanslick, E. (2018), *On the Musically Beautiful*, trans. L. Rothfarb and C. Landerer, Oxford University Press.

Hegel, G. W. F. (1853–8), "Vorlesungen über die Aesthetik," in H. G. Hotho (ed.), *Georg Wilhelm Friedrich Hegel's Werke*, vol. 10, 1–3, Duncker & Humblot.

Higgins, K. (2011), *Music of Our Lives*, Lexington Books.

Jackson, R. (1997), "Authenticity or Authenticities?—Performance Practice and the Mainstream," *Performance Practice Review* 10 (1): 1–10.

Jánkelevitch, V. (1961), *La Musique et l Ineffable* (Music and the Ineffable), Armand Colin.

Kant, I. (1790), *Kritik der Urteilskraft* (Critique of the Power of Judgement), Lagarde and Friedrich.

Kaufmann, H. (1968), "Thesen über Wertungsforschung" (Theses' on Judgement Research), *Österreichische Musikzeitschrift* 22:647–52.

Kerman, J. (1956), *Opera as Drama*, Vintage Canada.

Kierkegaard, S. (1843), *Enten—Eller: Et Livs-Fragment udgivet af Victor Eremita* (Either—Or: A Life-Fragment Edited by Victor Eremita), C. A. Reitzel.

Kivy, P. (1990), "The Profundity of Music," in *Music Alone: Philosophical Reflections on the Purely Musical Experience*, 202–18, Cornell University Press.

Klages, L. (1923), "Vom Wesen des Rhythmus" (On the Essence of Rhythm), in F. Hilker and L. Pallat (eds.), *Künstlerische Körperschulung*, 94–137, Ferdinand Hirt.

Klein, R. (2019), *Musikphilosophie zur Einführung*, Junius.

Leibniz, G. W. (1734), "Ad Christianum Goldbachium (17 January 1714)," in C. Kortholt (ed.), *Epistolae ad diversos theologici, juridici, medici, philosophici, mathematici, historici et philologici argumenti*, 241–9, Breitkopf.

Levinson, J. (1997), *Music in the Moment*, Cornell University Press.

Lyotard, J.-F. (1988), "Dieu et la marionette" (God and the Marionette), in *L'inhumain: Causeries sur le temps*, 165–76, Galilée.

Martinelli, R. (2019), *Philosophy of Music: A History*, trans. S. de Sanctis, de Gruyter.
Nägeli, H. G. (1826), *Vorlesungen* (Lectures), Cotta.
Nancy, J.-L. (2000), *À l'écoute* (On Listening), Galilée.
Naumann, B. (1990), *"Musikalisches Ideen-Instrument": Das Musikalische in Poetik und Sprachtheorie der Frühromantik* (Musical Ideas-Instrument: The Musical in Poetics and Language Theory of the Early Romanticism), Metzler.
Network for Nordic Philosophical Practitioners (n.d.), Nordic Pragmatism Network. Available at: http://www.nordprag.org/sida1.html (accessed July 23, 2023).
Nielsen, N. and M. Cobussen (2012), *Music and Ethics*, Ashgate.
Nietzsche, F. (1872), *Die Geburt der Tragodie aus dem Geiste der Musik* (The Birth of Tragedy from the Spirit of Music), E. W. Fritzsch.
Nietzsche, F. (2003), *Untimely Meditations*, trans. R. J. Hollingdale, Cambridge University Press.
Nietzsche, F. (2005), *Human, All Too Human: A Book for Free Spirits*, trans. R. J. Hollingdale, Cambridge University Press.
Perrakis, M. (2019), "Philosophical Practice for Musicians: A Short Report on TOM-Tool," *Philosophical Practice* 14 (3): 2416–19.
Perrakis, M. (ed.) (2020), *Musik und Lebensphilosophie*, Universal Edition.
Pollastri, N. (2007), *Consulente filosofico cercasi*, Apogeo.
Rilke, R. M. (1955–6), "Notizen zur Melodie der Dinge" (Notes on the Melodies of Things), in *Sämtliche Werke V*, Insel.
Rothfarb, L. (2011), "Nineteenth-Century Fortunes of Musical Formalism," *Journal of Music Theory* 55 (2): 167–220.
Rousseau, J.-J. (1781), "Essai sur l'origine des langues" (Essay on the Origin of Languages), in *Oeuvres posthumes de J. J. Rousseau*, le Pléiade edition.
Schopenhauer, A. (1819), *Die Welt als Wille und Vorstellung* (The World as Will and Representation), Brockhaus.
Seidl, A. (1907), *Vom Musikalisch-Erhabenen* (On the Musically-Sublime), Kahnt.
Spengler, O. (1923), *Der Untergang des Abendlandes* (The Decline of the West), C. H. Beck Verlag.
Spitzer, L. (1963), *Classical and Christian Ideas of World Harmony: Prolegomena to an Interpretation of the Word "Stimmung,"* Johns Hopkins University Press.
Spitzer, M. (2004), *Metaphor and Musical Thought*, University of Chicago Press.
Staude, D. (2017), "Aphorisms as Stimulation in Philosophical Dialogue," in L. Amir (ed.), *New Frontiers in Philosophical Practice*, 186–95, Cambridge Scholar Publishing.
von Hartmann, E. (1887), *Philosophie des Schönen: Zweiter systematischer Theil der Aesthetik* (Philosophy of the Beautiful: Second Systematic Part of Aesthetics), Duncker.

Watkins, H. (2011), *Metaphors of Depth in German Musical Thought: From E.T.A. Hoffmann to Arnold Schönberg*, Cambridge University Press.
Williams, B. (2006), *On Opera*, Yale University Press.
Wurth, K. B. (2009), *Musically Sublime: Indeterminacy, Infinity, Irresolvability*, Fordham University Press.
Young, J. (2023), *A History of Western Philosophy of Music*, Cambridge University Press.
Zöller, G. (2010), "Schopenhauer," in S. L. Sorgner and O. Fürbeth (eds.), *Music in German Philosophy: An Introduction*, trans. S. H. Gillespie, 121–40, University of Chicago Press.

10

Sculpting Space

Philosophical Practice Through Design

Lydia Amir

Introduction

Let me introduce the topic of this chapter by sharing four different stories, four cases of different approaches to a cherished deceased's belongings. While reading these short cases, we may ponder, are these belongings a vital part of the deceased or a material surrounding that should not outlive the dead person?

Case One: A professor dies. Nothing is kept from her belongings. Her library—usually the most cherished collection of items for an academic—is lapidated, although both loving daughters have space, one of them, a big house, where this library could have occupied a non-obstructive place in the second floor and be a source of excitement, interest, and curiosity for children and grandchildren alike, as well as a place of living memory of the grandmother. Although far from ignorant or resentful of studies, one of them tells me proudly about the decision to keep nothing, which the sisters shared, as if consensus were an argument.

Case Two: A mother dies. Her elderly son, too distraught to go over her things, asks a professional "disposer" to throw everything. Years later, he bursts into tears when he tells me this story on the following occasion: I am giving him the paintings that my mother drew to showcase in a permanent exhibition. He, to the contrary, never had the chance to go over the things that his own mother left; he tells me: It was too painful. Now he misses this experience and what it could have brought to him and deeply regrets his rush (re)action.

Case Three: One sister out of four children refuses to quickly let go of their mother's apartment and her belongings. She moves in, coming from another city and living now in a neighborhood she does not like, to be among the things that were part of her past, from birth to recent time. Her siblings consider her act weird and unnecessary except that it fits well with her personality and maybe, paradoxically, with the suffering she experienced from the relationship she had with her mother.

Case Four: An elderly person cannot get rid of any of her parents' belongings, from the smallest pin to the biggest piece of furniture. When they were alive, she did not think she would preserve anything, apart from two vases, but now, she combined her apartment with theirs, making her life impossible and obstructing anyone from coming to live with her. A terrible guilt, a senseless feeling of responsibility, comes over her when she attempts to throw anything. She is not allowed to go on except burdened by this past, her past, and her parents' past, which she carries with her.

The cases described here, as if of distant sources, were all personal stories of persons I know. Let me attempt to articulate what I learned from them about grieving, about life and death, and also about objects and their role in our lives. I believe that this articulation will demonstrate a new form of philosophical practice that I call "sculpting space."

When our parents die, we usually have to deal with their belongings while grieving. That, which makes it more difficult, we have to do while continuing living, working, and usually nurturing other people. The continual presence of death in life is particularly difficult when you want to put the experience to rest by focusing either on life (yours) or on death (your parents'). Rather than offering a resting place, going through their belongings is having the dead present, as if alive through their familiar things. The playing with death in life and life in death is particularly difficult as we touch the objects with which and in which they lived. Still imbued with their smell, they bring to mind memories as do the madeleine cookies in Marcel Proust's novel, *A la recherche du temps perdu*.

However, memories at this point are extremely difficult because each makes it clear that it is a memory, not a reality. Thus, at each moment, we are called to realize that what was is not and will never be and to experience this again and again, voluntarily, as if we were willingly torturing ourselves. For those who have to go to work and take care of children, this kind of torture is deeply debilitating. And, as modern society does not leave space for death, grieving creatively is a kind of luxury that not everyone can achieve and many do not even desire.

But we do not exist apart from things. Even the most remote tribes, we have recently found, put something on their naked bodies, even if just a red string. Since the biblical story of the forbidden fruit eaten by Adam and Eve, clothing, even elemental, is part of our original sin: the consciousness of our (shameful) nakedness. In most cultures, children did not see their parents naked (although in the 1970s, this norm has been challenged, especially in Scandinavian countries). As taking care of seniors is usually the task of professional strangers, the aging children may have never seen their parents without objects enveloping them. These objects left now like ghosts in an empty apartment, painfully point to the hole in them, their formlessness without the body, which cannot inhabit them anymore.

We do not bury today as we would in ancient Egypt or China. We are not allowed to take with us armies of living soldiers or copies of them nor the luxurious objects in/with which we lived. Yet these objects were crafted, sometimes bought, and in many ways esteemed and cherished as that which protect us, but from what, it is not always clear. They are meant to bribe, it seems, to be exchanged for goods, or safety, in this life and in the one that comes after it. Nakedness, once innocent, is a sin now, the sign of a hunted animal from which we are eager to differ.[1]

Most people die in the midst of their things, even if the actual death takes place in the hospital. We rarely saw them, if we used to visit, out of an armchair, a couch, away from a dinner table, or far from the television set; at the time, these were indifferent things to us; now they are cherished as if our life depended on them or shunned as death itself. Many more objects, ornaments, souvenirs, and pictures make a home, and to dismantle that delicate equilibrium between the person and their environment is to make sure the dead are dead, and the debris are liquidated so that no trace is left of the person who once lived in the midst of inanimate objects. Yet those objects received life and meaning, purpose and weight through those who "used" them. This may be one of the reasons that we appreciate antiques, other reasons being the beauty inherent in objects made sometimes with greater care and the strangeness of things that differ from what we are accustomed to.

Worries about consumerism; ecological concerns; smaller spaces; and faster, utilitarian lives have made our relationship with objects problematic. The functionalism of Danish designs and the minimalism of Japanese Zen-inspired attitudes have won the West. Rather than objects, space is the ultimate luxury. And spaces need to be clean and empty to be called spaces. We are told that less is more, and we are supposed to appreciate this paradox, although we normally do not understand the constraints of Japanese minimal spaces, nor the no-self theory of (Zen) Buddhism. Objects are seen as stuff, and stuff as clutter, and clutter as bad . . . mainly because it raises guilt feelings, we are told … and the rhetoric goes on and on …[2]

Should we throw perfectly good things that no one now cares to repair? Should we give away? Why not keep what we bought and like and cherish? Only to make place for new things? Are the interests of the economy the same as ours?

Objects in Our Lives

A first association with the important role that objects may play in human lives is magic. Objects have been endowed with a special power and have been used—in some cultures in the past and in others to this day—to embody albeit partly the identity of persons. These relics and artifacts crystallize the values, qualities, and flaws of the persons but also their aspirations and inner conflicts. Objects of magic are generally used to provide protection from danger and to communicate with the supernatural. They have their counterparts in psychology, where infants invest some objects (a blanket, a toy) with reassurance and are inconsolable when it is lost; getting through hardships in future life may be facilitated by some fetish objects as well as using some objects that are seen as embodying courage or faith or love, sometimes home, to help us in our attempts to overcome fears and phobias. Moreover, we regularly wear some tokens of love and faith on our bodies, symbolized through jewelry and religious artifacts. And we have been defined as *Homo faber*, the human being as maker, especially of tools, with the purpose of controlling the environment and, ultimately, one's fate.[3]

In the everyday life, objects play a significant role, while philosophic literature on this topic is hard to find,[4] though recent work has been done in the social sciences (Durand 2024, on clothes; Sacriste 2023, on the use of our objects in everyday life; Dassié 2010, on the ethnology of the intimate through objects we affectionate; and Dassié 2023, in a more personal account of the objects of her father, accompanied by photographs taken by Valérie Gondran), in history (Bartholeyns and Charpy 2021), and in psychiatry and psychology (Tisseron 1999).

These studies inquire into the question whether the objects of our lives—furniture; trinkets; books; cloths; collections; and, for some, our pans and cell phones—solely facilitate our everyday life and add to our comfort, or are they more than that? The question arises because we seem to be attached to the objects that share our everyday life. Historian Manuel Charpy tells us that this attachment followed the affective dimension we associated with objects through a very long process. It affirmed itself historically during the eighteenth century and manifested itself fully in the nineteenth century, with the development of industries and the serial and multiple objects. Within the collective phenomenon of multiple objects, a very individual relation to objects takes hold: writing one's history with objects. The notion of material heritage modifies the imagination. The affective relation to objects can be observed in heritage and moral testaments. From the middle of the nineteenth century, objects take a very important place: Jewels, for example, become carriers of stories (Bartholeyns and Charpy 2021).

Gradually, objects will no longer be kept for their financial value but for the value of the souvenirs they carry. Valérie Sacriste (2023) explains that this notion of attachment to objects evolved from the moment that individual relations were made possible by democracy, which equalized and averaged living conditions. An individual, singular attachment that was not possible in traditional societies, where only the privileged classes had material at their disposal, became gradually possible. It is with modernity that the equalization of conditions has generalized the attachment to everyday objects, which is present both in working-class and privileged circles.

Objects often mirror our individual and collective existence, as the background of the evolution of our society and epoch, our life, and our memories. Véronique

Dassié (2023) emphasizes all the symbolic force that an object comprehends from the moment it can tell thousands of stories about our lives. Objects resonate in all of our daily practices. Their value refers to key moments in our existence. The material dimension becomes significant when we cultivate an emotional value to objects; it is reinforced by the emergence of important events that mark our daily lives and of which objects become witnesses.

For Manuel Charpy, objects are authentic, real witnesses around which we build narratives. In each of our preserved objects, this historian tells us that all our individual stories resonate with our collective histories. The material nostalgia has an important collective meaning, which gives rise to a sensory experience such that it offers a return to oneself, to the fragments of our life in an increasingly dematerialized society (Bartholeyns and Charpy 2021).

Sacriste focuses on material attachment in the light of social dematerialization. She conducted a survey on the evolution of attachment to objects, in which she found that we now cultivate more and more an attachment to everyday objects and to which we attach no memorial value: What is significant in our lives is the attachment to objects that we consider essential, those that are existential supports of our existence. We are attached to habituation, like the use of the smartphone that we will only singularize for a while before changing it because of commercial logics and planned obsolescence. That is why, in this very uncertain social, cultural, and political context, the survival of objects from the past offers us a parallel sensory experience that no longer has to do with the current relationship to objects in a contemporary society that is part *of* a dematerializing logic. She explains that this is why we attach much importance to objects of the past, to a materiality that is no longer the reality of our experiences here. Objects have a very strong direct sensory dimension. The object of the preserved past is a source of life experiences that immortalize a much longer time in comparison with modern objects, those we can no longer master because they change all the time. Technology pushes us to constantly accustom ourselves to a perpetual renewal of objects to which one no longer has the time or the means to get attached.[5]

Thus, we should not wonder that in times of digital processing and virtual reality, voices arise that tell us that saving remnants of our past in material things is emotionally satisfying in ways not possible in virtual reality. Charles Spence (2020) makes this case for reading books. Although excessive attachment to things can be unhealthy, and hoarding has been defined by the DSM-5 (2013) as a distinct psychiatric disorder (Postlethwaite et al. 2019), many people keep things that are meaningful to them. These can be associated with bad as well as good experiences. Psychologist Krystine I. Batcho[6] remarks, based on Alexandra Niemyjska's (2019) study, that the emotions things elicit can differ as life circumstances change.

Batcho wonders if the shift away from material possessions has been completely beneficial or may have had unfavorable impacts on our well-being. The different types of value—financial, practical, and psychological—bear on the objects we choose. While most people are selective about what they save and what they discard, questions about the meaning and psychological significance of objects arise when we keep things that have no obvious practical value. Many people are reluctant to discard objects that carry memories. The things that matter most to us may well take their value from the person or people associated with them.

Somehow a photo of someone we love contains something of that person. Throwing away the photo can feel like we're discarding the person in the picture. It can feel disrespectful, unappreciative, or disloyal, says Batcho. In some cases, someone keeps something connected to a painful experience or one that ended badly. Someone might save a negative part of their past as punishment when they feel guilt, self-blame, or self-criticism. They might also want to learn from the past and believe that the reminder will prevent future mistakes. Objects associated with traumatic events can be saved as a tribute to those harmed by or lost to illness, injury, or violence or as a way of honoring their memory. Mementos of adversity can represent the hope that a commitment to never forget will ensure that the horror will not happen again.

Saving remnants of our past in material things is emotionally satisfying in ways not fully met in virtual reality. Psychologically distant, virtual reality doesn't engage our senses in the same way that physical objects do and leaves us unfulfilled to some degree. As virtual remains pristine, its unchanging nature robs it of a primary psychological function that special objects serve. Change conveys the passage of time and makes objects resemble us.

It is important for us to be able to let go of the past, both good and bad, Batcho advises. As the ticket stub or old hat loses its luster, it helps free us from the hold the past can have on us. It allows us to enjoy new experiences and grow without feeling guilty that we're abandoning the past that is so much a part of us. Putting the necklace or old letter in a drawer satisfies our obligation, yet wisely chosen special things to keep can be liberating.

This chapter addresses how our approach to the deceased's objects can be liberating and life enhancing, both for our lives and also, yes, for the deceased's earthly afterlife. If psychiatrist Serge Tisseron is right (1999), however, we invest objects with spirit. Locking our memories in the objects around us also means freeing our mind. The object not only extends some of our functions but also transforms the perception we have of ourselves; our ways of deceiving anxiety; and our ways of socializing or, on the contrary, isolating ourselves. Because our everyday objects are the support of expectations, attachments, and disappointments exactly similar to those we feel for human beings, Tisseron advises to never impulsively get rid of our belongings with the impression that we are mistreating the memories attached to them. Let's ritually separate ourselves from our things as if we were burying them, he says, and tells us stories to illustrate this strange relationship: the magic pan, the old armchair, the silk garment, the father's ring.

Grappling with Death

If philosophy is learning how to die, encountering death may ignite that interest in us. Who does not find himself philosophizing, even for the first time, when confronted with death? For Martin Heidegger ([1927] 1962), our own death is what matters in becoming authentic; the death of the other is of no consequence for us. For Emmanuel Levinas (1991), however, we think least about our own death; it is the death of the other that is foundational, as we feel guilty in front of his/her naked face and its infinite moral demands of us—the guilt of the survivor, which Levinas did feel as a survivor of a family that was exterminated (Nassif 2014).

Death is the time of the never more. Never will that kind of happiness be (or that kind of suffering). That absolute, which is death, is difficult for us to understand, for us who live in the relative, thus, to stomach . . . to comprehend.

In the third chapter of *Life and Death* (1992), Pojman describes the five classic views of death in the Western tradition: the Old Testament–Hebrew view that sees death as punishment; the Platonic-Christian view of immortality and resurrection; the Epicurean view of death, which he deems secular morality; the Stoic view of death, which he describes as creative resignation; and the existential view, which sees death as absurd. His treatment of the Epicurean and existential views may not be as balanced as we may wish, and thus, I do not mention these views to recommend this chapter. Rather, I point to the variety of ways of conceiving of death, even when we restrict the discussion to the West. This is relevant to the mourning process, as what is going on with the deceased deeply impacts our view of his/her death . . . and life. These opinions should be gently interrogated with the mourning person. As persons may become deeply religious, as Pojman did, in reaction to death, people brought up in religion may become doubters when actually encountering the experience or its circumstances.

Psychoanalysis, especially Sigmund Freud's (1914–16) work, "Mourning and Melancholia," has addressed mourning. His account should be supplemented by Karl Abraham's ([1911] 1927a, [1924] 1927b) and Melanie Klein's (1940) and, more recently, by Ulrike May's article, which recounts the conversation that Freud, Abraham, and Sándor Ferenczi had on "Mourning and Melancholia" (2019).[7]

Philosophers from Plato through the Stoics to Heidegger wrote about death (i.e., Brennan and Stainton 2009; May 2010), yet fewer wrote about grief. Notably, Socrates laughed at the grief of his students and family about his upcoming death because of our ignorance of the nature of death, if we believe the *Apology*, or because our soul is immortal, if we believe the Platonic view of the *Phaedo* (Plato 1997). The Stoics and Epicureans urged us to cure ourselves from our longing for immortality, which feeds our grief. Søren Kierkegaard considered grief a door to faith (Watkin 1983; Sweetman 2022); Martin Heidegger ([1927] 1962) viewed it as a way to give meaning to life (Earle-Lambert 2011); Emmanuel Levinas, as we have seen, considered it as ethically foundational; and Albert Camus ([1933] 1976) saw in grief the absurdity of it all. Contemporary philosophic contributions to the understanding of grief are not numerous. The religious philosopher C. S. Lewis (1961) gives us his account, while Michael Cholbi's (2022) *Grief: A Philosophical Guide* is a more recent and less personal attempt to treat this topic.

In the multidisciplinary anthology that Mikołaj Sławkowski-Rode (2022) edited on grief and mourning, he argues that despite their prevalence, there is no unified understanding of their nature and meaning. Katherine Ashenburg's (2002) *The Mourner's Dance: What We Do When People Die* is a lively account of grief and what we do to survive it. Yet it is Ruth Konigsberg (2011) who paved the way for a more creative approach to grieving by debunking the myth of the five stages of grief by culturally contextualizing grief and encouraging us to find our own style of grieving.

This is where memory intervenes. Following Giambattista Vico and others, including Henri Bergson, Dustin Peone (2020) has recently defended the view that there are various aspects of memory. He differentiates between three of them, which align with the understanding that the ancient Greeks had of memory: *memoria* (memory), which remembers the past; *fantasia* (imagination), which alters or imitates things remembered; and *ingegno* (invention), which puts things remembered into proper arrangement and relationships. *Ingegno* fabricates or discovers the necessary or inner order of things; thus, it requires a view of the whole and its parts, a view of the object's history as though upon a stage or a theater of memory. *Ingegno* is rooted in *fantasia* and the images of *memoria*; rather than a method, *ingegno* is playful: It does not have rules and procedures. For Peone, *ingegno* is the crown of memory, its philosophical aspect.

Akanaefu explains that Peone follows a Vichian understanding of memory as the instrument to repulse degradation (Akanaefu 2021: 44). Thus, he rejects Friedrich Nietzsche's view: On Nietzsche's account, memory is a harmful faculty that degrades the joyous state of forgetting that soothes all pains and attains ataraxia. Peone indicates various additional philosophers who acknowledge the creative power of memory. He notes that reflective philosophy cannot get inside the object and apprehend its essence; however, memory is a nexus between mind and matter, the arena in which an objective fact is transformed into a spiritual object for the thinking subject.

In other words, "memory allows us to contemplate the essence of an object, cancels otherness, and overcomes critical reflection" (Akanaefu 2021: 44). Bergson, who inherits this tradition of reflective philosophy, finds in memory the means for getting inside the object. Likewise, Peone notes how Karl Jaspers sees memory as the only means to preserve mental substance in the process of reconstitution.

Without necessarily endorsing all of Peone's arguments in relation to memory, it is this aspect of memory that he underlines—the playful, creative, and philosophical part of it, which will be encouraged for coping with grief in the way this chapter proposes.

It is now time to incorporate these thoughts on death, grief, and memory with our previous reflections on objects to discover what a philosopher can do to creatively capture and enact what best represents the life of the deceased as we hope or wish to remember it.

The Philosophical Practice of Sculpting a Space

Contemporary societies do not have a trusted practice of dealing with the material remains of the deceased. Time constraints, energy-saving devices, and fashionable approaches to space and minimalism make the objects left disposable, without guidance of what to do with them nor an answer as to why do this rather than that with them. The process of grieving through the repeated reenactment of the deceased through his/her familiar surroundings and personal objects, which I explore in this chapter, endows with value that which he/she left and allows for multiple encounters with the life that is now gone. Better than a disembodied memory, the working of remembrance through selected objects is most effective.

Yet the question now seems to be, which objects? If the above examples contributed anything to the discussion, it seems that sooner or later, we need to initiate a selection process, which, I believe, can be meaningful and enriching, indeed enlightening, insofar as the relation to the deceased, his/her character, and our memory of him/her is clarified. Though sobering because focused, this process can culminate in sculpting a space, big or small, in one's apartment or elsewhere, as in a permanent exhibit, a furnished or object-inhabited space, which more than telling the story of the person, gives us an impression of him/her: a living tribute to a form of life, to an experience of ours that we can rekindle every time we look at this space or sit in it or touch its constitutive objects.

This enduring impression can be captured if indeed the "essence" of the person is found and represented in a tangible way, indeed, if the actual artistic creation managed to get to the truth of the matter. Being both symbolic and creative, feeding on the past yet for the future's sake, this activity liberates knowledge of self, of self with other, and of other, but much more than that, it is a philosophical investigation into time, finitude, life, and death yet tailored to one's story, needs, and capacities—that is, it is a philosophical practice activity, which creates an art form with no name, except the provisional one I gave it: "sculpting space."

The process I am describing here begins by accompanying the grieving person to the apartment, sitting there quietly and sometimes at length, and letting the conversation flow. As we begin moving from one corner to the other, listening to the client's associations, memories intertwining joy and grief, laughter and tears arise, which fill our time together and the space between us with a commemorative experience.

We notice which corners matter most, and we engage in a discussion that reveals to us why this is so; we also note that some objects seem to be central to the experience the griever had with the deceased. From this initial shared experience, we let the client spend time in the deceased's place on their own, knowing that at the end of this search, someone is meeting them, and a common work begins, which softens the solitude of the grief (and the artistic creation).

The process I am following often involves reading sensitive material, such as old letters; disclosing family secrets and intimacies between spouses; stories of one's parents before one's birth; and unknown opinions about oneself as a child and an adult. One learns to know one's parents as individuals rather than parents, as single persons rather than spouses, and oneself as a being who did not always exist. As with the workings of all new knowledge, this relativization, or very concrete putting in proportion of one's self, together with the clearer delineation of the life of one's parents, makes the confusion that occurs with death, within life, less threatening. Meaning is restored to or created in the life of the deceased in a manner that enlightens the remaining life of the grieving. By better understanding those who begot us, we shed new light on our childhood and, from there, on our lives, and given the stillness of the actors involved, the drama can come to an end.

The objects left by the deceased are a gift to us. Or so I choose to see them. Yet they raise questions about time and its trashing power of divesting everything of meaning. The questions are deeply philosophical and are usually avoided because of that. The process of going through the objects clarifies not only what stays but, more importantly, what goes away. It enacts in advance our own death and the futility of the objects with which we shared our life. That which mattered to us will matter to no one else. What lesson for life can we take from that realization?

The discussions that follow the philosophic unpacking of the situation, sometimes accompanied by relevant readings, have as purpose to find out what is the nature of the thing that we would like to preserve: Is it an ongoing experience, a particular event, an atmosphere, an act, a feeling, or a thought? Is it supposed to provoke reflection, or emotion, and, if yes, of which kind?

Finally, we address the following question: Which object or objects would better represent that which we would like to enact and in which order or form? Why these rather than others? What is the space that we would like to fill? Is it an open space in the living room or a small place in a closet or a drawer that we can open at will, or maybe we would like to make it more public, as in an exhibition, where each family receives much to showcase their own cherished deceased?

The test of the success of the process is the experience one has when entering in contact with the sculpted space. If the experience that the design affords is vacuous, too powerful, or simply not agreeable, we should amend the result. And a new process can begin every few years, if some things are kept, as memory changes and the needs that the living have from the dead evolve. Children can be encouraged to sculpt their own grandma and grandpa spaces.

The purpose of the designed or sculpted space is to create an experience. Here lies the artistic creation. It differs from a process in which we choose one object, a book, a ring, or an ornament, which we keep. The experience is the process of grieving itself, which prunes the relationship, the deceased, and the living of that which is secondary to celebrate the essential. But the commemorative experience is joyfully repeated each time one gets into contact with this creation. Rather than a mausoleum, the design is a celebration of life but also a meditation on it. We are philosophers, after all, who do not take things lightly. Yet, by helping people disengage from death honorably through saving the life that remains and creatively giving it a new form, we enable them to make good of Benedict Spinoza's (1985) counsel, "The free person thinks least of all of death, and his wisdom is a meditation not on death but on life" (*Ethics* IV, Prop. 67).[8]

Coda: "My Brother, My Brother, Do You Refuse Me a Place?" (La Boétie, on His Deathbed, to Michel de Montaigne)

What is a place, and how is it related to what a person is? It seems that we need to address the question of what a person is to tackle the questions of death, memory, and the place the deceased may hold among the living.[9] This is an indication that the phenomenon of death, grieving, and remembrance is an opportunity to address most of our philosophic questions and thus that an account of this process outgrows this chapter's capacity.

Let me just say this then: Even if we do not have a fixed identity, as some philosophers believe,[10] a person is not solely the bearer of various identities projected onto him/her by relationships. The person is also a relation to self. As we do not see ourselves, except through objects, such as mirrors, our relation to self is also mediated by familiar objects. Some of them, which we call garments, we put on our bodies. Not only do we feel them all day, it is the first thing people see in or on us. Other objects come from status, family, memory, achievement, service . . . not only books but also loyal combs, humble pins, a bible, a cross . . .

Objects that we see on a regular basis or that we are used to contemplate reflect our gaze; there is an exchange between us; thus, the most ordinary objects that we utilize on a regular basis may become an extension of our selves, our identity. And so are they perceived by others, especially if they are all that is left of us *where ordinary life takes place.*

While writing this chapter, my sister-in-law died, relatively young. We went together for the first time to the apartment of my partner's deceased sister. I was not afraid. I knocked on the door and waited for permission to enter. I sat there every evening to befriend her, the things she shared her space with, the situation we call her life. I sat there till she disclosed her secret to me, the essence of her life as she saw it. I found a few cards saying in print, *Life is full of possibilities*, and an excerpt of Simone de Beauvoir that talked about autonomy, its price, and its wealth . . . she, too, wanted to be free! She, too, had her moment, her dance in the spring, her marriage, her husband and her husband's death, her own illness . . . yet she kept all clean and tidy and beautiful as long as she could, to the end.

What misery, her brother sobbed, to what a life is reduced, what little remains . . . He took the many paintings, all of them, and said, "I will feel better if we keep them . . . for a while, all together, even in storage." He looked at me and added, referring to my parents' death and my attitude to their belongings, "I did not get it . . . I understand you now."

I believe that we will sculpt a space for my partner's sister once we get a clearer view of who *she was*; who *she wanted* to be; who she was *for him*; and what he *wants her to be* for him, for me, for the rest of us, but also *independently* of *us*. By not hurrying to throw away carriers of memories, we will engage with the spirit of things and, vicariously, with hers. We may not call this process by this name, "sculpting place," or by any name, nor limit the time it will take, as the various partial identities will succeed each other till they crystallize in something that would abide.

Solon said, call no man happy till he is dead, a view repeated in Aristotle's (2016) *Nicomachean Ethics* (Book I, Chapter 10). Not only does a human life get interpreted only when it is completed, but it is only when a relationship is over, when the facts cannot be changed anymore—and what's more indicative of that than death—that it can begin to be evaluated. "The age of controversy is past," said George Santayana, "that of interpretation has succeeded."[11]

But we are sensual beings: Objects can be touched and seen in a way that death cannot, because to touch and see death is to encounter it in a way that is repulsive to us. We want to remember and, if possible, to celebrate life rather than death, hence the objects; yet a pile of objects won't do . . . thus, the idea of carving a meaningful space in our life that I call "sculpting space."

Notes

1 Georges Bataille has written on the vulnerability of the naked body (see Amir 2021, Chapter 1, and further references there), but mainly in the context of eroticism, which he associates with death.

2 For the best book on consumerism and ecology, see *The Best Books on Consumption and the Environment—Five Books Expert Recommendations*. That clutter is our enemy has been explained in many publications, such as Kerri Richardson's *What Your Clutter Is Trying to Tell You* (2017) and *From Clutter to Clarity:* Clean *Up Your Mindset to Clear Out Your Clutter* (2020); that the Japanese know how to solve this is hinted by Marie Kondo's *The Life-Changing Magic of Tidying Up: The Japanese Art of Decluttering and Organizing* (2014) and *Spark Joy: An Illustrated Master Class on the Art of Organizing and Tidying Up* (2017). That the Zen-like aesthetic is imbued with a certain vision of things is made clear in *Zen Buddhism: Selected Writings of D. T. Suzuki* (1996), and information on Zen and Danish designs is found with no difficulty. Finally, that philosophy is found in the arts, and the arts in philosophy, has been argued, among others, by Robert Pippin. See the collection of articles in Pippin (2021).

3 Originally introduced in Latin literature in Appius Claudius Caecus's *Sententiæ* to refer to the human ability to control his destiny and what surrounds him, "*Homo faber suae quisque fortunae*" ("Every man is the artifex of his destiny"), this view has been brought into attack in the twentieth century. It was ironically refuted in Max Frisch's novel, *Homo Faber: A Report* ([1957] 1959), and was given various philosophic meanings related to toolmaking and technology by Max Scheler, Hannah Arendt, and Henri Bergson. The latter defined intelligence in *Creative Evolution* ([1907] 1911) as the faculty to create artificial objects—in particular, tools to make tools and to indefinitely variate its makings.

4 On objects and their role in our life, very little is found in philosophy. Epicurus is a good place to begin, with his theory of artificial desires arising out of fear of death (2016); this idea is reprised by Ernest Becker, without reference to Epicurus, in *The Denial of Death* (1997).

5 https://www.radiofrance.fr/franceinter/podcasts/grand-bien-vous-fasse/grand-bien-vous-fasse-du-jeudi-02novembre-2023-9797112 (accessed November 8, 2025).

6 "Krystine I. Batcho, "Why We Keep Things That Matter—and Some That Don't. The Things We Keep Matter," https://www.psychologytoday.com/us/contributors/krystine-i-batcho-phd (accessed November 8, 2025).

7 For the most important critical bibliography on Freud's "Mourning and Melancholia," see May (2019, note 14).

8 I am grateful to Psychologist Dana Assaf who mentioned the work of psychoanalyst and daughter of Holocaust survivors, Lydia Flem, *The Final Reminder: How I Emptied My Parents' House* (2007). Similar work in relation to her father has been done by Veronique Dassié in *Les objets de mon père* (2023).

9 In some cultures, such as in traditional China, the lives of the living are lived under the gaze and in honor of the deceased, who live among us as ghosts.
10 For self-identity, see the seminal work by Derek Parfit (1971, 1984). See also Glover (1988). Jonathan Glover emphasizes self-creation, its viability, and how it is linked to recognition by other people.
11 At the end of the Introduction to *Life of Reason: The Phases of Human Progress* (Santayana [1905] 2011).

References

Abraham, K. ([1911] 1927a), "Notes on the Psychoanalytical Investigation and Treatment of Manic-Depressive Insanity and Allied Conditions," in *Selected Papers of Karl Abraham, M.D.*, trans. D. Bryan and A. Strachey, 137–56, Hogarth.

Abraham, K. ([1924] 1927b), "Melancholia and Obsessional Neurosis," in *Selected Papers of Karl Abraham, M.D.*, trans. D. Bryan and A. Strachey, 422–32, Hogarth.

Akanaefu, M. (2021), "Review of Dustin Peone, *Memory as Philosophy: The Theory and Practice of Philosophical Recollection*," *Sofia Philosophical Review* XIV (1): 42–51.

Amir, L. (2021), *The Legacy of Nietzsche's Philosophy of Laughter: Bataille, Deleuze, and Rosset*, Routledge.

Aristotle (2016), *Nicomachean Ethics*, trans. W. D. Ross with an intro. R. W. Browne, Digireads.com.

Ashenburg, K. (2002), *The Mourner's Dance: What We Do When People Die*, Vintage Canada.

Bartholeyns, G. and M. Charpy (2021), *L'étrange et folle aventure du grille-pain, de la machine à coudre et des gens qui s'en servent*, Premier Parallèle.

Becker, E. (1997), *The Denial of Death*, Free Press.

Bergson, H. ([1907] 1911), *Creative Evolution*, trans. A. Mitchell, Henry Holt.

Brennan, S. and R. J. Stainton (eds) (2009), *Philosophy and Death: Introductory Readings*, Broadview Press.

Camus, A. ([1933] 1976), "Losing a Loved One," in *Cahiers II: Youthful Writings*, trans. E. C. Kennedy, Alfred A. Knopf.

Cholbi, M. (2022), *Grief: A Philosophical Guide*, Princeton University Press.

Dassié, V. (2010), *Objets d'affection: Une ethnologie de l'intime*, Éditions du Comité des travaux historiques et scientifiques.

Dassié, V. with V. Gondran (Photographies) (2023), *Les objets de mon père*, Éditions d'Une rive à l'autre.

Durand, E. (2024), *L'envers des fripes—Les vêtements dans les plis de la mondialisation*, Broché.

Earle-Lambert, A. (2011), "Those Left Behind: Heidegger on Grief and Mourning," A Thesis Submitted to the School of Graduate Studies in Partial Fulfillment of the Requirements for the Degree Master of Arts, McMaster University, Canada.

Epicurus (2016), *Principal Doctrines*, Enhanced Media.

Flem, L. (2007), *The Final Reminder: How I Emptied My Parents' House*, trans. E. Powell, Souvenir Press.

Freud, S. (1914–16), "Mourning and Melancholia," in *The Standard Edition of the Complete Psychological Works of Sigmund Freud*, vol. XIV, translated from the German by J. Strachey, The Hogarth Press and the Institute of Psycho-Analysis.

Frisch, M. ([1957] 1959), *Homo Faber: A Report*, trans. M. Bullock, Harvest Books.

Glover, J. (1988), *The Philosophy and Psychology of Personal Identity*, Penguin Books.

Heidegger, M. ([1927] 1962), *Being and Time*, trans. J. Macquarrie and E. Robinson, Harper & Row.

Klein, M. (1940), "Mourning and Its Relation to Manic-Depressive States," *International Journal of Psycho-Analysis* 21: 125–53.

Kondo, M. (2014), *The Life-Changing Magic of Tidying Up: The Japanese Art of Decluttering and Organizing*, Ten Speed Press.

Kondo, M. (2017), *Spark Joy: An Illustrated Master Class on the Art of Organizing and Tidying Up*, Ten Speed Press.

Konigsburg, R. (2011), *The Truth About Grief: The Myth of Its Five Stages and the New Science of Loss*, Simon & Schuster.

Levinas, E. (1991), *Entre nous: Essais sur le penser-à-l'autre*, Grasset.

Lewis, C. S. (1961), *A Grief Observed*, Faber & Faber.

May, T. (2010), *Death*, Acumen.

May, U. (2019), "In Conversation: Freud, Abraham and Ferenczi on 'Mourning and Melancholia' (1915–1918)," *International Journal of Psychoanalysis* 100 (1): 77–98.

Nassif, P. (2014), "Que m'enseigne la mort de l'autre? Interview of François-David Sebbah," *Philosophie Magazine*, October 23.

Niemyjska, A. (2019), "When Do Keepsakes Keep Us Together? The Effect of Separation from a Partner on Directing Attachment to Inanimate Objects," *Personal Relationships* 26:262–85.

Parfit, D. (1971), "Personal Identity," *Philosophical Review* 80: 3–27.

Parfit, D. (1984), *Reasons and Persons*, Clarendon Press.

Peone, D. (2020), *Memory as Philosophy: The Theory and Practice of Philosophical Recollection*, Studies in Historical Philosophy, vol. 1, ibidem Press.

Pippin, R. B. (2021), *Philosophy by Other Means: The Arts in Philosophy and Philosophy in the Arts*, University of Chicago Press.

Plato (1997), *Complete Works*, ed. J. M. Cooper, Hackett.

Pojman, L. P. (1992), *Life and Death: Grappling with the Moral Dilemmas of Our Time*, John and Bardett.

Postlethwaite, A., S. Kellett, and D. Mataix-Cols (2019), "Prevalence of Hoarding Disorder: A Systematic Review and Meta-Analysis," *Journal of Affective Disorders* 256:309–16.

Richardson, K. L. (2017), *What Your Clutter Is Trying to Tell You*, Hay House.

Richardson, K. L. (2020), *From Clutter to Clarity: Clean Up Your Mindset to Clear Out Your Clutter*, Hay House.

Sacriste, V. (2023), *Nos vies, nos objets: Enquêtes sur la vie quotidienne*, Septentrion.

Santayana, G. ([1905] 2011), *The Life of Reason: Introduction and Reason in Common Sense*, critical edn, vol. VII, book 1, MIT Press.

Sławkowski-Rode, M. (ed.) (2022), *Meanings of Mourning: Perspectives on Death, Loss and Grief*, Lexington Books/Rowman & Littlefield.

Spence, C. (2020), "The Multisensory Experience of Handling and Reading Books," *Multisensory Research* 33: 902–28.

Spinoza, B. (1985), "Ethics," in *The Collected Works of Spinoza*, ed. and trans. E. Curley, vol. I, Princeton University Press.

Suzuki, D. T. (1996), *Zen Buddhism: Selected Writings of D.T. Suzuki*, ed. W. Barrett, Doubleday, The Leaves Press.

Sweetman, N. (2022), "The Concept of Grief: A Phenomenological Account with Continual Reference to Kierkegaard," Honors Undergraduate thesis, University of Central Florida. Available at: https://stars.library.ucf.edu/honorstheses/1274 (accessed November 8, 2023).

Tisseron, S. (1999), *Comment l'esprit vient aux objets*, Aubier.

Watkin, J. (1983), "Kierkegaard's View of Death," *Epopteia* 79: 399–408 (in Greek).

11

Art as Philosophical Practice

Ten Responses to Folly, Tyranny, and War

Lou Marinoff

Introduction

Is philosophical practice something only philosophers do? Demonstrably not.[1] We encourage our clients to philosophize, aspiring to awaken their "inner philosopher" (Ikeda and Marinoff 2012). So even though they may not be "card-carrying" philosophers in the pedigreed academic sense, they are fully capable of articulating philosophies of life and living according to their precepts. As Pierre Hadot's (1995) *Philosophy as a Way of Life* illustrates, love of wisdom is a broad path that can accommodate any walk of life, qua profession or occupation, by which one earns one's keep along the way itself. Leaders practice philosophy via policy; legislators, via law; activists, via action; artists, via art itself. Every significant work of art—be it a painting, sculpture, symphony, literary *magnum opus*, or architectural marvel—can be unpacked by an art historian to reveal foundational philosophical principles that inspired and motivated the artist—principles either at play in or at odds with—the given ethos that saw the work arise.

This chapter looks at ten examples of art as philosophical practice. In each case, the artist creates an *objet d'art* in his or her favored medium (e.g., painting, music, literature) that is also a transcendent vehicle for conveying that artist's philosophical commentary on the times, be it diagnostic or prognostic. Influential artists can be viewed as Nietzschean physicians to culture, not mere observers of it; they are practitioners, not pontificators.

The selected examples span Western civilization between 1628 and 1957. Their situational common denominator is wartime, whose circumstances invariably showcase the most destructive horrors that our species is capable of perpetrating while at the same time provoking our most intense emotional responses, vivifying our most cherished tenets, and animating our most authentic values. The selected exemplars are Thomas Hobbes; Francisco de Goya; Ludwig van Beethoven; Fernando Sor; Victor Hugo; Alfred, Lord Tennyson; Marcel Duchamp; George Orwell; Arthur Koestler; and Ayn Rand.

Thomas Hobbes (1588–1679)

Thomas Hobbes's (1651) *Leviathan* is a cornerstone of modern political philosophy and social contractarianism. While the circumstances of the English Civil War (1642–51) compelled him to write the *Leviathan* in exile in Paris, while tutoring a young Prince Charles II who would later ban his books, Hobbes had produced a much earlier work of historical literary art in a futile attempt to warn his countrymen of the calamities of civil war with the hope of thus averting it. An accomplished classicist, he brought out the first English translation of Thucydides' *History of the Peloponnesian War* in 1628 when he saw war clouds gathering on the English horizon. The thirty-year conflict between Athens and Sparta, viewed as a civil war within ancient Greece, destroyed Athenian power and devastated the Greek economy. Not wishing to see England meet a similar fate, Hobbes's translation of Thucydides was offered up "with the express intention of frightening his countrymen by an exhibition of the follies of democracy" (Lange 1925: 272). Although that mission failed, Hobbes did not undertake it as an exercise in classics but rather as a work of classic art in the service of conveying philosophical counsel to his compatriots: in other words, art as philosophical practice in a time of approaching civil war.

Hobbes viewed civil war as calamitous because its mutually hostile divisions inflame a polity even in the absence of overt violence, thus rupturing the social contract and compromising the commonwealth. By contrast, international conflicts can and do result in former foes becoming postwar allies and partners in trade and cultural exchange. Contemporary "follies of democracy" have been on full and shameless display in the "gender wars," "culture wars," and "woke wars" that have debilitated, destabilized, and polarized Western democracies for decades on end (Marinoff 2019). Note that while Hobbes insisted on law, order, and legitimate authority, he did not rule out representative democracy in favor of monarchy *per se*. His *Leviathan* described the institution of a commonwealth as occurring "when men agree amongst themselves, to submit to some Man, or Assembly of men, voluntarily, on confidence to be protected by him against all others" (Hobbes 1651, Chapters 17–18). This is perfectly consistent with the now widespread coexistence of elected heads of state in tandem with elected or appointed governance bodies.

It is also noteworthy that Hobbes risked his life in gifting the *Leviathan* to his student and patron, Prince Charles II. While it can be read as a defense of his then-embattled father, King Charles I, closet Catholics in the displaced English court—perhaps emboldened by their refuge in France—denounced it to the prince as an apology to Cromwell. This ostracized Hobbes from the court's protection in retaliation for his heretical repudiation of Saint Augustine's cardinal doctrine of original sin: "The desires, and other passions of man, are in themselves no sin," argued Hobbes (1651, Chapter 13). If that were not enough, Hobbes waxed polemical in Part IV of *Leviathan*, titled "The Kingdom of Darkness"—a polemic against the Roman Church. *Leviathan* was immediately placed on Rome's *Index* of banned books, while French clerics prepared to arraign him for heresy. In those days, he could have been tortured to death or burned at the stake. So he escaped back to England, where Parliament had already hanged Royalists for professing "Hobbesism."

Hobbes's theory of human nature entails political implications for worse and for better. Aware that publishing his work would put his life at risk in both England and France, he chose to offer counsel in light of his convictions and to disregard personal consequences. He descended into Plato's Cave, offering its prisoners invaluable works, only to receive death threats in return. Hobbes produced magnificent literary art as philosophical practice.

Francisco de Goya (1746–1828)

Goya is often regarded as both the last Old Master and the first Modernist: a colossus astride two eras. After a difficult coming of age, exacerbated by a wild spirit and melancholy temperament, he became a court painter to the Spanish Bourbons in 1784 and was appointed first court painter to King Charles IV in 1799.

Goya was a fearless witness to his epoch's follies and tragedies, whether mirroring the notorious characters of his royal and noble patrons in vivid portraiture, sketching the wretched conditions of inmates in lunatic asylums, or exorcising his own inner demons (Hughes 2003, *passim*). He beheld and painted the spontaneous uprising of Madrid's populace on May 2, 1808 ("El Dos de Mayo") against Napoleon's occupation of Spain and dethronement of the Bourbons; he likewise painted the heinous French reprisals of May 3: a slaughter of men, women, children, and priests alike.

These events sparked the tinderbox of Spain, whose popular resistance spread far and wide, in tandem with military campaigns by Spanish, Portuguese, and English forces against Napoleon's occupying army. Goya had no choice but to witness the mounting horrors of the Peninsular War (1808–13), which not only laid waste to Spain's populace, industry, and agriculture but also engendered ubiquitous episodes of looting, pillaging, rape, and slaughter by criminal elements from each and every army in the field as well as roving bands of Spanish deserters and brigands, who preyed on everyone—including their own compatriots—with equal opportunism (Gates [1986] 2001; Esdaile 2015).

Prior to the Peninsular War, Goya had already portrayed the follies of religious and political corruption in his series *Los Caprichos* (1797–9) and had moreover provoked the ire of the Inquisition by daring to paint nudes—groundbreaking profanity at that time—including his lascivious patron María Cayetana de Silva, the thirteenth Duchess of Alba. So even at this stage, Goya's art displayed his Socratic penchant to play the role of gadfly, stinging the horse of state and its citizens into awareness of truth and reality, however discomfiting or scandalous.

But in the wake of the escalating atrocities of the Peninsular War, Goya witnessed and captured horrific scenes of which nobody cared to be reminded, in a series of eighty-one etchings, titled *The Disasters of War*. While patriots are prone vociferously to condemn their enemies' crimes against humanity while muting if not lauding their own misdeeds—for war washes everyone's hands in blood—Goya's ghastly depictions played no favorites. They are soulful cries of humanitarian anguish, a "prodigious flowering of rage" (Connell 2004: 175) against the merciless tides of slaughter, rapine, and famine that inundated Iberia during 1808–13. That the series remained unpublished until 1863 (thirty-five years after Goya's death) attests to the stark contrast between the courage of Goya's outraged conscience and the perennial reluctance of rulers to entertain testimonials of truth to power.

Goya's poignant protestations against the acute excesses of the Peninsular War were but a prelude to his disillusioned desperation over its chronic repercussions. After Napoleon's formerly *Grande Armée* was bled white and driven from Spain in 1813, the victorious allies, led by Wellington and reactionary Spanish generals, reinstalled the Bourbon despot Ferdinand VII on the throne. King Ferdinand VII proceeded to repudiate Spain's liberal constitution of 1812, reinstate the Inquisition, and persecute, imprison, execute, or exile Spaniards who espoused Enlightenment values. This led to the distorted "branding" of Spaniards who favored social and political reforms, even if they supported the monarchy and the church, as *afrancesados*: Francophiles in the most pejorative senses—that is, Jacobins and traitors. There was no political middle ground on which to stand. Anyone who objected to the absolutist tyranny and medieval mentality of Ferdinand VII became guilty of treason. As a result, tens of thousands of liberal-minded Spaniards—including politicians, generals, bankers, intellectuals, artists, and ordinary citizens—were exiled (Marinoff 2021a). In contemporary terms, as described by Santiago del Rey (2021: xxiv), "It can now be said that they were rather patriots of another Spain: of a very different Spain, whose eventual birth would require much more time and suffer yet more labor pains."

This rift never fully healed. Its festering hostilities would boil over time and again in three subsequent Carlist Wars of succession and, in the twentieth century, in the catastrophe of what some historians would call the Fourth Carlist War, namely the Spanish Civil War (1936–9).

Meanwhile, the tyrannical reign of Ferdinand VII propelled Goya out of Madrid's inner circles and into an isolated farmhouse on its outskirts. Tormented by deafness, melancholy, and encroaching old age and driven to desperation over Spain's plight, Goya produced his fourteen so-called Black Paintings—murals in oil rendered on the crumbling plaster walls of the farmhouse (1819–22). The most shocking of these, "Saturn Devouring His Son," now hangs in the Prado Museum. It symbolizes the horror of the state devouring its own citizens, who are its political wards. Thus, portraying Ferdinand VII as monstrously cannibalizing his own subjects, the painting epitomizes Goya's artistic mission to depict truths, no matter how horrific. He painted immortal works from staunchly held principles: art as philosophical practice.

Ludwig van Beethoven (1770–1827)

Beethoven was not only a composer of immortal stature, and a bridge between the Classical and Romantic eras, but also an enthusiastic supporter of the humanistic ideals of the Enlightenment. Like many politically "progressive" intellectuals of the era, he applauded the principles that spawned the French Revolution but was appalled by the subsequent Jacobin terror and the criminals it empowered. So initially Beethoven admired Napoleon's restoration of order from chaos, approved his role as first consul of France, perceived him in a light with exemplary consuls of ancient Rome, and lauded his implementation of political and social reforms. Evidence of Beethoven's high regard for Napoleon is afforded by the composer's original dedication of his third symphony, penned in Italian on the cover of the score in early 1804: "Sinfonia intitolata Bonaparte"—"Symphony entitled Bonaparte."

The received account goes on to narrate that when Napoleon crowned himself emperor of France later that same year, Beethoven flew into a rage, declaring, "So he is no more than a common mortal! Now he, too, will tread underfoot all the rights of man [and] indulge only his ambition; now he will think himself superior to all men [and] become a tyrant!" (Lee 2018). Beethoven then scribbled over the dedication so furiously that he tore through the page, eradicating Bonaparte's name and retitling the work *Sinfonia Eroica—Heroic Symphony*. Although some historians challenge the authenticity of this account (Lee 2018), it resonates with Beethoven's humanistic aspirations and the enlightened philosophical spirit of the age.

Fernando Sor (1778–1839)

Sor sprang as a full-blown prodigy from Barcelona's middle class. After graduating from Montserrat's legendary choir school, he wrote an opera that became a local sensation, as did his sonorous tenor voice and unparalleled virtuosity on guitar. This led to sponsorship by the Duchess of Alba in 1800.

He and Goya met as fellow artists-in-residence at her Liria Palace in Madrid. Sor's compositions and performances became all the rage. When Napoleon invaded, Sor both fought for Spain and also wrote popular songs to help inspire resistance. But as years of carnage, horror, and privation ensued, tens of thousands of patriotic Spaniards, including Fernando Sor, began to believe that peaceful rule under a Napoleonic constitution would serve Spain and its people far better than this never-ending slaughter of Spaniards and devastation of their homeland, which had—through fate or poor governance—permitted itself to become a catastrophic battleground in a merciless clash of the British and French empires. His heart torn by the suffering of Spain, Sor and tens of thousands of his liberal compatriots swore allegiance to Joseph Bonaparte, whom Napoleon had installed on the Spanish throne after deposing and exiling the Bourbons.

Considering the political agenda of Bonaparte's chief adversary in Iberia, namely Arthur Wellesley, soon to be Duke of Wellington, one can readily sympathize with the Spanish liberal perspective. For while Wellington's military mission was to drive Napoleon out of Spain, his political goal was to eradicate democracy and reinstate medieval tyranny as a hedge against the spread of democratic revolutions beyond France and America. Even so, many liberal-minded Britons were torn between support for America's newly won independence and patriotism for their empire. But in Britain, they enjoyed a right to hold differing political opinions, whereas in Spain, they did not. Any Spaniard who supported a constitutional monarchy, in tandem with social and political reforms, was ruthlessly persecuted by Ferdinand VII. Sor loved his homeland but also loved liberty more than tyranny. So he joined the mass exile of so-called *afrancesados*, leaving his beloved Spain with a tearful song that concluded:

> O immense God, who reading the human heart,
> Sees what my feelings are,
> Unite the votes of Spain; cease the fierce dissension;
> Let us live as brothers, for this is how a nation prospers.
>
> —Sor (1814, trans. Jeffery 1994)

Yet Sor's exercises of musical art as philosophical practice were still in their inception. He had a lifelong knack for finding himself at the epicenter of political conflicts, starting with El Dos de Mayo in Madrid (where, recall, his patriotic music helped inspire popular resistance). Having sought refuge in Paris, Fernando experienced the "Hundred Days" of Napoleon's escape from Elba, and the ensuing chaos and cannon fire in the French capital. Relocating to London with his infant daughter, popular demand for his performances soared during the nail-biting run-up to the Battle of Waterloo (Marinoff 2021c, 69–70). Later, as court composer to Tsars Alexander I and Nicholas I in Russia, Sor was in residence at the Winter Palace when the Decembrists launched their ill-starred revolt in 1825 (Marinoff 2021b, 149–57).

Residing in Paris during his final creative period, Sor was about to give an evening recital to a packed hall when he was suddenly interrupted by the crack of muskets, the roar of cannons, and the rampage of mobs that signaled the outbreak of "Les Trois Glorieuses": the "Glorious Revolution" (July 27–29, 1830) that deposed King Charles X, the last Bourbon monarch of France. And what was Sor's response to that outbreak? He closed the windows, drew the drapes, and performed his program while the insurgency raged around the city.

If we seek a philosophical interpretation of Sor's performance not only on that momentous evening but also of his record of stellar performances in the eyes of historically cyclonic conflicts, it might be that art transcends bloodshed. Music uplifts the spirit and nourishes the heart, while savage conflict debases and dehumanizes them. And whereas musical compositions are immortal, strife cannot endure. On this view, Fernando Sor lived, breathed, and embodied his musical art with philosophical practice.

Victor Hugo (1802–85)

Hugo was the most influential French poet, playwright, and novelist of his time, even though he was overshadowed during his early career by the immense popularity of George Sand (Amantine Lucile Aurore Dupin), whom he greatly admired. Writing was his destiny. As a youth, he had vowed to become the next Chateaubriand or nothing. A contemporary of Sor's in Paris, Hugo was young enough to have been born into Romanticism and was driven into the arms of liberalism by the very same despotic excesses of Charles X that precipitated the July Revolution. But whereas Sor's art as philosophical practice was one of transcendence, Hugo's was one of imminence.

When the night of July 27, 1830, saw the outbreak of Les Trois Glorieuses, Hugo was still in the first flushes of success in his lengthy and distinguished career to come. Yet he had already revealed himself as a "man of the people," an author whose profound humanity, sincere social sensibility, and revulsion at the death penalty had impelled him to publish *Le Dernier Jour d'un Condamné* (*The Last Day of a Condemned Man*) in 1829. This strident call for the abolition of capital punishment in France would not be heeded until 1981, a century and a half later. Hugo's romantic play *Hernani* had just premiered at the *Comédie-Française*, in February 1830, while his classic romantic novel *Notre-Dame de Paris* (*The Hunchback of Notre-Dame,* 1831) was in the press.

So what did Victor Hugo do on the tumultuous summer evening of July 27, 1830, that imbued his art with philosophical practice? He took to the streets for three straight days and nights, wandering all over his beloved Paris—now festooned with barricades and littered with riots—bearing witness to this latest uprising in the name of liberty, equality, and fraternity. Scenes and characters that imprinted themselves indelibly on his mind would later be reconstituted in his *magnum opus*, *Les Misérables* (1862). Hugo's ever-burning ardor for social and political progress exerted seminal influence on other towering nineteenth-century novelists who likewise epitomized literary art as philosophical practice, including Dickens and Dostoevsky.

Toward the end of his life, in 1876, Hugo delivered a heartfelt eulogy for George Sand, embracing these egalitarian sentiments: "In this country whose law is to complete the French Revolution and begin that of the equality of the sexes, being a part of the equality of men, a great woman was needed. It was necessary to prove that a woman could have all the manly gifts without losing any of her angelic qualities, be strong without ceasing to be tender . . . George Sand proved it" (Thomson 1972).

Hugo willed a gift of 50,000 francs "to the poor," thus exercising the virtues of compassion and charity from beyond the grave.

Alfred, Lord Tennyson (1809–92)

Tennyson was poet laureate during much of Queen Victoria's reign, from 1850 until his death. His poetic arts ranged from powerful if sentimental short verse (as in *Break, Break, Break*, 1842) to classical mythological themes (e.g., *Ulysses*, 1842). His pithy stanzas still generate so much traction among literati that he is the ninth most often quoted writer in *The Oxford Dictionary of Quotations*. Examples still circulating include "Nature, red in tooth and claw," "Tis better to have loved and lost / Than never to have loved at all" (both from *In Memoriam A.H.H.*, 1849), "To strive, to seek, to find, and not to yield" (from *Ulysses*, 1842), and "Theirs not to reason why, / Theirs but to do and die (from *The Charge of the Light Brigade*, 1854).

As seen, philosophical practice can entail the exercise of one's virtue in a straightforwardly Aristotelian sense in addition to the "birthing" of another's virtue in the metaphor of a Socratic midwife. Tennyson's best-known poem reflects both. *The Charge of the Light Brigade* extols and inspires the virtue of courage as displayed in what amounted to a military cock-up over confusing orders issued in the Battle of Balaclava (1854), during the Crimean War.

Had it not been immortalized by a poet of Tennyson's stature, the massacre of a brigade of light cavalry charging headlong into a battery of cannon might otherwise have been covered up to spare the high command embarrassment or simply footnoted among the sanguinary annals of ever-mounting death tolls in nineteenth-century warfare. Napoleon had ushered in an age that engendered casualties on hitherto unthinkable scales, which ensued from employing tactics essentially unchanged since Alexander the Great on battlefields now blanketed by batteries of withering cannon fire.

So when Tennyson (1854) penned the celebrated stanza "Into the valley of Death / Rode the six hundred," he not only extolled the virtue of courage in the face of near-certain annihilation but also jangled patriotic nerve endings among citizens on whose empire the sun never set. *Love of one's country* (i.e., patriotism) is a far more delimited term than *love of wisdom* (i.e., philosophy) and therefore not lumped with classical virtues (wisdom, courage, temperance, justice). It seems more a value than a virtue. Patriotism nonetheless stimulates a deeply emotional and at times teleologically advantageous commitment to what formerly enhanced evolutionary survival value via passionate identification with one's tribe (symbolized by a local totem) but which had evolved by stages into passionate identification with one's empire (symbolized by a national flag gone global). And courage was traditionally wedded to patriotism—an arranged marriage—because both are of paramount importance in wartime and warfare.

Yet this time-tested matrimonial knot would unravel in twentieth-century wars, which bore witness to gratuitous slaughter on scales not merely unthinkable but altogether unimaginable. This unraveling was accompanied, if not heavily influenced, by "tectonic shifts" in art as philosophical practice, as we shall see in the following examples.

Marcel Duchamp (1887–1968)

Henri-Robert-Marcel Duchamp was a French painter, sculptor, writer, and chess player. He is strongly identified with post-Impressionism, Cubism, and Dada, movements that rejected "retinal art" in favor of noetic art, aligned with Duchamp's presupposition that art's influence should not be confined to the eye but rather should extend to the mind.[2] Dada itself, of which Duchamp was a foremost exponent, went on to exert a seminal influence on twentieth-century Bohemianism, the Beat Generation, and Hippie Counterculture. These were all unconventional movements that rejected or protested unquestioning mass acceptance of conformist values and norms—including "received" versions of patriotism—whose worldviews not only accommodated but also attempted to normalize the increasingly gargantuan slaughters and atrocities of World War I, World War II, and the Cold War's train of nuclear arms races and conventional proxy wars.

It should be recalled that Dada's epicenter is Zurich's Cabaret Voltaire (founded by Hugo Ball in 1916), so named in homage to Voltaire's *Candide*, a satirical critique of Leibnizian optimism via the ludicrous character of Dr. Pangloss (Voltaire 1759). Art as philosophical practice lies at the very heart of Dada, as formulated by Hugo Ball himself: "For us, art is not an end in itself … but it is an opportunity for the true perception and criticism of the times we live in."[3]

Ball, Duchamp, and their fellow Dadaists viewed World War I as the resultant of a constellation of ossified and obsolete political, economic, and social forces whose leaders and masses alike—stupefied by blind conformity—had somnambulated over the precipice of insanity and plummeted into the abyss of hell. From 1914 to 1918, generals far behind the front lines, stubbornly mired in nineteenth-century strategies and tactics, unmoved by grisly massacres, undaunted by poison gas, unperturbed by pestilential conditions in the trenches, and untouchable by accountability alike, continued to sacrifice millions of young men in well-advertised and futile frontal assaults that captured a few yards of barbed wire, cratered mud, and decomposing corpses, only to relinquish them in the next sacrificial counterattack. Dixon (1976) produced a sobering psychology of their military incompetence.

We can valorize courage in David versus Goliath or *The Three Musketeers* or three hundred Spartans at Thermopylae or six hundred horsemen at Balaclava. But when death tolls are scaled to the extravagance of World War I, moral compasses cry out for recalibration.

Duchamp's bold defacement of Da Vinci's *Mona Lisa* is emblematic of Dada's "wake-up call" to sleepwalking minds. Although easily misinterpreted owing to the prima facie "shock value" imparted by its crude vandalism and prurient mockery of female beauty, chastity, and mystique, its deeper message, *à la* Ball, appears to be a "true perception and criticism of the times we live in."

Consider that since 1804, the *Mona Lisa* has hung in the Louvre, seized from royal possession during the French Revolution and displayed for public viewing. Millions of tourists have since stood in line, waiting to pack the exhibition room in sardine-like fashion, jostling elbow to elbow and cheek by jowl merely to catch a glimpse of her as the herd surges slowly across the hall. Why? Not because they appreciate or exercise the virtues she purportedly represents but because of mass conformism to herd mentality and its prescribed behaviors. Visiting Paris but failing to view the Mona Lisa marks one as somehow "deficient"—at least according to the norms of bourgeois tourism.

But during World War I (1914–18), the same millions of men who had thronged to the Louvre to gawk at her now massed in the trenches, awaiting their turns to be brutally slaughtered over her possession as a spoil of war, while the same millions of women who had likewise viewed her in the Louvre now toiled relentlessly in factories, churning out arms and munitions for the selfsame war effort, which once again entailed possessing her as a prize.

On this interpretation, Duchamp's *Mona Lisa*—created in 1919—is neither a mockery of fine art nor a repudiation of female virtues but rather an indictment of conformity and insanity *en masse* and, as such, an iconic example of art as philosophical practice (Marinoff 2017: 4–33).

George Orwell (1903–50)

Orwell (born Eric Arthur Blair in British India) became so influential that his name is adjectivalized, a distinction shared by few modern authors. Orwellian "denotes an attitude and a brutal policy of draconian control by propaganda, surveillance, disinformation, denial of truth (doublethink), and manipulation of the past" (Gregório 2018).

In the aftermath of World War I, like many naive and disenchanted intellectuals of the period, Orwell held out romantic hopes that democratic socialism would save the day for humankind. When the Spanish Civil War broke out in 1936, he joined the International Brigade, serving with POUM (*Partido Obrero de Unificación Marxista*), which had links with Britain's Independent Labor Party. He served with courage and conviction but also with increasing disillusionment at the quarrelsome factionalism of the Left. He was shot through the neck by a sniper in May 1937 and was hospitalized. This probably saved his life, because in June 1937, the long arm of Stalin, operating through the Unified Socialist Party of Catalonia, declared the POUM a disguised fascist organization, and began to arrest its key members.

Orwell's wife, Eileen, alerted him to the danger, and they both escaped by train to France. In July 1937, the Tribunal for Espionage and High Treason in Valencia charged the Orwells with "rabid Trotskyism" as agents of the POUM. Accordingly, show trials of POUM leaders, and of the Orwells (*in absentia*), were held in Barcelona in October and November 1938. Orwell (2000: 31) wrote that they were "only a by-product of the Russian Trotskyist trials and from the start every kind of lie, including flagrant absurdities, has been circulated in the Communist press."

This led to Orwell's (1938) firsthand exposé of the plight of the Spanish people in *Homage to Catalonia*. As in the Peninsular War of 1808–13, Spain had become a proxy battleground between contending powers: in this case, the fascist dictatorships of Hitler and Mussolini backing the Nationalists versus the Communist dictatorship of Stalin backing the Republicans (while purging them for good measure).

Homage to Catalonia did not meet with the volume of readership that Orwell had anticipated. After reviewing Arthur Koestler's 1941 novel *Darkness at Noon* (to be discussed next), he realized that allegorical fiction had a larger impact than experiential fact in dispelling romantic Western delusions about Marxism in particular and totalitarianism in general. Thus, impressed by Koestler and informed by his own penetrating insight, Orwell crafted his two political masterpieces: *Animal Farm* (1945, a scathing satire on the Bolshevik Revolution) and *Nineteen Eighty-Four* (1949, an iconic anti-Stalinist dystopian novel).

A lifelong reviewer of books and influencer of larger literary culture, Orwell had lauded Charles Dickens in a 1940 essay as "a man who is always fighting against something, but who fights in the open and is not frightened, the face of a man who is generously angry—in other words, of a nineteenth-century liberal, a free intelligence, a type hated with equal hatred by all the smelly little orthodoxies which are now contending for our souls" (Brownell and Angus 1971: 576).

In sum, Orwell's stalwart defenses of liberty, opportunity, and hope against folly, tyranny, and war epitomize literary art as philosophical practice.

Arthur Koestler (1905–83)

Koestler (1941) was an eclectic Jewish-Hungarian author, journalist, ex-Communist, and activist, whose novelized condemnation of Stalin and Stalinism—*Darkness at Noon*—inspired George Orwell's immortal satires on the same theme.

Koestler's adventuresome life reads like a James Bond novel. Influenced by Zionism, he left Budapest in 1926, emigrating to Palestine to work on a kibbutz. But the austerity endured by *chalutzim* ("pioneers") of the day soon lost its romantic appeal. So he reinvented himself as a journalist, working as a stringer for German newspapers. After a stint in Paris, he established himself in Berlin in 1929 as a scientific editor and journalist for the *Vossische Zeitung*, a leading liberal newspaper. There he witnessed the collapse of the Weimar Republic's economy, which, devastated by the Wall Street crash of October 1929, suffered hyperinflation in tandem with ongoing crippling reparations for World War I.

These circumstances abetted Hitler's ascent to power in 1933, in the wake of escalating clashes between Nazis and Communists. Of this period, Koestler wrote, "Germany lived in a state of latent civil war, and if one wasn't prepared to be swept along as a passive victim by the approaching hurricane it became imperative to take sides" (Kirsch 2019). As a Jewish intellectual, Koestler's choice was self-evident: He joined the Communist Party in 1931.

Yet this was not strictly a process of elimination but rather more like a religious conversion. Marx's alluring ideology promised social equality and a "worker's paradise" here on earth: a secular religion that seduced many of the brightest young minds of the period, disenchanted by the bloodthirsty imperialisms of World War I, failings of capitalism, and invidious class distinctions. Brainwashed by Stalinist propaganda, Koestler threw himself into party work. Thus, as an important foreign journalist and trusted party member, he was given permission to tour the Soviet Union in 1932–3.

There he witnessed the realities of Stalin's totalitarian rule: widespread privation, famine in the Ukraine, destruction of the economy and lives via forced collectivization, and show trials that pretended to shift blame on "counter-revolutionaries"—including loyal Bolsheviks—for the catastrophes wrought by Marx's untenable theories in the murderous hands of Stalin's sadistic policies (Little 2022). The seeds of Koestler's awakening to truth, and his novel *Darkness at Noon*, were sown.

After Hitler's takeover of Germany in 1933, Koestler resettled in Paris and—notwithstanding his revelations about the realities in the USSR—persisted in the struggle against fascism. In 1937, he traveled to Spain to report on the Spanish Civil War for the *News Chronicle*, an anti-Franco British daily. He knew the risks and sure enough was captured by Nationalists and imprisoned in Málaga. He awaited execution for three months, listening daily to the firing squads outside his cell window. This somehow induced an existential calm and inspired his memoir *Dialogue with Death* (Koestler 1942). Fortunately, the British press intervened in his case, and ensuing public attention saw him spared in a prisoner exchange and returned to Paris as a stateless refugee.

In 1938, his antipathy to fascism was finally overmatched by his revulsion at Stalin's totalitarianism, so he quit the Communist Party. Even so, in early 1940, the French government arrested him as an "undesirable alien," but he was released following British government pressure. He escaped Paris and France before Hitler's May 1940 occupation by joining the French Foreign Legion, which he deserted in North Africa. Making his way to Portugal, he sailed to England but was promptly arrested there for not having an immigrant permit.

Ironically, Koestler was still in jail in Brixton when *Darkness at Noon* was published in 1941. His English girlfriend, sculptor Daphne Hardy, had translated it from German while they were together in Paris. Hardy had made her way to London with a single-minded determination to see it into print. Its publication brought him a measure of celebrity and financial security along with liberty and UK residency. It also led to his friendship with and literary influence on George Orwell. The bestselling French edition of *Darkness at Noon* may also have tipped the scales against Communism in the elections of 1946.

Koestler wrote many engaging books on a variety of topics, but *Darkness at Noon*'s powerful repudiation of Stalinism remains a shining beacon of literary art as philosophical practice.

Ayn Rand (1905–82)

Rand (born Alisa Zinovyevna Rosenbaum in Saint Petersburg, Russia) exemplifies literary fiction as philosophical practice. She experienced civil war in her youth, having witnessed the outbreak of the 1917 October Revolution at age twelve. Her parents were middle-class Russian Jews, and her father—a pharmacist—saw his business nationalized (i.e., confiscated) by the Bolsheviks. He relocated with his family to the Crimea, still under the control of White Russians. There she completed high school. Her family then returned to a renamed Petrograd, where they faced privation and near starvation. She enrolled in Petrograd State University, was expelled in a purge of bourgeoisie, and was reinstated after foreign students protested. Graduating from the renamed Leningrad State University in 1924 with a degree in history, she studied for a year at the State Technicum for Screen Arts.

Rand obtained a visa to visit relatives in Chicago in 1925 and never returned to the USSR. She married actor Frank O'Connor in 1929 and became a US citizen in 1931. Following minor ups-and-downs with films in Hollywood, plays on Broadway, and novels in New York, she became friends with conservative journalist Henry Hazlitt and Austrian School economist Ludwig von Mises. Her philosophy of Objectivism received public attention and acclaim with the publication of *The Fountainhead* in 1943. This success set the stage for the creation of her *magnum opus*, *Atlas Shrugged*, published in 1957. It has since sold more than ten million copies, vaulting her earlier works into prominence as well. Cumulatively, her books have sold more than thirty-seven million copies as of 2020, a staggering number that belies their widespread exclusion from academic reading lists. In terms of popular sales, Rand achieved a status comparable to Victor Hugo, whom she idolized.

Rand's life and works of fiction are in many respects mirror images that reflect an apparent paradox. How can such an impactful female author, who professes an original philosophical outlook, be all but ignored by academia, especially in an age when reverse-sexist norms emphatically favor women over men? One encounters excuses, but not answers, in the weeds of knee-jerk criticisms. Mainstream philosophers reject her nonfiction as lacking rigor, betraying autodidacticism, exhibiting oversimplification, and so on. While such charges are not frivolous, mainstream academia has gleefully embraced postmodern newspeak, delusional anti-realism, and progressive propaganda in place of erudition (e.g., Gross and Levitt 1998). Larger mainstream culture, having been commandeered by a congeries of increasingly rabid neo-Marxist ideologies, is committed to toppling Objectivism's very pillars: methodological individualism, self-determination, individual rights, property rights, enlightened self-interest, laissez-faire economics, and meritocracy—and to replacing them with their opposites: groupthink, identity politics, group rights, decriminalization of theft and looting, mob rule, centrally planned economics, and incompetence.

What truly rankles Western Marxist and neo-Marxist sensibilities is that Rand is an authentic, native-born refugee of Marxist–Leninist–Stalinist totalitarianism and therefore an incontrovertibly credible witness to its atrocities. What really arouses the American Left's antipathy toward Rand is that she possessed the temerity and perspicacity to expose the horrors of neo-Marxism in a distinctively and definitively American context. To her everlasting delight, Ludwig von Mises once called her "the most courageous man in America" (Burns 2009: 114).

What would happen, she asks rhetorically in *Atlas Shrugged*, if the world's mightiest industrial power, most prodigious economy, and greatest defender of liberty were commandeered by self-hating, morally bankrupt, and functionally incompetent parasites, who resent ability and achievement, brand them as "evil," and brim with Nietzschean *ressentiment* while pretending to represent the interests of "the people"? Beyond that, she asks what would happen if the competent went "on strike" against the incompetent, removing themselves from the reach of ideologues who cannot create wealth but only destroy it, who cannot sustain prosperity but only sabotage it?

At the very core of *Atlas Shrugged*, Rand's female protagonist Dagny Taggart, proud daughter of a railroad baron, is desperately striving to save her family's enterprise from a government of saboteurs and "looters" (as Rand chillingly calls them), when she encounters the greatest philosopher of the age, Hugh Akston, working as a short-order cook in a remote diner. He had resigned from his Ivy League university after the curriculum itself had been sabotaged. Akston then gives Taggart what amounts to philosophical counseling, opening her eyes to the only way to defeat the saboteurs: by allowing them to loot the economy until it collapses from the untenable untruths of their delusional ideology. He counsels her to shelter from the storm and then rebuild (Marinoff 2022, Chapter 13).

Rand's philosophy of Objectivism—and its responses to folly, tyranny, and civil war—is powerfully portrayed in her prescient literary fiction. Thus, she created and epitomized art as philosophical practice.

Conclusion

As each of these foregoing exemplars illustrates, the motivation, creation, and celebration of influential art are inseparable from the artist's conscientious engagement with and principled response to recurrent vicissitudes of the human condition. When masses are afflicted by folly, tyranny, or war, art's mission is not merely to provide entertainment, distraction, or temporary escape from dire circumstances but rather to speak truth to power, proffer diagnosis, offer counsel, suggest remedy, and inspire action. In such cases, art becomes a prominent vehicle for philosophical practice.

Notes

1 Thanks to Jeanette Bresson Ladegaard Knox for inviting this contributed chapter.
2 For example, see https://www.metmuseum.org/toah/hd/duch/hd_duch.htm (accessed September 10,2023).
3 "Dada," https://www.moma.org/collection/terms/dada/a-catalyst-for-creativity (accessed July 16, 2025).

References

Brownell, S. and I. Angus (eds) (1971), *Orwell: Essays, Journalism and Letters*, vol. 4, Mariner Books.
Burns, J. (2009), *Goddess of the Market: Ayn Rand and the American Right*, Oxford University Press.
Connell, E. S. (2004), *Goya: A Life*, Counterpoint.
del Rey, S. (2021), "Introduction," in L. Marinoff, *Fernando: Beethoven of the Guitar. Book One: Youth, Celebrity & War*, xxv–xxviii, Waterside Productions.
Dixon, N. (1976), *On the Psychology of Military Incompetence*, Jonathan Cape.
Esdaile, C. (2015), *The Peninsular War: A New History*, St. Martin's.
Gates, D. ([1986] 2001), *The Spanish Ulcer: A History of the Peninsular War*, De Capo/ Perseus Books.

Gregório, C. (2018), "Are We Living in an Orwellian Dystopia?" [Blog], September 13. Available at: https://angry.ventures/blog/are-we-living-in-an-orwellian-dystopia/?ref=academy.gopax.co.kr (accessed July 16, 2025).

Gross, P. and N. Levitt (1998), *Higher Superstition: The Academic Left and Its Quarrels with Science*, Johns Hopkins University Press.

Hadot, P. (1995), *Philosophy as a Way of Life*, trans. M. Chase, Wiley-Blackwell.

Hobbes, T. (1651), *Leviathan*, printed for Andrew Crooke, at the Green Dragon, in St. Paul's Churchyard. Available at: https://www.gutenberg.org/files/3207/3207-h/3207-h.htm#link2H_4_0205Facsimileedition (accessed September 17, 2023).

Hughes, R. (2003), *Goya*, Harvill.

Hugo, V. (1829), *Le Dernier Jour d'un Condamné*, Charles Gosselin.

Hugo, V. (1862), *Les Misérables*, Lacroix, Verboeckhoven & Ce.

Ikeda, D. and L. Marinoff (2012), *The Inner Philosopher: Conversations on Philosophy's Transformative Power*, Dialogue Path Press.

Jeffery, B. (1994), *Fernando Sor: Composer and Guitarist*, 2nd edn, Tecla Editions.

Kirsch, A. (2019), "The Desperate Plight Behind 'Darkness at Noon,'" *New Yorker*, September 23. Available at: https://www.newyorker.com/magazine/2019/09/30/the-desperate-plight-behind-darkness-at-noon (accessed September 22, 2025).

Koestler, A. (1941), *Darkness at Noon*, trans. D. Hardy, Macmillan.

Koestler, A. (1942), *Dialogue with Death*, trans. Trevor and P. Blewitt, Macmillan.

Lange, F. (1925), *The History of Materialism*, trans. E. Thomas, Kegan Paul, Trench, Trübner.

Lee, A. (2018), "Beethoven and Napoleon," *History Today* 68 (3). Available at: https://www.historytoday.com/archive/music-time/beethoven-and-napoleon (accessed September 2, 2023).

Little, D. (2022), "Koestler's Observations of Soviet Totalitarianism" [Blog], November 27. Available at: https://understandingsociety.blogspot.com/2022/11/koestlers-observations-of-soviet.html (accessed September 26, 2025).

Marinoff, L. (2017), "Dada as Philosophical Practice, and Vice-Versa," in L. Amir (ed.), *New Frontiers in Philosophical Practice*, 4–33, Cambridge Scholars Press.

Marinoff, L. (2019), *On Human Conflict: The Philosophical Foundations of War and Peace*, Rowman & Littlefield.

Marinoff, L. (2021a), *Fernando: Beethoven of the Guitar. Book One: Youth, Celebrity & War*, Waterside Productions.

Marinoff, L. (2021b), *Fernando: Beethoven of the Guitar. Book Three: Glory Finale & Legacy*, Waterside Productions.

Marinoff, L. (2021c), *Fernando: Beethoven of the Guitar. Book Two: Exile, Favor & Triumph*, Waterside Productions.

Marinoff, L. (2022), *Essays on Philosophy, Praxis and Culture*, Anthem Press. Essay #13, "Atlas Shrugged, Akston Counseled: How Ayn Rand Reinvented Philosophical Practice."

Orwell, G. (1938), *Homage to Catalonia*, Secker & Warburg.

Orwell, G. (1945), *Animal Farm*, Secker & Warburg.

Orwell, G. (1949), *Nineteen Eighty-Four*, Secker & Warburg.

Orwell, G. (2000), *Facing Unpleasant Facts*, Secker & Warburg.

Rand, A. (1943), *The Fountainhead*, Bobbs-Merrill.

Rand, A. (1957), *Atlas Shrugged*, Random House.

Sor, F. (1814), *Donde Vas, Fernando Incauto?*, Benoist.

Tennyson, A. L. (1854), *The Charge of the Light Brigade* [Poet]. Available at: https://www.poetryloverspage.com/poets/tennyson/charge_of_light_brigade.html (accessed September 27, 2023).

Thomson, P. (1972), "George Sand and English Reviewers: The First Twenty Years," *The Modern Language Review* 67 (3): 501–16. https://doi.org/10.2307/3726119.

Thucydides (1628), *The History of the Grecian War*, trans. T. Hobbes, John Bohn.

Voltaire (1759), *Candide, ou l'Optimisme*, Cramer.

Index

Contributors

Lydia Amir is a professor in the Philosophy Department at Tufts University, USA. Her long international practicing career culminates in serving as president of a national association, adjunct director of the APPA, scientific board member of IGPP, and founding editor of this series. A board member of various journals and the founding president of IAPH, she has published numerous articles and essays and, in philosophical practice, both monographs (2017; 2018; forthcoming in Lexington) and edited collections (2015, with A. Fatic; 2017). On related topics, she has edited *Handbooks* (2025; 2025) and *Companions* (both forthcoming) and founded three additional book series.

Vaughana Feary, PhD, taught philosophy and women's studies at Fairleigh Dickinson University in Madison, New Jersey. She is former president of the American Society for Philosophy Counseling and Psychotherapy (ASPCP) and is vice president and a founding board member of the American Philosophical Practitioners Association (APPA). She is program director and a founding board member of Excalibur: A Center for Applied Ethics. She does consulting work for corporations, correctional facilities, hospitals, and museums and is the author of numerous publications.

Pia Houni, PhD, is an adjunct professor who has worked at various universities, the Theatre Museum, the Finnish Institute of Occupational Health, and the Arts Promotion Centre Finland. She is a philosophical practitioner, writer, and conceptual artist. For more than twenty-five years, her research has focused on the fields of art, culture, social science, and humanism. She is a member of the American Philosophical Practitioners Association (APPA) and a founding member of the Finnish Philosophical Counselling Association. Houni has published widely across multiple media, including academic journals and books.

Jeanette Bresson Ladegaard Knox is associate professor of health humanities and ethics at the University of Copenhagen's Faculty of Medicine. She holds a PhD in philosophy and degrees in theater and religious studies. She is former president of the Danish Society for Philosophical Practice (2011–18), acting vice president of the Danish Society for Clinical Ethics (2012–), and a member of the Clinical Ethics Committee for Pediatrics at the University Hospital of Copenhagen (2012–). Knox has published widely, edited several anthologies, and writes fiction alongside her work on philosophy, art, and health.

Lou Marinoff, a commonwealth scholar from Canada, is professor and former chair of philosophy at the City College of New York. He is the founding president of the American Philosophical Practitioners Association (APPA) and editor of its journal, *Philosophical Practice*. Marinoff has authored fifteen books, including *Plato Not Prozac*, translated into twenty-seven languages, and over seventy journal articles and book chapters. He serves as pro bono faculty for global leader communities like the World Economic Forum (Davos) and Horasis (Zurich) and lectures internationally on philosophy and its practical applications.

Tomoko Masaki is a retired professor from the Faculty of Education at Seiwa College in Japan. She specializes in picturebooks, particularly their history in both England and Japan, and has run her own voluntary library in Osaka for fifty years, sharing picture books, poems, and stories with children. She has been awarded two PhDs for "A History of Victorian Popular Picture Books" from the University of Roehampton in England, for which she was awarded the Harvey Darton Award by the Children Books History Society in England and for "Merleau-Ponty and Phenomenology of Children and Picturebooks" from the University of Osaka.

Luis de Miranda is senior research fellow in the Department of Philosophy of the University of Turku, Finland, a Marie Skłodowska-Curie Fellow at the Turku Institute for Advanced Studies, and affiliated research fellow at the House of Innovation of the Stockholm School of Economics, Sweden. A PhD in philosophy, he is the author of books translated in various languages, both essays and philosophical novels, for instance, *Being and Neonness* (2019),

Philosophical Health (2024), or *Paridaiza* (2020). He has engaged in action research as a philosophical counselor worldwide, with individuals, institutions, and corporations, thanks to the methodologies he designed and developed.

Manos Perrakis is an academic researcher, writer, and translator based in Vienna, Austria. He holds a PhD in philosophy from Humboldt University of Berlin. He works mainly on the interface between aesthetics and practical philosophy. He was Lise Meitner Research Fellow of the Austrian Science Fund at the University of Music and Performing Arts in Graz, Austria, where he led the project "Music as Life-Affirmation. The Value of Music in Life-Philosophy." Perrakis is member of the International Society for Philosophical Practice (IGPP) and its professional association (BV-PP). He translates German classics and has published two books of prose and poems.

Ann S. Pihlgren, PhD, research director at the Ignite Research Institute, has worked as supervisor, principal, vice principal, and teacher educator at Stockholm University. She is involved in school development projects and leadership training. She is a consultant to the Swedish National Board of Education on students' philosophizing and reading abilities and a practicing member of the Swedish Association for Philosophical Praxis. Her doctoral dissertation "Socrates in the Classroom," awarded "Swedish Dissertation of the Year" in 2008, was a thorough investigation of the Socratic traditions in education—a phenomenological analysis of the interplay of youngsters philosophizing as part of their education.

Sebastian Rehnman is professor of philosophy in the Department of Care and Ethics and member of the research group Life Phenomena and Caring, the Faculty of Health Sciences, at the University of Stavanger, Norway. He holds doctorates from the University of Oxford and Oslo University. Rehnman is a philosophical practitioner, teacher, and supervisor in the Norwegian Society for Philosophical Practice; counselor, supervisor, and scientific board member of the Swedish Society for Existential Psychotherapy; therapist and board member of the Norwegian Society for Existential Therapy; and philosophical practitioner in the Swedish Society for Philosophical Practice. He runs his private practice Dialogikos.

Detlef Staude studied philosophy, German language and literature, communication sciences, and psychology in Munich and Freiburg im Breisgau. He was a high school teacher in philosophy and German for many years. Since 1997, he has headed the philosophical practice *philocom* in Bern, Switzerland. He has been president of the Swiss Network for Practical Philosophizing since 2002 (please consult the homepage, philopraxis.ch). Over the years, Staude has published several books on philosophical practice. His latest book is on the history of philosophy: *Turntable of Philosophical History: Philosophical Thought in and from Switzerland* (2022).

www.ingramcontent.com/pod-product-compliance
Ingram Content Group UK Ltd.
Pitfield, Milton Keynes, MK11 3LW, UK
UKHW020216290926
15470UKWH00001B/226

9 781666 94700